The
Extramarital
Affair

The Extramarital Affair

Herbert S. Strean

THE FREE PRESS
A Division of Macmillan Publishing Co., Inc.
NEW YORK

Collier Macmillan Publishers
LONDON

The Free Press
A Division of Macmillan Publishing Co., Inc.
866 Third Avenue, New York, N. Y. 10022

Collier Macmillan Canada, Ltd.

Library of Congress Catalog Card Number: 79-55937

Printed in the United States of America

printing number
1   2   3   4   5   6   7   8   9   10

Library of Congress Cataloging in Publication Data

Strean, Herbert S
   The extramarital affair.

   Bibliography: p.
   Includes index.
   1. Adultery. 2. Sexual ethics. 3. Marriage.
I. Title.
HQ806.S86 1980   306.7'3   79-55937
ISBN 0-02-932180-8

Acknowledgments

Excerpt from *How to Save Your Own Life* by Erica Jong. Copyright © 1977 by Erica Mann Jong. Reprinted by permission of Holt, Rinehart, and Winston, Publishers.

Excerpt from *The Affair* by Morton Hunt. Copyright © 1969 by Morton Hunt. Reprinted by arrangement with The New American Library, Inc., New York, N. Y.

Excerpt from "I Want a Girl Just Like the Girl That Married Dear Old Dad" by Harry Von Tilzer and William Dillon. Copyright 1911 by Harry Von Tilzer Music Publishing Company. Copyright renewed. International copyright secured. All rights reserved. Used by permission.

Excerpt from "I Can Dream, Can't I" by Irving Kahal and Sammy Fain. Copyright © 1937 by Chappell and Co., Inc. Copyright renewed. International copyright secured. All rights reserved. Used by permission.

Excerpt from "Dream" by John H. Mercer. Copyright renewed 1962 by John H. Mercer. All U.S.A. rights controlled by Mercer Music.

Excerpt from "Stardust" by H. Carmichael. Copyright © 1929 Mills Music, Inc. Copyright renewed. All rights reserved. Used by permission.

Title "Release Me." Used by permission of Four Star Music Co., Inc.

Excerpt from *When We Were Very Young* by A. A. Milne. Copyright 1924 by E. P. Dutton and Co., Inc. Copyright renewed 1952 by A. A. Milne. Used by permission.

For Marcia

The love between the sexes is undoubtedly one
of the first things in life, and the combination of
mental and bodily satisfaction attained in the enjoyment
of love is literally one of life's culminations. Apart
from a few perverse fanatics, all the world knows this
and conducts life accordingly: only science is too
refined to confess it.

Sigmund Freud, "Observations on Transference Love" (1915)

Contents

III. Responses of the "Injured Party"

IV. The Professionals' Response

Prologue

The past few decades have witnessed vast changes in accepted sexual practices in our culture. Premarital sexual intercourse and cohabitation without marriage, once decried, are widely accepted today. "Swinging," "switching," and group sex among the married are far from taboo in many sectors of society; it has been estimated that as many as eight million couples have participated in the practice of exchanging partners for sexual purposes (Breedlove and Breedlove, 1964). Homosexuality, once considered morally reprehensible and symptomatic of mental illness, is now tolerated, even legitimized as a way of life, and the American Psychiatric Association has recently struck homosexuality from its list of psychiatric disorders. Many dynamically oriented therapists now advocate premarital and extramarital sex as avenues to mental health (Fine, 1975).

Because there has also been an immense change in what is permissible to say and print, sociologists and other professionals have been studying and reporting on all forms of sexual behavior, including extramarital sex. Yet, there is virtually nothing of substance in the professional literature that examines the extramarital affair from a psychoanalytic perspective. Psychoanalysts have long contended that behavior in and of itself cannot be fully understood unless the individual's unconscious wishes, history, superego admonitions, defenses, fantasies, dreams, and the like are taken into account; otherwise, the meaning of his or her behavior can at best be only hypothesized. The psychoanalytically oriented therapist is not ready to say upon immediate observation that sex not practiced within the marital relationship is "neurotic," "acting out," or "maladaptive"; neither is the therapist willing to term the behavior "mature," "healthy," or "adaptive."

The aim of this book is to review the major psychodynamics of men and women involved in extramarital affairs and to offer a psychoanalytical explanation of their behavior. By utilizing live clinical examples in which the person's history, unconscious wishes, anxieties, dreams, defenses, and fantasies are described in detail, we will be able to appreciate not just the rationales that people offer for their extramarital activity but its deeper and more significant unconscious meaning to them.

In my own practice and in the practices of psychoanalysts whose work I supervise, I have witnessed a sharp rise in the incidence of extramarital affairs. In the past ten years I have studied over seventy-five of these phenomena in the consultation room and in supervisory discussions. The individuals involved were men and women who sustained their marriages while they were concomitantly involved in extramarital relationships of a few months' to several years' duration. Some sought psychotherapy because they were consciously conflicted about their extramarital relationship, while others wanted therapy for other reasons.

There is much ambiguity about the term "extramarital affair." Marital infidelity ranges from what novelist Erica Jong has called the "zipless fuck" (Jong, 1973), a sexual encounter with limited emotional overtones, to what journalist Morton Hunt refers to as the "grand amour" (Hunt, 1969). The subject of this book is extramarital activity as manifested in an intense and sustained relationship with a member of the opposite sex; "one-night stands" and other manifestations of casual sex are not considered here because their meaning to the person is often quite different from that of a prolonged extramarital relationship.

As I have studied the unconscious meaning of psychoanalytic patients' prolonged extramarital activity, it has become quite clear that in each case there was a conflicted marriage. When I could comprehend better why the patients under study married whom they did and what neurotic and healthy gratifications they derived from their marriages, it occurred to me that my observations could lead to an enriched understanding of the modal married person who is involved in an extramarital relationship.

My data, as well as the findings of others (Ziskin and Ziskin 1973; Hunt, 1969; Block, 1978; Bartusis, 1978) indicate that breaking up a marriage to marry or live with a lover is rare. It does appear that there is a unique cluster of men and women in our society who want to preserve their marriages but at the same time experience the need to engage in extramarital relationships. It is these people who are the subjects of this book.

The objection might be made that patients in psychoanalytic therapy are a skewed sample and that the findings of my research are not applicable to those not in psychoanalytic treatment. My answer would be that although individuals who seek psychoanalytically oriented therapy and stay in it for a while are usually more mature, courageous, and less defensive than the rest of the population, they probably share more similarities than differences with those who do not wish or who fear to examine their unconscious minds.

Psychoanalysis has uncovered the conflicted nature of the human being. The struggle, as Freud described it, is between the pleasure principle, which constantly seeks gratification, and the reality principle, which takes into account self-preservation and the voice of the superego, or conscience (Freud, 1923). All of us have dreams involving extramarital activity even if we do not act out these fantasies in waking life. Furthermore, it has been observed (Freud, 1939) that sexual dreams rarely involve one's spouse as partner. This book will attempt, in part, to explain this phenomenon further and also why, although all married individuals at one time or another fantasize having extramarital affairs, as much as 50 percent of the married men and women in our population actually do so (Spotnitz and Freeman, 1964; Bartusis, 1978).

Most psychoanalysts and social scientists agree with Margaret Mead (1967) that monogamous heterosexual love is probably one of the most difficult, complex, and demanding of human relationships. This is probably why some professionals contend that an extramarital affair can help a married couple sustain their marriage with less tension. In chapter 1 we will examine some of the often overwhelming demands of modern marriage that can propel a married person into extramarital activity.

An extramarital affair is of course only one possible means of escape from the conflicts of marriage. One can seek escape from marriage through an "affair" with his or her work, spending hours and days away from the spouse by being a workaholic. Similarly, one can compulsively engage in a hobby, organizational work, or travel in order to cope with the demands of marriage. Why some individuals choose to react to the conflicts of marriage by becoming involved in an extramarital sexual relationship is the major concern of this book.

Psychoanalysis has its own unique perspective on sexuality. From a psychoanalytic point of view, one who can enjoy a sustained and relaxed sexual relationship has resolved certain "psychosocial tasks" (Erikson, 1950). According to Erik Erikson, in order to enjoy an intimate and loving sexual relationship in marriage, the individual must resolve certain conflicts that arise in the normal course of development—for example, trust versus mistrust, autonomy versus self-doubt, identity versus identity diffusion. In chapter 2, we review and examine these psychosocial tasks and their relationship to sex and marriage.

It is the thesis of this book that when psychosocial tasks are resolved, one can enjoy a monogamous marriage and cope with its frustrations but that when these tasks are not mastered, there is a neurotic choice of mate (the theme of chapter 3), the marital relationship induces anxiety, and the individual will seek to escape from it in one way or another.

Chapters 4 through 8 discuss various types of conflicted marriages and demonstrate why an extramarital affair seemed to be an inevitable outcome for the individuals involved. Chapter 9 examines some of the characteristic responses of the "innocent" spouse who becomes aware of the marital partner's "affair," and the final chapter discusses the question of when and if an extramarital affair can ever be considered healthy and adaptive.

As the reader travels with me in an exploration of marital conflict and the extramarital affair, he or she will note that I have referred to authors as disparate as the founder of psychoanalysis, Sigmund Frued, and the novelist J. D. Salinger. The reason for this range of citation is that many psychoanalytic ideas that I espouse have already been intuitively incorporated in the folk culture. Very frequently, a novelist, poet, or song writer has articulated a psychoanalytic concept with more sensitivity and clarity than the psychoanalyst.

All of the individuals described in this book are very real people. Their names, occupations, and other identifying features have been disguised in order to protect confidentiality. I am grateful to them for helping me to reach a better understanding of the unconscious meaning of extramarital activity.

Part I

Marriage, Sex, and Mate Choice

Chapter 1

Modern Marriage
and Its Discontents

PATTERNS OF OUR CULTURE

Rapid social change is one of the most conspicious features of twentieth-century culture. Our societal norms are questioned in the media almost daily. Social critics like Alvin Toffler (1970) and Vance Packard (1968) describe Americans as suffering from severe disorientation and inability to cope with the stresses induced by the continual flow of cultural change in contemporary society.

The most notable shift in interpersonal relationships has been in the interaction between men and women. Today more than half of all married women work outside the home. As they move into parts of the economic orbit traditionally restricted to males, contemporary women are actively competing with men and are repudiating their formerly subordinate roles. Rather than submit to the authority of their husbands in all matters, married women in Western society are attempting to expand their personal horizons. Some groups in the women's movement argue that a woman who commits herself to one man is collaborating in her own oppression (Durbin, 1977) and that traditional marriage is a form of serfdom or slavery (Smith and Smith, 1974). Many writers emphasize masturbation or lesbianism as acceptable routes to sexual gratification for women, and some (e.g., Hite, 1976) find them in some ways superior to heterosexual intercourse.

Until quite recently many women had a tendency to suppress their wishes for pleasure, autonomy, and status. In the 1960s women began to assert their rights and demand that men make a new accommodation to them. Anxious over the loss of some of his traditional privileges and immunities and threatened by the new competition from women, many a man in contemporary society copes with his fears by feeling and acting hostile toward his wife and often toward women in general.

One result of men's fears and women's growing independence is that the United States today is experiencing a divorce epidemic; there are approximately 1.6 divorces for every three marriages (Ziskin and Ziskin, 1973), or just about one divorce for every two marriages. Many married couples that are not divorced are feuding and/or separated. The newspaper columns of Ann Landers, Rose Franzblau, Joyce Brothers, and others amply testify to the prevalence of marital unhappiness.

To some extent marital discord is a reflection of more wide-spread discontent. In the professional literature one reads of "the emerging character type torn from family commitments by the demands of urban living" or of "modern man alienated from himself and from others" (Deburger, 1978). In sociologist C. Wright Mills' terms, the modal personality today is a "cheerful robot" (Mills, 1959) and according to social psychologist David Riesman he is the "other directed" (Reisman, 1956). In psychoanalyst Erich Fromm's formulation, the twentieth-century man or woman is unable to love intimately because of an obsession with becoming a "personality package," an exchangeable commodity to be sold for success (Fromm, 1956). Marriage as seen by popular writer Jane Howard has become "a chancy, grim, modern experiment instead of an ancient institution" (1978).

Because of the blurring of gender roles, husbands and wives are unsure about what the rules and regulations of married life should or can be. Every day another book or article appears that attempts to instruct people on how to conduct heterosexual transactions, particularly the inevitable fights in married life. The proliferation and popularity of books such as *The Intimate Enemy: How to Fight Fair in Love and Marriage* (Bach, 1969) are testimony to the fact that the norms that are supposed to govern marital behavior are shifting and vague in most individuals' minds. A good example of how sexual differences have become blurred is the growing similarity of the sexes in dress and grooming. A booth I saw at an amusement park recently bore the sign "Guess your Sex."

Advertising, a medium that reflects society's values, constantly emphasizes the opportunities for sexual, economic, social, and psychological success available to those who use the product being touted. These "come-ons" constantly whet the appetites of men and women and frequently induce the thought that all kinds of sexual and social conquests are possible.

As psychiatrist Hyman Spotnitz and writer Lucy Freeman have noted:

> . . . Pause before any newsstand and peruse some of the magazine covers. You will be staring at an arrogant array of completely nude females who made the New Guinea ladies look modest indeed. Once only burlesque houses offered the female in naked form to the public eye. Now Hollywood stars permit themselves to be photographed bare . . . if not in photographs or real life, then in descriptions on the printed pages which go far beyond any picture. Words of lust, infidelity and adultery pour from newspapers, magazines and books to excite and titilate. . . . We are now swirling in the vortex of the sexual sell, which has led many into believing that any behavior in which they wish to indulge is permissible under the banner of sexual freedom. [1964, pp. 20–21]

Today's husband and wife are constantly being stimulated by the lure of so many potential pleasures. Eroticism in both advertisements and the popular media is flooding the market, promising increased happiness, self-esteem, and joy to those who heed the message. When appeals to narcissism, grandiosity, and omnipotent fantasies are ubiquitous, frustration tolerance tends to decline. Washing the dishes, listening to the details of a spouse's day, and resolving conflicts among the children are boring or unpleasant tasks when contrasted with the Garden of Eden that seems within reach.

We now live in a psychologically sophisticated era that puts considerable emphasis on the right of the individual to personal emotional satisfaction and to a sense of fulfillment. A public widely disillusioned by wars and scandals shares the belief that good times should be sought here and now (Williamson, 1977). The traditional commitment to lifelong monogamy, "for richer or poorer, in sickness and in health," is a frequent casualty of today's hedonistic creed.

Many individuals have been led to believe that life can be

ecstatic and that one can be loved and admired most of the time
provided that one learns the right methods to achieve the promised
state of bliss. Self-help books insist that happiness is to be achieved
by self-aggrandisement, that the desires of others are important only to the extent that they contribute to one's own well-being, and
that involvement in social or altruistic causes is a waste of time
unless it demonstrably enhances one's success. Many psychotherapists claim that nothing one does or does not do should be
considered wrong or immoral unless it gets him or her in trouble.
As the late Allen Wheelis (1958), a California psychoanalyst,
noted in *The Quest for Identity*, most people today are experiencing a decline in the strength of the superego or
conscience; guilt seems to be no longer regarded as an appropriate response to any kind of behavior. In the film *An Unmarried
Woman*, when the distraught wife tells her therapist (played, in-
cidentally, by a real-life therapist) that she feels very guilty
because she believes she provoked her husband to leave her for
another woman, the therapist orders her to "take a rest from
guilt!" — choosing not to help her patient with the anger and
other feelings and fantasies that created her guilt.

The expanding opportunity structure and constant stimulation
by the media have increased most people's primitive desires. Instead of dying for a cause or sacrificing for an institution, individuals in current Western society are preoccupied with how
they are going to discharge their accumulated tension. Married
men and women, like everybody else, are eagerly looking for a
paradise that does not seem to exist in the confines of marriage.
Marriage is experienced by many as mundane, irritating, and too
demanding.

Many married people feel deprived because they are convinced
that much more gratification is available outside marriage. This is
one of the reasons that occasional fantasies of divorce are a near-
universal phenomenon and why so many people so often think
about some form of escape from marriage. More and more people
are contending that married love is rarely able to provide more
than a part of what they hunger for. In a popular film of the late
1960s, *Bob and Carol and Ted and Alice*, two married couples
were hungrily, albeit ambivalently, seeking to swing and switch.
The best-seller *Please Touch* (Howard, 1970) offered a guided tour

of the human potential movement, describing how thousands of people pay millions of dollars annually to have indiscriminate, aggressive foreplay.

Herbert Hendin (1975), a psychoanalyst who has studied the impact of cultural forces on individual behavior, has dubbed our current era "The Age of Sensation." According to Hendin, we are living in a time when most people want what they want when they want it and are furious when they don't get it. He contends that the high rate of divorce and disruptive family life reflect the cultural trend toward replacing commitment, involvement, and tenderness with self-aggrandizement, exploitativeness, and titilation.

Given the pervasive narcissistic preoccupations and feelings of deprivation, it is not surprising that violence is at an all-time high. Psychoanalyst Reuben Fine (1975) has referred to our society as "a hate culture" and has pointed out that most individuals harbor a great deal of distrust and suspicion in their interpersonal relationships. Competition is more valued than cooperation, and there is more self-centeredness than genuine concern for others. In a hate culture, marital interaction reflects what is dominant in the society—frustration, anger, competition, and self-centeredness.

An American Tragedy

In today's society, in which we all want a lot, a married woman is expected, and expects herself, to be a combination of orgastic playmate, intellectual stimulator, emotional empathizer, and cathartic absorber for her husband—plus a strong and independent person. Many women have been aspiring to become a cross between Madame de Pompadour and Madame Curie! Not only does the wife of the 1970s expect a great deal from herself, she expects as much, if not more, from her husband. He should be a willing and abundant provider of material goods and yet encourage her gainful employment; he should be a sparkling conversationalist, yet respect his wife's needs for solitude and privacy; he should help with domestic chores, yet have a stable role as a masculine father; he should be an appetizing sexual partner but should tolerate his wife's flirtations with other men.

The modern husband is in tremendous conflict because he, too, is often plagued by unrealistic expectations; he must be an accomplished sexual athlete, a source of profound wisdom, and a provider of plenty of money. If his inevitable failure does not lead to obsessive self-beratement, he is frequently preoccupied with the fantasy that life could be more fulfilling if his wife were more motherly, tender, supportive, and "feminine"—and at the same time ecstatically erotic, decisive, and brilliant. Married people seem to expect their spouses to be embodiments of the omnipotent parental figure who gives all, knows all, and can anticipate needs and wishes before they are verbalized. Yet, despite the hunger for parenting by the spouse that most marital partners exhibit, they also want to be admired for their strength, praised for their autonomy, and rewarded for their independence. Given the demands that husbands and wives place on themselves and each other, it is surprising that approximately 50 percent of the marriages in Western society survive.

Much of married life is a paradigm of discontent because of the reduced capacity of men and women to give and feel protective and loving toward each other (Hendin, 1975). The institution of marriage as it now exists, rather than promoting the excitement that can sometimes be found in extramarital affairs, long and short-term, challenges our more mature ego functions—high-level judgment, object-related interaction rather than narcissistic joy, frustration tolerance rather than instant pleasure, mature reality testing and deferred gratification, acceptance of criticism rather than adulation. These are demands that most married individuals resent in an age of sexual freedom and "doing one's own thing." The extramarital affair, which appears to be an oasis of sexual and emotional bliss, excitement, and devilish abandon, seems to be a welcome respite for many married people and a fantasy for almost all of them. While it lasts, unhappy married people can feel understood, loved, and listened to, particularly when they complain about their unsympathetic and unstimulating spouses.

THIS SIDE OF PARADISE:
THE ROMANTIC IDEAL

Any social scientist or psychoanalyst who has studied the conflicts inherent in contemporary married life has commented on the discrepancy between what people expect and what is realistically attainable in marriage.

Marriage in our culture owes much to the notion of romantic or courtly love developed in the twelfth and thirteenth centuries among the nobility of France and later encouraged throughout Europe by the wave of romantic individualism that swept the continent. Romantic love is characterized by total fealty to and idealization of the beloved, and particularly by asexuality. The chivalrous romantic lover, although always intensely idealizing his beloved, never demonstrated his passion physically, even by a kiss or a hug (Montagu, 1956).

The courtly ideal derives from the medieval cult of the Virgin. Early English Puritans, notably John Milton, wrote about intense relationships that combined a high degree of idealization, dedication, selflessness, and tenderness (Hunt, 1969).

Romantic love as described in the literature was not always requited and often was not even acknowledged. This is best exemplified in the relationship between Cyrano de Bergerac and Roxanne. Far from confessing his devotion to Roxanne, Cyrano even wooed her successfully for another man. When romantic lovers do have sexual contact, the contact is usually limited in frequency; physical distance and legal and moral constraints serve to keep them separated. Further, it is often followed by death or some less drastic punishment. In the case of the guilty lovers Tristan and Isolde, consummation was followed by death and transcendence, which, of course, restored the relationship to an idealistic, asexual plane.

In many respects romantic love is totally antithetical to marriage. First, it should be noted that many of the famous romantic lovers of history never shared a domestic life. Romeo never saw Juliet in curlers and Juliet didn't see Romeo putting out the garbage. Roxanne and Cyrano did not have to quarrel about the family budget, and Tristan and Isolde kept their trysts without being interrupted by a telephone. Since the essence of romantic love is idealization of the beloved, it cannot withstand the confrontation with reality that day-to-day married life entails.

Romantic love in our own day is usually characteristic of adolescents and preadolescents, for it protects the lover from having to participate in a sexual and emotional relationship that he or she is not ready for. Like many other phenomena of adolescence, romantic love is egocentric and a product of many unrealistic fantasies. The romantic lover often idealizes the beloved to a point where he or she is almost unrecognizable. This is well illustrated in the film "The Story of Adele H." in which the central character is obsessively "in love" with her seducer. At the climax of the film, Adele is so consumed by her own egocentric and ecstatic passion that she fails to recognize her lover when she passes him in the street.

Despite the fact that romantic love is illusory, its pursuit is still encouraged by the advertising media, the florist lobby, and wedding gown manufacturers, to name just a few.

Tender is the Night — Psychological Factors in Romance

From a psychoanalytic perspective, one of the features of romantic love is that the lovers project their "ego ideal"—i.e., their concept of the perfect person and what they wish they themselves could be—on to the loved one. The qualities ascribed to a loved one during the spiritual and aesthetic experience of romantic love are almost always far beyond whatever real qualities the loved one possesses. The psychoanalyst distinguishes between "being in love," which has unrealistic and obsessional characteristics and therefore is a neurotic state, from "loving," which is personalistic, based on reality and not too egocentric (Fine, 1975). Anthropologist Ralph Linton (1936) contrasts the mature loving individual with the "ecstasy and madness" of the person in love, which he describes as like an epileptic fit.

Freud (1939) likened the romantic lover to the fond parent who projects his own ideal on to his child to substitute for the lost narcissism of childhood. He pointed out that what the lover wishes he could have been, he fantasies his beloved as being. To the psychoanalyst, the romantic ideal is an irrational, immature, and unrealistic form of love based on the re-awakening of family romances of childhood. The loved one is made into a father or mother figure and becomes the recipient of fantasies that emanate from the lover's childhood. Just as the idealized parent of one's childhood was sexually inaccessible, so romantic love seems to flourish when there is limited physical contact.

In the "honeymoon" stage of a requited romance the lover, having overidealized his or her partner, is emotionally convinced that this is the best person on earth and that they really are in the

Garden of Eden. The lover lives only for giving to the beloved; the paradox is that the partner demands little but gets everything, inasmuch as he or she is at the same point—giving all and asking nothing but to bestow love on the other.

The essence of the romantic ideal is exclusivity—the wish to feel that one is fulfilling the beloved's needs so completely that he or she does not and could not have any romantic or sexual interest in anyone else. Said Juliet to Romeo, "The more I give the more I have, for both are infinite."

The intense overidealization that is part of romantic love is dramatically portrayed in some of Sigmund Freud's own letters to his fiancée, Martha Bernays:

> What I meant to convey was how much the magic of your being expresses itself in your countenance and your body, how much there is visible in your appearance that reveals how sweet, generous, and reasonable you are. . . .
>
> Once the smoothness and freshness of youth is gone, then the only beauty lies where goodness and understanding transfigure the features, and that is where you excel. . . .
>
> In your face it is the pure noble beauty of your brow and your eyes that shows in almost every picture.

According to his biographer, Freud likened Martha "to the fairy princess from whose lips fell roses and pearls, with, however, the doubt whether kindness or good sense came more often from Martha's lips" (Jones, 1953, p. 103).

Romantic love carries the seeds of its own destruction in that eventually reality begins to assert itself. Then a strange phenomenon occurs. Lovers who were originally sufficient unto each other are no longer so. They begin to perceive each other in terms of their real characteristics. As the demands of living intrude, each partner begins to give less, to focus more on his or her own needs and to expect more of the mate. It is the coincidence of giving less and expecting more that punctures the romantic ideal and sparks many conflicts between spouses (Ables, 1977).

Another force that frequently disrupts the romantic complex is sex. Because romantic love is idealized, the lovers' sexual yearnings for their romantic object often induce guilt and anxiety. Novelist Anatole France (1933) in *Penguin Island* pointed out that when the penguins turned into human beings they lost their virtue only when they put on clothes—that is, when they hid the rejected realities of their bodies. So frequently does the taboo on sex influence romantic lovers. Rejecting their own bodies, they feel that their love is degraded by their participation in an "animal act."

Despite all the evidence that the romantic ideal is a false illusion, many people still think that marriage will solve their problems and bring them lifelong bliss (Neubeck, 1969). This myth, to psychoanalysts, emanates from a fantasy that there really is an omnipotent, omniscient, perfect parent who can supply eternal bliss. This fantasy is a residue of the belief that most children hold but eventually outgrow: "My mother (father) is the greatest. She (he) is most brilliant, all powerful, can give all and has no needs of her (his) own!" In a culture that stimulates erotic hunger and encourages us to "do our own thing" as much as possible, it is inevitable that some members will want to regress to the infantile position, where there were no responsibilities and all wants and needs were gratified by a parent who seemed godlike.

In *Emotional Security*, psychiatrist Milton Sapirstein (1948) points out that romantic love, like overwhelming grief, seems to be a temporary state, and sooner or later has to be replaced by a working relationship suitable for effective living on an adult level. Sapirstein adds that many couples who start off on a high romantic level feel "out of love" when this normal transition begins and therefore feel the need to wreck their marriages. Their insistence that their love shall not change in quality, despite increasing maturity and sexual experience, forces them back to the emotional problems of adolescence.

Many couples find it very difficult to acknowledge that a perpetual honeymoon is an impossible dream and that things cannot stay the way they were in the early days of the relationship. A honeymoon is most difficult to recapture but the childish wish lingers on, and many a husband or wife contends, "If you really loved me you would know what I need and devote all your efforts to meeting my needs." When the spouse is unwilling or unable to satisfy this demand, the lover often goes into a state of angry disbelief and disillusionment. Shakespeare captured this feeling in *Cymbeline*, act 5, when the forsaken lover laments:

> *Mine eyes were not in fault for she was beautiful*
> *Mine ears that heard her flattery!*

Another expectation of marriage derived partly from the romantic ideal is that if two individuals love each other they will want to be with each other as much as possible. Many a married person feels extremely threatened by his or her own wish for autonomy and becomes even more upset if the partner has other interests and relationships that are not shared. In many people love and romance seem to stimulate the wish to achieve once again the perfect symbiosis of childhood, when mother and infant are psychologically one. Just as many parents and children feel terrified to be apart, many mature adults react similarly when they feel separated emotionally from their spouses. Many married people have the unrealistic expectation that they can and should get everything they need from the marital partner. Thus they resent the partner's close attachments to relatives and friends. Similarly, many a married individual feels guilty about enjoying a relationship or activity apart from the marriage because he or she still clings to the notion that all pleasure *should* be derived from the marital relationship.

It is often difficult for married people to acknowledge that one cannot do everything for the mate or expect the converse. In the play, *After the Fall* (Miller, 1964), the wife says, "If you really loved me, you would do much more," and the husband answers, "No one loves that much, except maybe God."

Still another characteristic of the romantic ideal is the premium placed on physical beauty and youthfulness. The potential for disillusionment and marital conflict is enormous when the spouses eventually recognize that physical attractiveness plays a very small role, if any, in determining the fate of the union.

As our popular songs, movies, and novels attest, the romantic ideal, though elusive and in many ways unrealistic, to many people is still worth pursuing. Rare is the person involved in an extramarital affair who does not speak with enthusiasm about the romance of the relationship. Because "romance" is lacking in marriage, he or she feels that an extramarital affair is necessary in order to be fulfilled.

After he had been married for two years, Ken began to pursue one woman after another, claiming that he could not "resist the compulsion of romance." He would fall "happily in love, just like I did with my wife," feel enormously fulfilled for a few weeks, and then get bored and irritable. When he tried to stop his "escapades" he felt "so empty" that he had to seek another lover. At the point when he entered analysis he had been through four romances in 19 months.

Even if romantic fantasies do not preoccupy a married couple, husbands and wives in contemporary society have to cope with shifting expectations of marital roles. The traditional expectations of a marital partner have been loyalty, respect, and caring. Psychoanalysis, the human potential movement, women's liberation, and other movements have introduced additional expectations such as companionship, sexual satisfaction, and support in resolving personal and interpersonal problems. Psychiatrists Grunebaum and Christ (1976) have pointed out that to be a best friend, a favored bed-companion, and a "therapist" are difficult tasks, especially "through sickness and health, for richer and poorer, for better or worse." Stability, loyalty, and dependability are qualities which do not easily coexist with stimulation, excitement, and variety.

LISTENING WITH THE THIRD EAR: THE PSYCHOANALYST'S VIEW OF MARRIAGE

A happy marriage is composed of two happy people. This may appear at first to be a simple statement. However, many wives, husbands, and even some marital counselors and therapists argue vociferously that the unhappy spouse is a victim of circumstances and that if he or she had a different partner the suffering would disappear. In some ways, this is a residue of the romantic notion that the beloved is a kind of savior who can and will resolve all the lover's hurts and problems.

The late Dr. Lawrence Kubie stated:

> Psychoanalysis may well be able someday to contribute a great deal to the prevention of marital problems, but only after young folk have learned that they can never marry themselves out of their neuroses, and that whenever two unhappy young people marry, each adds the problems of his own neurosis to those of the other. From these experiences comes the hard but inescapable conclusion that we must earn our right to marry by solving our individual problems first. [1956, p. 32]

Marital conflict is like any other neurotic symptom. Just as the person who fears heights or sweats profusely on an airplane would like to believe that the cause of his distress is external—that is, that it is the "unsteady" building or "poorly constructed plane" that causes his difficulty—so too the unhappy spouse invariably feels that the marital distress is caused by the partner.

When psychoanalysts subject patients' marital complaints to examination and study the analysand's dreams, fantasies, and histories, they learn that almost every complaint about a spouse is an unconscious wish. The husband who laments that his wife is sexually unresponsive may unconsciously have chosen an asexual partner in the first place to protect him from experiencing frightening incestuous wishes. The wife who complains that her husband is unaggressive and unassertive may reveal in her fantasies and dreams that she receives unconscious gratification from criticizing and weakening a man.

Psychoanalysis takes the position that people, in many ways, write their own scripts. If a person consistently complains about a spouse's unresponsiveness, coldness, or competitiveness, analysis will generally reveal that this is what the complainant unconsciously wishes.

That a spouse's derogatory remarks about his or her marital partner are expressions of unconscious wishes becomes apparent when we observe how the spouse conducts him or herself as a patient in the psychoanalytic relationship. Almost always the patient will experience the analyst in the same way that the marital partner is experienced. For example, the husband who claims that he is "put down" by his wife will feel "put down" by the analyst; the wife who says her husband is cold and rejecting will eventually perceive her therapist the same way; the spouse who thinks his or her marital partner is stupid will at some point in the analysis label the analyst stupid, and on and on!

Mary Ellis had been in psychoanalytic treatment for about a year when she blurted out in a session that her husband, Joe, was "a cold, insensitive, unfeeling ox who is afraid of intimacy." On her birthday, she complained, "All Joe got me was some stinky perfume. He's afraid to have me smell nice cause then he'll feel close and that scares him!"

After discharging a great deal of anger, Mary began to cry. In

between her sobs she said that she was very capable of an intimate relationship with a man but that Joe would not or could
not reciprocate her wishes for "closeness, tenderness, and warm
sex." Then Mary fell silent for several minutes. When the analyst
asked what she was thinking about during the silence, Mary said,
"I'm feeling very close to you now. I feel you understand me. I
feel warm inside. . . . I'm fantasizing that your arm is around me
and that you are lying with me on the couch. . . . Now I have a
fantasy of throwing a chair at you. You affect me too much, you
bastard! Go away!"

Mary was afraid to feel close to her analyst. She protected herself from warm, sexual feelings toward him by fantasizing that she
would hurt him with a chair. Psychologically, this was precisely
how Mary coped with Joe; she attacked him in order to ward off
close feelings toward him. When, later in treatment, Mary expressed the wish to seek out another analyst although she still felt
very close to her regular therapist, she was able to understand
some of her motives for arranging the extramarital affair in which
she had been involved for several months.

Mary's case illustrates that when a person complains that the
spouse is emotionally or sexually inhibited (and the spouse very
well may be), the complainant unconsciously wants it that way.
That the complaint is a manifestation of an unconscious wish is
verified when the same phenomenon is observed in the patient's relationship with the analyst. Analysts call this "transference."*

Happy People
Dr. Reuben Fine (1971) has postulated that a happy human being is
one who pursues love; seeks pleasure guided by reason; has sexual
gratification; has a rich, feeling life, a role in the family and social
order, a sense of identity; and can communicate with others and be
creative. This "analytic ideal" is what the therapist has as a goal
when treating a patient psychoanalytically.

Happy people (discussed in more detail in chapter 2) have

* In supportive therapy or other nonpsychoanalytic treatment, where
the therapist does not take a neutral stand toward the patient's produc-
tions, this phenomenon is less likely to occur.

resolved several psychosexual tasks. They are able to trust another person without feeling guilty about being dependent. At the same time, they have a sense of their own identities and can take care of themselves if the other person is not available. They can enjoy feeling independent without resentment because they have a realistic sense of their own capacities; they are not busy doubting themselves.

One of the reasons that happy people can sustain their good feelings about themselves and others is that they have overcome childish narcissism and feelings of omnipotence and strive to achieve what is realistically possible. They have some tolerance for frustration and realistic judgment; they can compete without wanting to destroy or hurt others and achieve without guilt or fear of retribution. Happy people realize that their failure to seduce one or both parents is no reflection on their capacities. They can enjoy their own sexual identities. Having resolved romatic fantasies, they are free to love and devote themselves to a member of the opposite sex.

The ability to commit oneself to another person and trust him or her evolves from the early mother-infant relationship, when attachment was the major source of pleasure. However, mature and happy adults can attach themselves to another person without making excessive demands or seeking symbiosis. They can admire the loved one without being infatuated; they can enjoy sex without using it defensively to prove their adequacy; they can enjoy intimacy and devotion without engulfing or fearing that they will be engulfed. In effect, the psychoanalyst views people as happy and mature when they can enjoy a love relationship with a member of the opposite sex that is characterized by mutual commitment, admiration, enjoyable sex, intimacy, and devotion.

The happy man or woman will probably choose a happy and mature marital partner and enjoy loving and being loved. The unhappy person usually chooses an unhappy partner to complement his or her neurosis (see chapter 3) and an unhappy marriage is the result.

Unhappy people are, in many ways, like egocentric children. Consequently, they cannot love in a wholehearted, intimate, and devoted manner. Either they must compete with, avoid, or attack the partner or risk being abused, avoided, or attacked. Although immature or neurotic people usually arrange to have neurotic marriages, more often than not they do not recognize how they have unconsciously written their own self-destructive scripts. Usually they feel very misunderstood, indignant, and self-righteous. Divorce, separation, even murder may follow. In some cases, the attempt to escape an unhappy marriage leads to an extramarital affair.

Unlike men or women in a troubled marriage who can say, "Enough is enough, I'll go it alone or look for someone else," the individuals involved in extramarital affairs want to continue marital relationships that they do not fully enjoy. At the same time, they have only a part-time relationship with their lovers. Unlike happy and mature people, they cannot comfortably and fully devote themselves sexually or emotionally to one person, whether their spouses or their lovers. They need two part-time partners to whom they can relate and whom they can love only partially.

In the chapters that follow I will try to demonstrate that sexual infidelity is usually, if not always, a neurotic form of behavior that will be observed only in an unhappy and immature man or woman. A husband or wife involved in an extramarital affair is unable to relax in a mutually dependent relationship because of fears of rejection, abandonment, or engulfment; to accept frustration without feeling sadistic or masochistic; to enjoy sex without being bombarded by competitive, incestuous, or homosexual fantasies; or to admire and be admired without overidealization.

In contrast to the happy and mature husband or wife who enjoys and demands an exclusive sexual relationship with the marital partner, the person involved in an affair unconsciously fears a monogamous marriage. Tormented by feelings of distrust, self-doubt, inferiority, a shaky self-image, and uncertain sexual identity, he or she needs a lover to bolster low self-esteem.

Although it is an unpopular point of view today, I intend to demonstrate in the remaining chapters of this book that, for adults, anything other than a monogamous marriage is immature and unhealthful. While many people aver that the institution of marriage is outmoded, it is my contention that these individuals prefer to criticize an institution rather than face the fact that loving and being loved in a monogamous marriage frightens, humiliates, and angers them. Unable to cope with strong but unacceptable dependency wishes, fearful to confront their unconscious desires for power struggles, and helpless to face their forbidden incestuous and homosexual fantasies, many married men and women need to engage in a prolonged extramarital affair because they are poorly equipped to master the tasks that a monogamous marriage entails. They stay in their unhappy marriages because they fear autonomy and cannot cope with separation anxiety.

The husband or wife in a sustained extramarital affair must be distinguished from one who from time to time engages in casual extramarital sex. In contrast to the occasional participant in casual sex, the individual in a prolonged extramarital affair needs the extramarital partner desperately. Whenever the idea of ending the affair presents itself, the individual begins to feel an underlying depression, latent homosexual fantasies, or repressed sadism or masochism. An occasional "one night stand" can be a fairly harmless regression, but a sustained extramarital affair is a form of neurotic compulsion in a person who is too immature to cope with the emotional and interpersonal tasks of marriage.

To understand the psychodynamics of the extramarital affair more fully, we will first review how psychoanalysis explains psychosexual conflicts (chapter 2) and what unconsious factors work together in the choice of a marital partner (chapter 3).

The Agony and The Ecstasy: A Psychoanalytic View of Psychosexual Development

In his *Three Essays on the Theory of Sexuality* (1905) Freud demonstrated very convincingly that the sexuality of adult men and women is strongly influenced by their developmental experiences as children. Whether or not an adult is able to enjoy a sustained and loving sexual relationship depends on how well he or she has resolved the psychosexual tasks appropriate to the various stages of childhood. This chapter will be a review of the stages in human growth through which every child must pass and will also indicate how failure to cope with the demands of any of these maturational stages can lead to certain conflicts in the individual's love and sexual life.

In the Prologue mention was made of the "maturational task" as formulated by the psychoanalyst Erik Erikson. By "maturational tasks" Erikson meant the universal "psychosocial crises" which occur throughout the life cycle and which must be resolved at appropriate developmental points. Erikson uses the term "crisis" to connote not a threat or a catastrophe but a turning point and a crucial period of increased vulnerability and heightened potential (Erikson, 1950). He phrased the tasks in terms of opposing pulls or choices.

The first maturational task that all children must confront Erikson calls "trust versus mistrust." If children can learn to trust themselves and their environment during the first year of life, they are ready in their second year to cope with the next task, "autonomy versus self-doubt." Feeling an inner certainty and a relaxed independence, they can move during the third to the sixth years of life to the task "initiative versus guilt." If children learn to assert themselves without much guilt, they will be better prepared during their seventh to eleventh years to cope with the task "industry versus inferiority." As youngsters are able to be industrious and creative with their peers and feel themselves as equal, they slowly begin to want identities of their own. Erikson referred to the maturational task of adolescence as "identity versus identity diffusion." During the teenage years young people struggle with achieving a sexual identity and making an occupational choice.

When young people feel comfortable with their sexual identity and secure about their choice of occupation, they, according to Erikson, are emotionally ready to consider marriage. The task of people in their twenties is "intimacy versus isolation." If adults enjoy loving a member of the opposite sex and derive satisfaction from work, they will resolve the task "generativity versus self-absorption"—i.e., they will derive pleasure from living rather than being excessively preoccupied with conflicts. When people can resolve the various life crises, they will experience a sense of integrity in their later years and will not feel desperate. Erikson referred to the last conflict in living as "integrity versus despair."

Erikson's maturational tasks have also been referred to as "The Eight Stages of Man." They are similar in many respects to Freud's psychosexual stages of development, which will be considered in detail in this chapter—the oral, anal, phallic, oedipal, latency, pubertal, adolescent, and genital periods of development.

THE ORAL STAGE

One's experiences during the first year of life in many ways influence how comfortable one is when involved in an intimate sexual relationship, how trusting one feels, how expressive one is, and how much pleasure one derives.

Freud called the first phase of maturational development "the oral period" (Freud, 1905) because the needs and interests of the infant center around the mouth; to be fed and made comfortable through the nursing process are overriding wishes at this time. It has been well documented that in addition to food the infant also needs generous doses of spontaneous fondling and affection. The feeling of being wanted, loved, and played with is an important part of the infant's diet, and the intake of nourishment and the intake and acceptance of good will should proceed simultaneously (English and Pearson, 1945).

The attitude that the mother demonstrates in the feeding process is the attitude that the child is likely to associate with food, feeding, and the nursing process. Furthermore, the child's orientation to the outside will be heavily influenced by the responses he*has met in these first experiences with life. Psychoanalyst Karl Abraham (1927) pointed out that the adult who is inclined toward optimism has been well fed and nourished in the first few months of life, while the pessimistic adult as a child was left crying in hungry frustration on many occasions. If a child is held frequently and finds himself in a state of well-being, these first interpersonal experiences lead him to expect that other people as well as his parents will be emotionally receptive (Ribble, 1943).

The tenderness and bodily closeness in sex recapitulate the closeness of the early oral period. Lovers frequently refer to each other in oral terms ("honey," "cookie," "sweetie pie") and often call each other "babe" or "baby." Frequently, the individual who cannot trust another human being in a sexual relationship has been extremely frustrated during the first few months of life. Being close and intimate with another human being conjures up unconscious associations to the early nursing period. If one has angry memories of his mother, he will probably displace these hostile feelings onto the sexual partner and distrust the partner. Frequently the man or woman who perceives sex as a battle of wills is one who still has strong feelings of murderous rage toward the first interpersonal partner, the mother (English & Pearson, 1945). The person is unable to trust the sexual partner because he has never overcome the trauma that resulted from this first and most crucial human encounter.

* In this and subsequent chapters, "he" and "his" are used in a generic sense, to refer to both males and females, so as not to interrupt the flow of the argument.

During the oral phase of development the infant has a strong sucking impulse. If it is gratified, as an adult he can enjoy the oral dimensions of sexual foreplay—kissing, fellatio, cunnilingus, expressing love verbally, etc. Just as the child who is frustrated at the breast will express discomfort and aggression by biting or withdrawal, the adult who has not had an enjoyable first year of life will tend to make "biting" remarks, "chew out" his partner, or ignore the partner altogether.

Oral Frustrations

During the oral period every infant experiences frustrations. Dominated by the "pleasure principle" and therefore wanting instant gratification of all desires, he is inevitably going to be rebuffed. The infant may desire continued sucking when his biological equipment makes weaning to the bottle and other foods possible. He may want to be carried when his musculature enables him to crawl, toward the end of the first year of life. As is well known, weaning and other frustrations are prerequisites for healthy maturation. Although discomfort and aggression are inevitable responses to frustration, they are also necessary, for they help the child to develop new skills for living in an imperfect world. As the child experiences these frustrations in small doses, he derives pleasure from learning to eat a greater variety of foods, to walk instead of being carried, and to talk instead of expressing his needs through crying and thrashing.

If a child has been indulged and not appropriately weaned, emotionally and physically, in adulthood he will tend to approach a love relationship as a demanding baby. Very narcissistic and seeing himself as the center of the universe, the child-adult is unable to empathize with his partner's desires. When he is not catered to, he thrashes, has temper tantrums, and may even physically hurt the partner, much as a baby bites and hits whomever and whatever is in sight when his demands to be gratified pronto are denied.

Freud described the infant as "His Majesty, the Prince" (Freud, 1914). The baby, by definition, is an extremely narcissistic person who has strong omnipotent wishes. If the parents of the child do not help him tame these wishes, as an adult he will have the tendency to demand that the spouse or lover treat him like royalty.

When the normally developing child begins to realize that he is not omnipotent and cannot control his universe, he tends to project his desires onto his parents and believe that they have the power to do almost anything. Parents who are afraid to say "no" and unable to provide limits and restrictions encourage the child's belief that they are omnipotent, omniscient gods. This conviction can persist to adulthood, so that the sexual partner is believed to be an all-powerful god. When the adult ascribes unrealistic power to his spouse, he begins to feel powerless himself, is easily intimidated, often feels hurt and criticized, and is baffled when his spouse is unable or unwilling to gratify his every whim and ease every frustration.

If the adult invests his sexual partner with omnipotence, emotional or physical distance from the partner induces the same kinds of emotional responses that are observed in a baby when separation occurs. Psychologist John Bowlby (1973) has described the sequence of protest-despair-detachment when a child is threatened with loss of his mother or in fact loses her. Many adults demonstrate the same emotional reactions when confronted with the possible loss of their spouses or lovers, even if the loss is temporary. It has often been observed that when adults think their marriages or love relationships are about to break up they react with loss of appetite, insomnia, depression, and desolation.

Stages of Growth During the Oral Phase

The infant progresses through three predictable phases in the first year of life: the autistic, symbiotic, and separation-individuation stages. If biological development and maternal care are adequate, the infant moves from primary narcissism through need-gratification to "object constancy" (Hartmann, 1958). In the autistic stage, which occurs in the first few weeks of life, there is no perceptual differentiation of the mother from the self and sensory awareness is focused primarily on the body. The infant does not distinguish the initial ministrations by his mother from his own tension-reduction efforts such as coughing and sneezing.

In the symbiotic stage the foundation for an individual's ability to trust others is laid down. This requires a mother who is sufficiently responsive to the signals sent out by the infant. As a result of reliable gratification, images of the "good" mother are formed which, in turn, form the foundation for basic trust (Erikson, 1950).

Progression to the third stage, separation-individuation (Mahler, Pine, and Bergman, 1975), also depends on the nature of the mother-child relationship. If sufficient closeness has evolved, a gradual process takes place whereby the infant disengages from the mother and establishes his own individuality and autonomy.

The degree of success in accomplishing these developmental tasks has major implications for problems posed in marriage. For example, a constant need for reassurance through frequent contacts with the spouse may result from an incomplete resolution of symbiotic ties. An individual whose mother discouraged and disapproved of disengagement because she perceived it as rejection may have difficulty in asserting his individuality in marriage, fearing that emotional separation may bring loss of love. The individual may believe that love and approval can be achieved only by denying his own needs and subjugating himself to others (Ables, 1977).

When the child's symbiotic wishes are prematurely frustrated, he often erects defenses against them. A need to renounce one's symbiotic wishes often precipitates the desire to initiate an extramarital affair because the constant separations inherent in an affair do not activate the individual's anxiety over his dependency wishes. This will be discussed further in chapter 4.

In marriage, couples must constantly deal with aspects of coming together and being apart, which involve their identity, autonomy, interdependence, separation, and mutuality; the interplay of these variables can be seen in the sexual act. Coming together sexually should provide gratification, but for individuals who have not successfully separated from the mother, the sexual union may provoke anxiety and fear of being consumed by or merging with the other (Ables, 1977; Blanck and Blanck, 1968).

Some authors have contended that the child's deep and early attachment to the mother is one important reason that monogamy has existed as an ideal in men's minds (Spotnitz and Freeman 1964). According to Melanie Klein (1957), when a child experiences his mother as cruel and unloving, he is likely to have a dual image of "the good mother" and "the bad mother," which may persist throughout life.

If a mother has been cruel and unloving her son is likely to reject monogamy when he grows up. If she was the "bad" mother one moment, the "good" mother the next, he may refuse to settle for one woman, for his childish fantasy is that two women took care of him, one "bad," the other "good," and he will seek to find another two, then another two. [Spotnitz and Freeman 1964, p. 31].

What Spotnitz and Freeman have said of the boy is also true for the girl, because all love relationships for both sexes recapitulate the early mother-infant interaction to some extent. The oral phase establishes a lasting association between affection, the need for others, and oral activity. If the child has received consistent, warm, and empathetic mothering, as an adult he will be more inclined to trust himself and his partner in a loving relationship (Erikson, 1950). However, if the oral period has been characterized by ambivalent and inconsistent mothering and abrupt weaning, the adult will be most suspicious of his sexual partner, feel strong hostility toward him or her, and anticipate rejection. When an individual can trust himself and his world, he is less inclined to be narcissistic and omnipotent in a love relationship and therefore his partner will be able to appreciate him more.

A consistent and mutually gratifying mother-infant relationship leads the child to seek out emotional attachments to people for the rest of his life. If his first emotional attachment has been emotionally gratifying, he will have resolved the first psychosocial task and thus will later be able to enjoy mutually gratifying love relationships.

THE ANAL STAGE

If the infant has received adequate emotional and physical gratification in the nurturing process of his first year and if he has been appropriately weaned, he is ready during his second year of life to leave one level of adjustment and explore a higher one. This does not imply that the activities of the oral period have ceased; in fact, the activities and needs of the oral period continue in some form as long as life lasts (English and Pearson, 1945). Maturation does not mean an abandonment of satisfactions from particular zones of the body; rather, it implies that the individual is able to derive satisfactions from a wider and more diverse range of intra- and interpersonal experiences.

If tasks at higher levels of maturation activate anxiety, the child or adult will return to less mature satisfactions. When this phenomenon occurs, we speak of *regression*. For example, the child who cannot cope with the demands of toilet-training might regress to orality by compulsively sucking his thumb to bind his anxiety. The adult who cannot deal with the rigors of a work situation might regress by habitually drinking alcohol.

Psychoanalytic theory postualtes that the psychic structure of every human being includes what Freud called the *id*. The id represents the instinctual forces of libido and aggression which are always clamoring for gratification. The infant, according to Freud, is dominated by the pleasure principle, as opposed to the reality principle, and therefore is virtually "all id" (Freud, 1932). The parents' job is to help the child, at the appropriate point in his maturational timetable, to renounce certain id pleasures, take on some frustration, and grow.

The dilemma faced by the child in his first learning situations, which is a forerunner of future learning situations, is that on the one hand he wants to express his primitive wishes—to cry when he wishes to cry, kick when he wishes to kick, soil when he wishes to soil, i.e., stay as he is and remain a baby; on the other hand, there is an impetus to establish his own identity, somewhat separate from mother, and to experience the pleasures that come with mastering some of life's tasks. Furthermore, the child wants the love and approval he receives from his parents when he controls himself; however, he also wishes to retain the pleasures of throwing, kicking, defecating, and urinating at will. The old habits still present a very alluring attraction, yet the child wants to give mother or father the gift of seeing him defecate appropriately in the toilet bowl or hearing him say to himself, "Don't break it!" or "Don't touch!"

It is difficult for the child to mature. The baby who has been "all id" is not always eager to change; he strongly resists growing up—and why shouldn't he? He has been the recipient of bounties for a whole year and then suddenly, during his second year of life, a dramatic change occurs in his environment. Instead of being a receiver, he is asked to be a giver. Instead of being completely irresponsible, he is asked to take on some responsibility. It is understandable that the patient in psychotherapy cannot readily give up some old gratifications no matter how dysfunctional they are.

Conflict and Ambivalence

A great deal of ambivalence is characteristic of the child during the learning and training period of the second year. He is still dependent on his parents for his physical and psychosocial survival but resents them for the control that they must and do place on him. The child often wishes to kill his parents for their impositions and therefore he often feels "bad." It is not uncommon to see a child of 20 months or so slapping himself or herself and saying "bad boy" or "bad girl." The child is beginning to curb his instincts with the help of an internal censor or what Freud called the *superego*. By superego, Freud referred to that part of the psychic structure that contains the internalized voices of the parents, forbidding unacceptable id thoughts and wishes and insisting that the individual obey ethical imperatives. To mediate between the voice of conscience, the superego, and the instinctual demands of the id, Freud formulated the notion of the *ego*—that part of the psychic structure that judges, reasons, defends against anxiety, and relates to the outside world.

The psychic structure is often compared to an automobile, with the id as the engine, the ego as the driver, and the superego as the backseat driver.

The pain emanating from overt control by the parents and his own developing superego induces irritation and aggression in the child. He wants to please his parents and live in peace with them, but he also wants to express his hatred for their impositions and controls. Attempts to control his angry impulses so as to preserve his love relationship with his parents often take the form of games and rituals, such as the familiar chant, "Step on a crack, break your mother's back." The game involves jumping over the seams in a sidewalk, coming as close as possible to the "cracks" without stepping on them. Thus the child expresses his wish to defy mother (at the risk of "breaking her back") and at the same time his ability to control this impulse so as to retain her love.

Toilet Training

Freud referred to the period from the beginning of the second year
of life up to the end of the third year as the anal period (Freud,
1905). It was his contention that the former eroticization of the
mucous membranes of the mouth is displaced to the anal area so
that during this period of psychosexual development the child
becomes interested in his excretory functions.

Learning to meet the environment's demands for cleanliness is
not an easy process. It is very frustrating for the child to learn to
regulate his bowel movements and excrete them in a toilet. Many
parents, failing to understand their child's normal resentment of
the new restrictions they must place on him, attack him for rebelling. Thus power struggles often occur at this time between the
parent, who wants the child to be toilet-trained, and the child, who
wants freedom of expression. The child withholds from the parent
what the parent wants; he rebels against the pressure to do his "duty."

The power struggles that characterize many marriages derive in
large part from unresolved difficulties in the anal period. Many a
spouse experiences giving love or pleasing the partner as "doing
one's duty," feels humiliated by it, and, like the child who resents
feeling subordinate to a seemingly tyrannical parent, wishes to
defy and rebel. It is such power struggles between marital partners
that often precipitate extramarital affairs (see chapter 5).

If a child has been toilet-trained prematurely or too harshly, one
can probably assume that his parents handled other learning situations in much the same way. Usually this kind of parental treatment results in the development of a demanding and punitive
superego; the child feels that he must perform regardless of what
his inclinations and whims are at the moment. As an adult this
individual feels an enormous obligation to please the spouse but
unconsciously resents it. The resentment is strong because the individual is not spontaneously loving the spouse but is angrily "doing his duty" for fear of reprisals if he does not comply.

In sharp contrast to the child who has been harshly and
prematurely trained is the one who has been indulged and not expected to master the tensions of toilet training and other learning
situations. As an adult he "shits all over others" and rarely is

mature enough to cooperate with a spouse. He expects the partner to cater to him and submit to his narcissistic wishes. In sex he finds it difficult to empathize with the partner and does little or nothing to bring the partner pleasure. Sex is all for him; in his mind the partner, like the parent of the past, has no needs of her own except the obligation to minister to him. If the spouse does not meet his exact expectations he may seek an extramarital partner who will. Just as the child experiences toilet training and other demands placed on him as threats to his freedom and libidinal pleasure, many individuals who have failed to learn that being and feeling frustrated are facts of life experience marriage as a threat to their freedom. They perceive the spouse not as an enricher and a stimulator but as one who curbs their instinctual lives.

Many adults have a distorted view of sex, as if they were submitting to the demands of an arbitrary parent. To them sexual relations are not occasions for mutual pleasure but are seen as "putting out" and being exploited. Like the child who refuses to defecate or urinate in the toilet because, in his mind, "it's all for my parents," such an adult sees "nothing in sex for me." Sexual intercourse, if it is to be culminated successfully, requires the individual to discharge his sexual tensions in an orgasm. Adults who have not resolved conflicts of the anal period feel that sex is "dirty," like urine or feces. It is as if they are urinating or defecating on or in their partner or as if their partner is defecating or urinating in or on them.

Many sexual problems of adults are related to unresolved problems of toilet training. Not only are the organs of excretion the same or close to the sexual organs, but many people are brought up with the idea that sex is a form of evacuation. Many young children who have observed the primal scene describe it as "Father pissed in Mother's peepee place!" As adults, such individuals may be unable to separate the feelings of shame and guilt connected with the toilet from the sex act.

Because bowel and urine training is the first strong demand for control which the parents place on the child, conflicts are bound to ensue. The outcome of these conflicts will determine whether the individual will be cooperative with the spouse and others or obstinate, defiant, and rebellious.

Erikson (1950) describes the conflict of the second and third years of life as one of autonomy versus shame and doubt. If the anal period has not been too conflictful, the individual will be able to give and take in a love relationship. He will not be troubled by self-doubt and guilt and therefore will not feel revengeful, spiteful, or expoited.

THE PHALLIC-OEDIPAL STAGE

As the child gradually resolves the conflict between the urge to express his instinctual wishes and the desire to maintain the security of his relationship with his parents by conforming to some of their demands, he becomes less narcissistic. At about the age of three, the youngster should begin to give love as well as receive it. While at first the child loves both parents indiscriminately, between the ages of three and six the child turns his affection with greater intensity to the parent of the opposite sex (Freud, 1905).

The erotically tinged relationship that the child fantasizes and aspires to have with the parent of the opposite sex is known as the Oedipus complex, a name derived from a Greek myth concerning Oedipus, the son of Laius, King of Thebes. When it was prophesied that the boy would grow up to kill his father, to avert the tragedy, Laius gave him to a shepherd with instructions to leave the boy on a mountain to die. Instead, the child was permitted to grow to manhood. He eventually met his father and, unaware of his identity, slew him. Oedipus then returned to his birthplace and, in return for solving a riddle, was given the queen, Jocasta, to be his wife. When he finally learned that his wife was his mother, in his guilt he tore out his eyes and was later completely destroyed by the avenging deities. The theme of incest, guilt, and punishment has been associated with the name "Oedipus" for some time.

Although there is ongoing debate as to whether the oedipal conflict is a biological phenomenon or evolves because of familial and social arrangements, the evidence seems clear that it is found in all human beings and in all cultures. The anthropologist Malinowski, who studied familial patterns in several cultures, concluded:

By my analysis, I have established that Freud's theories not only roughly correspond to human psychology, but that they follow closely the modifications in human nature brought about by various constitutions of society. [1923, p. 431]

Inasmuch as the nuclear family is close to a universal phenomenon (Murdock, 1949a), the sexual partner who seems to be the most accessible is the parent of the opposite sex. Against such a choice the taboo of incest has been set up by all known societies.

The Oedipal Conflict in the Boy

From birth the boy has been primarily dependent on his mother for comfort and security. While the object of love, his mother, does not change during the oedipal period, the nature of his relationship to her does. The boy continues to value his mother as a source of security, but he now begins to feel wishes toward her of a more romantic and sexual nature. In much the same way that he notices his father loving his mother, the boy between three and six years of age wants to be his mother's lover. As he competes with his father, the father becomes a dangerous rival for the mother's affections. The boy fears his father's disapproval, anger, and punishment because of his competitive fantasies toward him and also he usually feels guilty about his sexual wishes directed toward his mother.

The boy fears castration by the father because of his wish to supplant him and this fear becomes reinforced when he notices the absence of a penis in his mother, sister, or girl friends. Often the boy reasons that these females have been castrated and that the same catastrophe can befall him. Just as the mythical Oedipus lost his eyes as punishment for his sexual and competitive wishes and actions, so the oedipal boy reasons, "An eye for an eye, a tooth for a tooth." The so-called talion principle is revealed in the nightmares of children and adults who have strong guilt feelings about their oedipal wishes.

Retaliation for his hostile feelings is only one part of the oedipal conflict that creates anxiety for the boy. Because the boy needs and loves his father, he often feels like a "bad boy" for wishing to displace him. This is why Freud spoke of an *inverted Oedipus complex* as part of the maturational process (Freud, 1905). Inasmuch as the boy fears his father's retaliation and concomitantly loves him, he submits to father for a while and psychologically imagines himself as father's lover. He becomes ingratiatory and compliant with him. Unless he is helped to feel less guilt and less fear of punishment for his oedipal wishes, he can remain fixated in this position and may later become a latent or overt homosexual.

A common means of handling the oedipal conflict is by repressing hostile wishes and displacing them to other objects such as non-parental figures or animals. This is what usually occurs in the phobias of children between the ages of three to six. They fear attack not by the parent but by a horse or a burglar. In this way they preserve the love relationship with the parent of the same sex by taking the oedipal battle elsewhere. This was clearly demonstrated in Freud's famous case of a five-year-old boy, Little Hans (1909). Hans had strong wishes to "penetrate his mother with his 'widdler' and get rid of his father." Because Hans feared retaliation from his father, he displaced the conflict onto a big, naked, and aggressive horse. Instead of fearing father's retaliation, Hans worried that the horse would trample all over him. He could not leave his home because he was emotionally convinced that he would be hurt by a horse if he went outside to play. He received "secondary gain" from his neurosis by staying at home and conversing with mother while father was at work.

Contributing further to the boy's oedipal conflict is his small size compared to his father's. Father is such a big and tall adversary; consequently, the boy begins to wonder whether the battle is really worth it. Added to these doubts is the fact that the mother usually is not seduced by her son's amorous advances and does not move away from father. After a while, the boy feels like a loser and does not wish to chance defeat any further. Feeling inadequate in the face of a very tough battle, many boys compensate by trying to exhibit their toughness through the use of toy guns and other phallic symbols or by playing at being "Superman" or "Batman." Thus they fantasize themselves as phallic strong men.

The most common and the healthiest resolution of the Oedipus conflict for the boy is to identify with the father, incorporate his values, and look forward to marrying a girl "just like the girl that married dear old Dad." In introjecting father's values, identifying with his standards, and curbing his oedipal wishes, the boy strengthens his developing superego. By identifying with his father and renouncing his mother as a lover, the boy can escape from the intensity of relationships created by the domestic triangle.

Many men experience marital problems due to unresolved oedipal conflicts. Because they often fantasize the wife as the incestuous mother, sex becomes forbidden, and impotence can be the result. A man may experience getting married as a hostile triumph over his father and unconsciously provoke punishment for himself. He may make his wife his punitive superego and feel that she will punish him for libidinal pleasure. Or he may renounce his wife as he renounced his mother during the stressful oedipal period of his boyhood, form an inverted Oedipus complex, and go out with "the boys" and join them in blasting their wives. These residues of an unresolved oedipal conflict can also give rise to extramarital affairs which can dilute oedipal anxiety and offer some libidinal pleasure. (See chapters 6, 7, and 8.)

Oedipal Conflict and Penis Envy in Girls

Although there are many similarities in the oedipal conflicts that boys and girls experience, there are differences as well. The girl's oedipal conflict is usually more difficult for her than the boy's is for him. In contrast to the boy, who continues to rely on his mother as a source of love and security, the girl, in directing her libido toward her father, becomes a rival with the parent who has been her main emotional provider, her mother. Inasmuch as the dependency gratification coming from the mother has usually been so great, the girl is caught in a powerful dilemma—whether to give up the dependence on her mother which has been so gratifying all her life or pursue her father and risk the disruption of a positive relationship with her mother.

Unresolved oedipal conflicts in a woman create conflicts in marriage. If the woman unconsciously is still seeking father, she may experience sex and intimacy as incestuous and forbidden. She may repudiate her husband for not being her unconscious ideal, i.e., her fantasized father. The woman, like the oedipal man, may experience marriage and motherhood as an oedipal victory, feel guilty about her fantasized triumph, and regress to an inverted Oedipus complex, spending her time and energy with women and enjoying being derogatory toward her husband and other men.

As we discussed earlier, all children have omnipotent fantasies and want what they want when they want it. Therefore, all boys fantasize having the privileges and pleasures of women. They want babies, breasts, vaginas, etc. Similarly, when the girl turns toward father, she has fantasies of wanting a penis. It is a part of father, whom she treasures, and also, like all children, she wants to own everything in sight, particularly if it belongs to somebody else.

Although Freud believed that penis envy was a biological phenomenon, many contemporary psychoanalysts believe that it is a byproduct of culture, exacerbated by a male-dominated society. Some feminists argue that girls (and women) covet a penis because they want the special status and privileges that its possessors seem to enjoy.

Whatever its source, in adulthood, penis envy is normally buried in the unconscious and becomes manifest only through its derivatives—for example, in low self-esteem, lack of self-assertiveness, or through reaction formation, a defense mechanism which operates by accentuating the qualities that are the very reverse of low self-esteem and lack of competitiveness. In marriage, a woman with unresolved problems of penis envy may take a very subordinate role with her husband or, through reaction formation, constantly deride him (Marasse and Hart, 1975).

In child rearing, if the parent of the same sex is too permissive and is intimidated by the child's competitiveness and hostility, the youngster either becomes overwhelmed by impulses that are insufficiently controlled or else unrealistically feels that he is entitled to everything he wants in relationships with the opposite sex. If as a child he was overwhelmed by his impulses and has never resolved this distortion, as an adult the individual feels that he is constantly overwhelming the spouse and feels uncomfortable next to the marital partner. If he was never frustrated as a child, e.g., never appropriately toilet trained, he will demand that the spouse take limited or no interest in others because that is just the way life should be.

Punitive responses by parents to oedipal competition can stimulate the development of a harsh superego and lay the groundwork for sexual inhibitions. The child feels that his sexual wishes are "bad" and does not chance much intimacy with the opposite sex.

According to Erikson (1950), the maturational dilemma to be resolved in the oedipal period is taking initiative versus feeling guilt. The child who feels guilty about his sexual fantasies and activities may become docile and passive. However, if the phallic-oedipal period has been essentially conflict-free, the maturing child will enrich his capacity to achieve and to love—he will be able to form an enjoyable, trusting attachment as a carryover from the oral stage, to be cooperative and yet feel autonomous because the anal stage was successful, and to admire his loved one and take initiative with him or her, without feelings of guilt.

THE LATENCY STAGE

If the child has resolved most of his oedipal conflicts, he is able to move from the close and intense tie to his family toward the social world of his peers for many of his emotional investments and outlets. While he cannot feel safe and secure in the school, neighborhood, club, or gang without the continued protection and guidance of his parents, the child between ages six and ten should gradually be able to become part of a group. Feeling some security in his own identity as well as reinforcement from his parents, the child should be more and more capable of foregoing childish impulses, sensing the needs of others, and giving to them (Josselyn, 1948).

Freud termed the period from six to ten "the latency period" because the force of the child's instinctual impulses is temporarily subdued. The child during this time, impelled by the threat of castration or the anguish of penis envy, is attempting to renounce erotic attachment to the parent of the opposite sex and also to reduce competition with the parent of the same sex (Freud, 1905). The child diverts his libidinal energies into socially acceptable channels such as Boy Scouts and Girls Scouts, clubs, gangs, and other peer group activities. The activities chosen are consistent with the standards of his emerging superego, which is being more and more consolidated by the internalization of parental values and prohibitions. He thus achieves discharge of his id desires by way of a process called sublimation, i.e., gratifying id wishes through socially acceptable channels.

The degree of withdrawal from sexual preoccupation during the latency stage depends on the sexual climate of the particular culture in which the child is being socialized. Consequently, the degree of sexual activity in latency varies widely (Roheim, 1932).

As the child's superego is strengthened and his Oedipus complex is outgrown, early in the latency period (age six or seven) he has his first love affair with a youngster of the opposite sex. It seems that few, if any, human beings can give up an important love object except by substitution of another. From mother the child moves to father. From father the child moves on to another child, with whom he forms a love relationship that is similar to the love relationship of his parents, as he perceives it. A child who does not experience this first love affair with a peer has not succeeded in liberating himself from his parents, with dire consequences for later personality formation (Fine, 1975).

During the latter half of the latency period (eight to ten years of age), most boys and girls confine themselves to same-sex groups and often express much contempt and resentment toward members of the other group (English and Pearson, 1945). The cruelty and anger of this battle of the sexes make the observer wonder if the participants are not protesting too much.

Much of the sexual antagonism and aggression of this period can be better understood if we consider where the latency child is maturationally. In his attempts to renounce the oedipal situation, the child often uses defenses like reaction formation. Rather than acknowledge that he feels sexually inadequate, rather than admit his attraction to members of the opposite sex, which might reactivate the power of sexual impulses, the child proclaims to his sexual counterpart, "I don't love you, I hate you!"

As society places further demands and controls on the child, as he is required to renounce the expression of more sexual and aggressive drives, the child's superego manifests itself in the emphasis on "right" and "wrong" and fair play. In the games that latency-age children play, their concern about rules and regulations becomes quite intense. Because they are tempted to revert to the old days and attempt to satisfy their wishes at any cost—i.e., to violate the rules of the game—latency-age children are quick to tattle or "squeal" on the child who is doing the very thing that they wish to do but find forbidden. The child who regresses and violates rules is frequently labelled a cheater and scapegoated by his peers.

When the child experiences difficulty emancipating himself from his parents, this separation anxiety often is recapitulated in his interpersonal relationships as an adult. Thus he clings to his spouse and feels very jealous of her other relationships or activities.

When oedipal anxieties are intense and sexual feelings are experienced as forbidden, the latency child often avoids close, one-to-one relationships. He may utilize the gang or community group as protection. If his anxiety is not resolved, as an adult he will frequently want to escape from the intimate marital relationship (if he marries at all) and will become active in political and social clubs or professional organizations. He can permit himself pleasure and excitement in group activity, which seems safer than the man-woman interaction that conjures up oedipal associations. Frequently, married couples who are involved in switching and swinging are individuals who cannot tolerate the anxiety they feel in a one-to-one relationship with its oedipal overtones and dissipate it through group sex.

Marriage, like the latency period, requires the individual to take on many new responsibilities. Just as the six-year-old child moves from the rather free life of prelatency and is required to adapt to a host of new rules and regulations in school, likewise, marriage places many curbs on the partners' lives. The child who enters school, like the adult who enters marriage, has to share more than he did before rather than be concerned almost exclusively with his own interests. Like marriage, school and club affiliation in latency requires frustration tolerance, mutuality, compromise, negotiation, and problem solving. Many adults handle their marital frustrations in the same way that the latency child deals with his now unacceptable impulses—by "squealing" on another who is doing the very thing he wishes to do but finds forbidden. Thus many husbands and wives enjoy collecting injustices and relish pointing out that their partners are "unfair," "not playing the game" or doing their share. A favorite preoccupation of some married individuals is to find out who is "the cheater" among them and gossip about him or her. This achieves the same psychological purpose for adults as similar activity does for latency children. Discussion of somebody else's sexual or aggressive activity is stimulating for the discussants and at the same time, because someone else is the culprit, the conscience or superego is placated.

The maturational task of the latency period is to resolve the conflict between "industry" and "inferiority" (Erikson, 1950). The adult who has resolved the tasks of this state feels relatively sure of his internal resources. Feeling confident and not inferior, he is freer to love.

ADOLESCENCE

After a period of relative quiescence, the child moves into puberty and adolescence. Puberty refers to the glandular changes that take place from about age 11 or 12 to about age 15. Adolescence connotes a phase of development beginning approximately at the time puberty commences and lasting until age 18 or 19. Adolescence, although a social and cultural construct in part, is always characterized by psychological changes in mood, role, peer activity, and modified relationships with parents and other significant adults.

Anatomical, physiological, emotional, intellectual, and social factors combine to make adolescence a turbulent and unstable stage of development. As the hormonal changes define the onset of puberty, the adolescent storm begins. Sexual and aggressive drives express themselves with greater intensity. The teenager wants to be treated like an independent adult in many ways, yet with so many changes occurring, he feels a strong yearning for parental direction. Consequently, the teenager is a remarkably ambivalent person, vascillating in mood with frequent rebellious tirades, impulsivity, and unpredictability.

Adolescents are usually quite egoistic, and yet at no time in later life are they capable of so much altruism and devotion. They form the most passionate love relations only to break them off as abruptly as they began them. While they can throw themselves enthusiastically into the life of the community, they also have an overpowering longing for solitude. They can oscillate between blind submission to some self-chosen leader and defiant rebellion against any and every authority (A. Freud, 1937).

Very few teenagers consciously realize what makes their burgeoning sexuality so anxiety-provoking. Their strong yearnings to hug, touch, and explore friends' bodies and their own conjure up memories of where and when these activities largely took place for the first 12 or 13 years of life—with mother and father, grand-parents, uncles, aunts, and siblings. Much of the young person's self-consciousness surrounding bodily contact stems from the teenager's concern about whether he or she is a young child again. Particularly among boys, verbal and physical expressions of affec-tion are often considered signs of weakness or unmasculine behavior. One of the most painful conflicts for many adolescents is the dilemma between wanting to give and receive warmth and have emotional contact with another person, on one hand, and the need to repudiate this wish, on the other, because emotional and physical closeness is frequently experienced as childlike depen-dency and this must be derogated (Blos, 1953).

Anyone who has lived or worked with teenagers has noticed their struggles on all levels of development. Oral conflicts appear in the tendency to hoard food or abstain from it, in peculiar preferences and food mixtures. Anal-sadistic activities are fre-quently observed in the use of "foul" language and the disregard of, or excessive preoccupation with, clothes and cleanliness. Phallic and oedipal interests are embodied in "crushes" on heroes of film and television (Strean, 1970).

The intensification of the sexual urges during adolescence threatens the barriers previously established against the incestuous impulses of the oedipal period. Many young people "fall in love" with a movie hero or heroine, a teacher, or a sports idol. Sexual impulses receive some gratification in fantasy, but because the beloved is beyond reach, the adolescent does not have to worry about meeting the demands of a real and intimate relationship. A crush on a distant object such as a movie star provides some outlet for emotional tension while protecting the young person from hav-ing to confront the source of his fantasy (Josselyn, 1948; English & Pearson, 1945).

During adolescence, there is a resurgence of oedipal fantasies, and the young person again feels rivalrous with the parent of the same sex. This usually manifests itself not only in the direct rela-tionship with the parent but also with other figures of authority and with peers. Frequently, the adolescent attempts to minimize the importance of the parent of the opposite sex by deriding and deprecating him or her. By defending himself in this way, he can deny the dangers of competing with the parent of the same sex and other adults.

Just as the oedipal youngster often finds his rivalry with the parent of the same sex too intense and defends himself by means of an inverted Oedipus complex, a transient phase of homosexuality during adolescence can frequently be noticed. Friendship frequently disguises the homosexual element, but it is not uncommon for youths between 12 and 15 to "experiment" sexually with each other. Often, the inverted oedipal defense takes the form of a real attachment to an older person of the same sex, such as a teacher. Many of these relationships are free from any overt sexual response, and the love is a desexualized one. However, sometimes the dependency wishes fuse with the sexual ones, become eroticized, and express themselves in overt homosexual activity.

Adolescent Rebellion

Because of the biological urge to establish himself sexually and the wish to free himself of childish feelings activated by instinctual sensations, the teenager has a strong desire to emancipate himself from subjection to his childhood affectional ties, and from the domination and protection of his parents. Because in his mind to agree with his parents signifies submitting to a childhood status, he is frequently argumentative. Yet the adolescent simultaneously fears complete independence with all of the attendant tasks that are assigned to an adult. Hence, the adolescent by definition is very ambivalent and frequently vascillates back and forth on decisions and opinions, reflecting his basic indecision about dependence and independence (Cameron, 1963).

In his rebellion the young person may appear to his parents as ungrateful, callous, and senseless; to himself his behavior seems justified even though he may at times regret it. Although eventual emancipation and independence are necessary in our culture, the fantasies attached to them, which exist in both parents and offspring—such as fear of permanent abandonment and loss of love—complicate the maturation process. This is why some adolescents never really succeed in emancipating themselves and remain very much attached to their parents and other parental figures and why others are chronically rebelling without recognizing against whom or what they are rebelling.

Inasmuch as adolescence recapitulates all of the previous stages of psychosexual growth, if the young person does not resolve the conflicts and face the tasks of this period, he will find it difficult to function in a marriage. He will feel rebellious when he is asked to cooperate; he will assume a pseudo-independent facade to deny his dependency, and he will be unable to cope with a sexual partner if he has not resolved oedipal rivalries and incestuous wishes. As Erikson has pointed out, the man or woman who has not mastered the tasks of "identity versus identity diffusion" and "intimacy versus isolation" will not be able to enjoy himself or herself in marriage.

MATURE LOVE AND SEXUALITY

By the time an individual has reached the age of 18 or 19 he should be able to enjoy a mutually gratifying relationship with a member of the opposite sex. This, as mentioned above, rests on the satisfactory resolution of the earlier stages. A period of free sexual experimentation in adolescence is optimal for the development of the individual. The anthropological evidence is overwhelming that this makes for healthy growth (Fine, 1975).

The period of sexual experimentation during adolescence should be followed by an intimate relationship with one person of the opposite sex. This intimacy should include a mutual interchange of feelings, hopes, attitudes, memories, and everything else that makes a relationship worthwhile. Here, for the first time, the person can feel that he is an adult (Erikson, 1950; Fine, 1975).

In any sexual relationship, the history of individual psychosexual development is recapitulated in condensed form. Each person follows an inner script, and that is why handbooks on sexual technique have only limited value. If the individual, as a child, has successfully progressed through the various psychosexual stages, he will be able to form an attachment and trust himself and his partner in it. The mature person will want to cooperate with his partner and feel autonomous as he does so. He will admire his sexual partner without feeling any loss of self-esteem. He can initiate love making without feeling uncomfortable because he has a sense of identity. The mature person can allow passivity in himself without feeling threatened. The mature person enjoys intimacy and devotion without feeling self-sacrificial about it. He enjoys giving and receiving because symbiotic wishes, hostilities, and destructive competition are all at a minimum (Fine, 1975; Erikson, 1950).

Only a minority of individuals can engage in a devoted, intimate sexual relationship where they freely admire the loved one and where the attachment is not threatening. Rather, as every psychoanalyst has observed, love can be and is expressed in a variety of neurotic ways. Most of these neurotic forms become manifest in unhappy marriages (Fine, 1975).

IMMATURE FORMS OF LOVE: A SUMMARY

Love as Dependency
Here, the individual is consistently submissive to the loved one, saying overtly or by implication, "I will do anything for you; just love me in return." There is a strong quest for a symbiotic relationship reminiscent of the oral period and the individual feels very unsure of himself when the loved one is not reassuring him. Frequently, the dependent lover or spouse becomes quite depressed because the merger he fantasizes is never attainable. Feeling that the symbiosis would be available if he tried harder, the dependent individual becomes more and more masochistic and self-sacrificing. Unconsciously, the very dependent lover or spouse does not trust himself or his partner and is incapable of being autonomous, independent, and separate. Out of anger and a low sense of self-esteem, he often seeks an extramarital partner to bolster him (see chapter 4).

Sadistic Love
Sadism can be expressed in oral, anal, and oedipal terms. Oral sadism derives from a chaotic mother-infant relationship where the frustrated child has strong feelings of rage, contempt, and murder toward his ungiving mother. In a marriage or love relationship, the spouse is chosen so that she can become an object of abuse—abuse that the person felt he could not direct at his mother because as a child he needed her and could not risk alienating her.

Anal sadism is expressed in those many marriages and love relationships that are characterized by pervasive friction and one-upmanship fracases. Cooperating with the loved one is experienced as a form of humiliating submission. Consequently, the sadistic person is forever trying to get his partner to suffer, feel weak, and, in effect, become the powerless child that the sadistic person felt *he* was as a child.

Another reason the sexual partner is debased emanates from the oedipal conflict. Children frequently find it hard to believe that their parents willingly engaged in sex; hence, they split people into the asexual and the sexual—the loved mother (father), who is chaste, and the hated mother (father), who is sexually promiscuous (Klein, 1957). As an adult, such a child may need to perceive his spouse as asexual and hence deserving, while the extramarital partner is experienced as a sexual object. If the spouse manifests sexual interest or excitment, he or she is debased and derogated.

Love as a Rescue Fantasy

In Freud's *Contributions to the Psychology of Love* (1910a) he describes a form of love that is usually found among men but is seen in women as well. The man wishes to rescue the woman from her unhappy lot. Hence, he chooses a woman who is in fact unhappy. This form of neurotic choice derives from the boy's perception of his mother as an unhappy victim of father's brutality—i.e., she was forced to have sex with him.

When a woman (or man) enters marriage in an unhappy state, the unhappiness will become manifest in the marriage. The rescuer begins to regret his sacrifices, and his negative attitude toward sexuality asserts itself in the marital encounter.

Love for the virgin, while buttressed by cultural mandates, derives from an oedipal conflict where the boy or girl (more often the boy) splits his internal image of the mother into the "loved mother" and the "hated mother" and can only love a nonsexual mother. This neurotic anxiety extends to only loving a virgin, but in some cases people forbid themselves to love somebody who has been previously married.

Homosexuality and Compulsive Sex

Although homosexuality is not regarded as a neurotic problem by the American Psychiatric Association, Freudian psychoanalysts consider it a form of neurosis because the individual is avoiding the anxiety he or she feels when near the opposite sex and is compelled to seek out partners of the same sex.

The individual who engages in obsessive sexual activity with the opposite sex but without much pleasure is attempting to prove, to himself or others, that he is not homosexual. Through his active engagement in compulsive sexual activity, the person is negating and denying his homosexual fantasies.

Regardless of frequency, if it is pleasurable, sexual activity should not be regarded as Don Juanism or nymphomania.

Love for the Unattainable Object

Many individuals still seek the perfect father or mother. The more unattainable the love object, the more lovable he seems. This neurotic perspective usually evolves from an unresolved oedipal conflict in which the unattainable object is a substitute for the fantasized mother or father of the past. As soon as the individual succeeds in attaining the love object, it loses its fascination, and a deep disillusionment sets in (Freud, 1910b).

All of these immature forms of love of course make for unhappy marriages. In the following chapters we shall examine various forms of immature marital relationships and demonstrate how the extramarital relationship serves as a defense to protect the individual from unrecognized anxiety in his or her marriage.

Chapter 3

Great Expectations: On Choosing A Mate

Many centuries ago the Greek poet Homer wrote that "the best thing in the world [is] a strong house held in serenity when man and wife agree. Woe to their enemies, joy to their friends." Although a fulfilling marriage may be a rarity, the desire for one persists, as is evident from the popularity of mass entertainment based on idealized family life, such as "The Waltons."

Perhaps one of the reasons that a harmonious marriage is unusual in our society is that there is a lack of understanding of why mates select each other. Researchers on marital choice generally agree regarding the influence of such variables as age, socioeconomic status, geographic propinquity, race, previous marital status, and educational level. If two people are similar in these respects they are more likely to marry and to have a successful marriage than if there are wide differences between them. Researchers have also demonstrated that these variables are not independent of each other but tend to interact; that is, the likelihood that two people will marry each other and be happy together increases when they have similarities on several of these variables (Murstein, 1976).

The psychological factors involved in choosing a mate are more difficult to describe than these social variables because they are subtle and unconscious. Although most of us like to conceive of marriage as a result of free, rational choice, writers who have investigated the phenomenon note the strong unconscious determinants in the decision (Blanck and Blanck, 1968; Eisenstein, 1956; Bolton, 1961). According to psychoanalytic theory, mate choice is never an accident; the prospective marital partners are always influenced by unconscious and frequently irrational motives. Psychoanalysts contend that, when marriages founder, it is usually not because the couple has incompatible interests but because they are ignorant of the unconscious purposes that determined their respective choices.

The psychoanalyst Carl Jung believed that the search for a mate was completely unconscious: "You see that girl. . . . and instantly you get the seizure; you are caught. And afterward you may discover that it was a mistake" (Evans, 1964). Similarly, the philosopher, George Santayana, described the process of falling in love and wanting to marry as "that deep and dumb instinctive affinity." The ancient Romans described "falling in love" as a form of madness: *Amare et sapere vis deis conceditar* ("the ability to keep one's wits when in love is not granted even to the gods").

Love in the words of Romeo is "A madness most discreet,/A choking gall, and a preserving sweet." The "madness most discreet" is a state of passionate love that psychoanalysts have compared to a psychosis where reality is obliterated as the lover lives in a dream world. "Choking gall" describes the intense agony the lover feels when he or she is rejected. Yet, love is a "preserving sweet" in that the feelings between lovers sustain and nurture them (Spotnitz & Freeman, 1964).

MARITAL CHOICE AND COMPLEMENTARITY

In examining the psychological factors involved in marital choice, Freud (1914) referred to "the romantic ideal" which we discussed in chapter 1. He pointed out that no individual is exempt from being influenced by unconscious childish fantasies in mate selection.

Freud contended that there were two types of marital choice. The narcissistic choice is patterned after oneself as object; that is, the person falls in love with someone like himself. Love for a substitute mother is called the anaclitic choice; that is, one loves someone who can be depended upon for nurturance and support. Freud thought that men were more likely to make anaclitic choices whereas women were more inclined to make narcissistic choices. Within each of these types, Freud pointed out that there are several paths to a choice of partner:

1. The narcissistic type may love:
   a. what he is himself—someone whose personality seems to be very similar to his own;
   b. what he was once—someone who reminds him of himself as a child;
   c. what he would like to be;
   d. what once was part of him—someone who reminds him of parents or siblings.
2. The anaclitic type may love:
   a. one who feeds;
   b. one who protects.

In determining mate selection, the complementarity or "fit" of the two individuals is of enormous importance (Lutz, 1964). Psychoanalysts have for some time noted the complementarity of the sadist and the masochist, the dependent alcoholic and the nurturing spouse, and the deceiver married to the naive individual who enjoys, albeit unconsciously, being deceived (Waelder, 1941). Emotional pathology may sometimes be a binding factor if it provides for complementarity in the marital interaction.

Psychoanalysts have been able to determine that, regardless of how much a spouse criticizes a partner's sadism, competitiveness, compulsive sexuality, or alcoholism, unconsciously he admires it and receives vicarious gratification from identifying with the spouse as she rants and raves, is sexually promiscuous, or gets drunk. Psychoanalysts have also observed that though the overt behavior of spouses may differ considerably, the mates frequently share similar unconscious fantasies. In the film The Days of Wine and Roses, although the wife was appalled by the behavior of her alcoholic husband, it turned out that she was addicted to chocolate bars. Like her husband, she had strong oral cravings which were difficult to control. Eventually it became clear that she derived unconscious gratification from watching her husband imbibe.

As the psychoanalyst listens to marital arguments, he learns that the spouses unconsciously share very similar values despite the fact that they overtly disagree with each other. I recall a former analytic patient who became furious when her husband watched wrestling matches on television. She declaimed the viciousness of wrestlers, their barbaric habits, and their lack of humanity. She came a little closer to understanding her unconscious identification with her husband's interest in wrestling when one day, while arguing with him about his "wrestling addiction", she bellowed, "Anybody who watches such a brutal sport ought to be shot!"

That husbands and wives receive vicarious gratification from the very behavior of their spouses that they condemn also becomes apparent when only one member of the marital dyad is in therapy. Although one member of a couple urges the spouse to enter psychotherapy to resolve sexual inhibitions, unassertiveness, a need to nag, etc., when the partner in treatment improves, the one not in treatment frequently becomes very threatened by the partner's changes and then insists that the mate stop seeing the therapist. Usually the spouse who is not in treatment is unaware of the anxiety aroused by the partner's more mature behavior. For example:

Bob Underwood was in analysis because he was sexually impotent. At his first consultation interview he said he was "driving [his] wife crazy" by his inability to satisfy her and feared that she would leave him.

After a few months of treatment Bob became more potent with his wife. One night, after a mutually satisfying sexual experience, Rena turned to Bob and asked, "How come your penis is so much smaller than most guys'?"

Using his wife as a superego, Bob then attacked himself again and told his analyst he was not good enough for Rena. It took many months for Bob to realize that he *wanted* and *needed* a wife who experienced him as weak and that she *wanted* and *needed* to weaken a man.

It often appears uncanny how prospective husbands and wives become sensitized to their mutual fears, wishes, defenses, and history, all of which provide for a complementarity in their marriage.

Although Jack and Barbara Abels had similar educational and social backgrounds and shared many interests and values, there was always a great deal of tension in their interaction. When Barbara desired sexual relations, Jack was usually impotent; when Jack was potent and took some initiative sexually, Barbara resented his "sloppiness and ineptness." She also complained about Jack's "arrogance" and said he constantly "puts me down." Jack complained about Barbara's persistent efforts to "castrate me."

As a youngster, Jack was very much attached to his mother and very competitive with his authoritarian father. He had conscious wishes that his father would die. At the age of 13, Jack's father died of a heart attack, and Jack blamed himself for his death. He became very depressed and withdrew from most people, including his mother.

Barbara, as a child, was her father's favorite and had a strong erotic attachment to him; her relationship with her mother was very ambivalent. She consciously felt that her sexual feelings toward her father upset him and unconsciously experienced his death as punishment for her sexual fantasies.

Because both of the Abels had strong incestuous wishes which induced guilt, they both had to defend themselves against enjoying themselves sexually. Acknowledging their own individual anxiety and guilt was too difficult for them; consequently, they unconsciously chose each other for their sexual incompatability.

One of the major demands of a marriage from a psychoanalytic perspective is coping with one's own and one's mate's unresolved childhood neuroses. Both Barbara and Jack, viewed psychosexually, were frightened children trying to act as mature adults. Although they complained bitterly about each other, unconsciously both wanted an asexual spouse to defend against the anxiety that stemmed from their incestuous wishes.

Needs that are obscure to the young husband and wife often take forms that are clear to their intimate associates. Yet, when friends or relatives point out neurotic patterns to the couple, they frequently resist facing the emotional truth. The title of a Broadway play, borrowed later for a film with a totally different plot and characters, is Lovers and Other Strangers.

Jane Banting was a very intelligent and highly educated woman. Despite her many accomplishments, she had low self-esteem and a poor self-image. She belittled her achievement and felt that if she were a man, she would "be somebody." To compensate for her low self-esteem, she married a well-known athlete who was intellectually limited. Despite his athletic successes, Dick felt very fragile and often referred to himself as a "patsy." He thought Jane's brilliance would present a good front to the world.

It did not take Jane and Dick long to discover that marriage never cures a neurosis. Their needs for reassurance were much too strong for either of them to support the other adequately and both became depressed, irritable, and hostile toward the other. Dick experienced Jane's wish for sex as a demand and frequently became impotent. Jane perceived Dick's reaction as a personal rejection and became angry and more demanding. A vicious and unhappy cycle developed.

Like the Bantings, many individuals consciously seek as a spouse someone who they believe will help them to overcome feelings of low self-worth. Instead of being supported and strengthened by the partner, they frequently find that they themselves are expected to support, parent, and strengthen their spouse. The Bantings expected each other to be omnipotent and perfect, to relieve each other's suffering. Each was always disappointed in the other and their unconscious resentment was expressed in disguised ways— Jane by her demands and Dick by his impotence and withdrawal.

RETURN OF THE NATIVE: LOOKING FOR A PARENT

Many people marry with the unconscious purpose of finding a parent. Thus, the woman may seek an older man or the man may seek an older woman. Sometimes the individual is unconsciously attracted to the fiancé's father or mother even more than to his future spouse. During the courtship, while the marriage is still in the offing, any vague feelings of resentment or discontent are balanced by the reassuring hope that fulfillment merely awaits the wedding bells (Kubie, 1956).

In many societies there is a strong cultural pressure on women to marry older men and on men to marry younger women. This is overwhelmingly the norm in American society. Nevertheless, it is by no means uncommon for a man to experience his much younger wife as a mother figure. Age, as is well known, is only one of many motherly or fatherly characteristics that appeal to prospective marital partners.

Sarah Campbell, 26, had been left fatherless when she was three years old. As an adult she went steady with several men who were much older than she; finally she married a man who was a year older than her father would have been had he lived. In spite of Paul's age, he wanted a mother as much as Sarah wanted a father. Each felt very deprived, and this led them to voice much anger toward each other.

To most psychoanalytically oriented therapists the concept "neurotic choice of mate" (Eidelberg, 1956) connotes a marital selection that interferes with enjoyable interaction so that displeasure exceeds pleasure. When such an error in judgment occurs it can be hypothesized that it was caused by the individual's neurosis. It is then necessary for the therapist and patient to amass the evidence that will establish with relative certainty how the unconscious is interfering with the individual's adaptation.

A neurotic choice of mate may be the result of various unconscious defense mechanisms; thus, defenses may be directed against an awareness of oral, anal, or phallic-oedipal wishes. The man or woman chooses a mate to avoid recognition of the infantile wishes he or she fears—e.g., the wish to merge, to punish and be punished, or to have incestuous gratification. According to psychoanalyst Ludwig Eidelberg,

> . . . whenever a neurotic choice is made, the patient, instead of choosing a person with whom he could be happy, has selected an object he needs in order to avoid recognizing what he is afraid of. The defense mechanisms used to achieve this aim lead to various pathological formations. [1956, p. 58]

As was mentioned earlier, the individual seeking help for marital conflict usually describes himself as a victim of the spouse's problems. Just as the person who suffers from a phobia, compulsion, or psychosomatic problem often does not realize how he is unconsciously arranging for a good part of his plight, so the unhappy husband or wife who feels exploited rarely recognizes his own contribution to the marital woes.

Irving Dodson came for psychotherapy after his third divorce. He had many rationalizations to account for his failures, but it was only through an investigation of his fantasies and history that he was able to ascertain the cause of his troubles. Irving had a strong unconscious wish to be close to a mother figure and transformed any woman to whom he was married into an incestuous object. After a jubilant love affair he would become sexually impotent and guilty and seek out other women. He experienced his extramarital choices as nonincestuous objects, so he could be relatively comfortable with these women. But whenever a woman showed interest in him and wanted him for a husband he first became excited, then anxious; eventually his impotence returned.

CHOOSING A PARTNER TO CONCEAL INADEQUACIES

Just as the choice of a spouse may be influenced by the need to defend against certain instinctual impulses, it can also be made to cover up a weak self-image.

Dorothy Flint, 30, had always been convinced that there was "something wrong" with her. Consequently, she was a very private and secretive person. Although she had been engaged several times to men her family and friends thought were admirable, she had to break up each engagement in order to avoid the exposure of physical intimacy.

Dorothy was finally able to go through with a marriage to a man for whom she cared very little. She reasoned, "Because I don't really love him or value his opinion, what he thinks won't bother me." Furthermore, her fiancé, David, had a job in a small African country and this also protected Dorothy, because she felt she would be hidden away in Africa. Dorothy did not realize how much her marriage to David was motivated by the need to protect herself until David's employer wanted to arrange for him to return to the United States. The idea of living with David in the United States frightened Dorothy so much that she had to break up her marriage. She became acutely anxious, felt very unprotected, and eventually sought treatment.

When a person chooses a marital partner to hide some real or fantasized fault in himself, the utility of this defensive maneuver is soon disrupted. In day-to-day married life, the partner will eventually be resented because the person feels deprived. For example, Dorothy Flint would, no doubt, have come eventually to resent living in Africa for she would have had to give up many pleasures to remain permanently hidden in a foreign country.

The person who chooses a partner to hide some fault in himself also feels deprived in another way. Most people experience their choice of marital partner as a reflection of themselves, and they resent saying to the world, in effect, "This is all I am, and all that I am good for" (Kubie, 1956).

When the source of self-doubt is unconscious, the need to prove one's adequacy becomes insatiable. Therefore, men and women try to cope with lifelong feelings of rejection by getting an unloving spouse to love them. Groucho Marx's statement, "I wouldn't join a club that would have me as a member" reveals how a self-hating person strives for self-acceptance by trying to get withholding and rejecting people to accept him. Psychoanalysts note daily that when men are unsure of their potency or women are not confident of their lovableness, they may seek to prove themselves adequate by trying to overcome the aloofness of a hostile spouse. Just like people who have to prove their physical courage by enormous feats, so men and women who need to prove that they are potent or lovable may feel that they have achieved their goal if the attempt was made in the face of great resistance (Kubie, 1956).

The appeal of a misogynist lover to an insecure woman is legendary. In *Rebecca* and *Jane Eyre*, both main characters reason, "If he loves me when he hates every other woman, I must be quite acceptable."

UNCONSCIOUS REVENGE IN CHOOSING A PARTNER

The need to erase an old pain can influence marital choice, usually in destructive ways.

Boris Grant, age 25, had an intensely hostile relationship to an older sister. He felt inferior to her and thought she surpassed him in every conceivable way. Boris married Eva "to show her off to my sister so that I wouldn't have to fight with her any more." Because he felt that Eva was superior to his sister in every way, he thought that his marriage would stop him from feeling jealous and angry toward his sister.

Although Boris felt triumphant when he became engaged to Eva, Eva soon became sensitive to Boris' wishes and angrily declared that she wanted a lot more from her relationship with Boris than to be used as a weapon.

Boris and Eva began to feel much misunderstood by each other. Eventually they became angry and depressed. At this point they sought therapy.

The fate of a marriage is decided long before the marriage occurs. The human psyche is formed early in childhood and the result is enshrined in the person, often without his conscious knowledge. Marriage does not create anything new in the partners; the reproaches one partner heaps upon the other become much clearer when one understands that the mate was unconsciously chosen to repeat childhood conflicts. Inasmuch as the pattern is unconscious, the indignation that is felt consciously is understandable. However, there are few if any innocent victims of marital disasters; the "chance" misfortune was unconsciously arranged and self-perpetuated (Bergler, 1963).

Psychologist Joel Block (1978) speaks of the complex process of choosing a marital partner as follows:

> Few of us marry out of mature love. We marry out of hope, and we hope that our fantasies will spring to life. We dream of love, but developing a loving relationship is another matter. Marriage, involving two complex and everchanging adults and, in most instances, one or more equally complex and rapidly changing children, precludes continuous and perfect harmony. . . . A man may want a hostess, a mother, an accessory, a centerfold, a sister, a slave, or a tyrant. A woman may crave a father, a son, a savior, an escape from home. . . . [Although it is possible] to achieve a reasonably nurturing, loving, and workable relationship despite the inherent flaws of the institution, most marriages unfortunately, do not achieve this; they are more often characterized by discord and destructiveness. [p. 106]

Part II

Types of Marriages and the Extramarital Affair

Chapter 4

The Winter of Discontent: The Trust-Mistrust Marriage

An enjoyable and enduring marital relationship requires acknowledgment of mutual dependency by both partners. If the husband and wife cannot permit themselves to be somewhat dependent on each other, the marriage will be in serious jeopardy.

Many married people cannot tolerate their own dependent wishes or their spouse's dependency on them. When the psychoanalyst works with such individuals, he learns that they have a great deal of unresolved conflict from the oral or trust-mistrust period of life (Erikson, 1950; Fraiberg, 1977). Some of these people were so frustrated during the first year of life that they still feel huge quantities of rage, which often becomes directed at their marital partner, whom they experience as withholding and frustrating. Often the individual who was left hungry at the breast develops "a paranoid orientation to living" (Klein, 1957)—i.e., a distrust of virtually everyone he deals with—and in marriage he becomes very suspicious of the spouse.

PARADISE LOST: THE DISTRUSTFUL SPOUSE

A person who has suffered a great deal of trauma during the first year of life and is very distrustful of an intimate relationship may nonetheless marry. Like the child who has experienced much rejection from his mother but would like to believe that if he tries harder mother will love him, the depressed and distrustful adult who gets married has kept alive the fantasy that somewhere there exists a mate who will finally meet his emotional needs. However, as we discussed in previous chapters, marriage never resolves a neurosis nor can it ever compensate for a miserable childhood. A person who has been acutely frustrated during the oral period may seek a mate to make up for his past deprivations; when the spouse inevitably "fails" to do so, he may pursue an extramarital affair.

Husbands and wives who have been acutely deprived during infancy harbor a great deal of murderous rage, but they keep their hateful feelings suppressed most of the time. Inasmuch as their self-images are very poor, they do not have the confidence that they will be listened to empathically, particularly when what they have to say is hostile. Because these people are emotionally convinced that nobody wants to have anything to do with them, they spend much of their time alone. They liken almost all of their relationships to the one they experienced with their mothers and perceive most other people as cold, hostile, selfish, and ungiving.

Distrustful spouses frequently display a propensity for injustice collecting. They complain that their marital partners are not assuming their appropriate responsibilities. Wives tend to point out to their husbands that they are poor breadwinners, inadequate sexual partners, and inept conversationalists. Husbands are frequently indignant because they perceive their wives as ungiving, unloving, and uncaring.

Distrustful spouses feel most anxious when emotional intimacy becomes an issue. Repelled by their own desires for love, they frequently project these desires onto their marital partners and criticize them for being "infantile," "dependent," and "demanding."

People who have not experienced a warm, empathetic relationship with a nurturing mother as children tend to develop a paranoid orientation to living. They become very suspicious of another person's warmth and often are contemptuous of one who appears loving. As one suspicious husband said to his therapist in commenting about his wife, "Every time she smiles I wonder, 'How does she want to manipulate me this time?'" At a later session he said, "Her love is poison and I don't want it. If I take it in I'm a sucker."

Usually a suspicious man marries a suspicious woman and the

two people, because of their mutual fear of dependency, often compete to see which is the less needy, which the more clinging. This constant dispute serves two purposes: both partners feel stronger and independent while battling and at the same time they gratify their secret and unconscious wish to be with each other.

Marital partners of the distrustful type rarely acknowledge their wish for contact. Rather, they work overtime to keep at a distance from their mates and justify their rejecting behavior by accusing their partners of being unlovable. Sometimes they use an extramarital affair as a means of saying to themselves and their spouses, "I'm not the one who is a poor mate; you are. See, I can make it with somebody else."

Jackie Phillips, age 22, sought psychotherapy six months after her marriage. She had met her husband, Steve, at work. She admired him for his quiet composure and dedication to his job and concluded that he would be a loyal husband and father. Although both Jackie and Steve had had virtually no sexual experiences before they met each other, and although there were virtually no physical demonstrations of affection during their courtship, the couple rationalized their sexual inhibitions and thought that after they were married sex would not be a problem.

No sooner were they married than Jackie became acutely depressed. When Steve approached her sexually, she broke out in hives and vomited. After a while he ceased taking any initiative in sex, but this did not help Jackie. Not only did she continue to dread physical contact with Steve but she began to express hatred toward him. She complained that he did not make enough money and did not have sufficient intellectual sophistication. She began to feel more and more deprived in her marriage.

When Steve threatened to leave her, Jackie sought therapeutic assistance. Her history revealed that her mother had died of cancer when Jackie was three years old. Although she had few memories of her mother, she did recall that her mother appeared sick and depressed most of the time and did not talk to her very much. Her father worked sporadically and was often drunk. While Jackie did well as a student, she had few friends and had only one or two superficial relationships with young men prior to meeting Steve.

As was discussed in chapter 1, one of the features of psychotherapy is transference; that is, the patient tends to behave toward the analyst in much the same way that he or she behaves toward significant persons in "real life" (Eisenstein, 1956; Giovachinni, 1972). Thus the angry husband will find things about the analyst that anger him; the detached spouse will find reasons to be isolated from the analyst; the dependent person will want to cling to the analyst. In her transference relationship with her analyst, Jackie was extremely quiet and shy. In the early months of treatment, she would break out in hives and feel acutely nauseous as soon as she entered the consultation room.

With encouragement from the analyst, Jackie was eventually able to talk about what she "could not stomach." "You are an unfeeling dope who doesn't give me a damn thing!" she charged her analyst during the fifth month of treatment. She compared him to her "stupid husband" and later to her "ungiving mother."

After she had discharged a great deal of rage for being deprived by her mother, husband, and analyst, her hives and nausea abated and she was able for the first time to have some sexual foreplay with Steve. However, her distrust continued. In her dreams, her husband and analyst appeared as monsters or witches whom she always compared to her "monstrous mother."

During one session Jackie reported a fantasy in which the analyst had died and she attended his funeral. The fantasy could be seen as her wish that the analyst would die, but it also demonstrated some warm feelings toward him because in the fantasy she experienced grief, weeping at his burial. As she looked at her developing feelings of closeness toward her therapist, Jackie also began to experience a yearning for her mother. She was finally able to emotionally acknowledge her desire to be loved by a mother. With this discovery she was able after two years of therapy to have sexual intercourse (without orgasm) with Steve.

Although Steve was overjoyed by Jackie's progress, she did not enjoy her changes very much. She began once again to feel quite contemptuous toward her analyst and toward Steve as well. She viewed her increased ability to enjoy sex as "feeding" her analyst and husband while she got very little for herself. She had dreams of depriving her analyst and her husband of food and clothing and enjoyed her feeling of hostile triumph.

Jackie was clearly expressing and feeling her revenge toward her mother. By depriving her analyst and husband of food and comfort she was placing them in the same psychological position that she had occupied when she was a child. As she continued to express her hostility, she began an extramarital affair with George, a colleague at work. She contrasted George to Steve and the analyst. "George really feeds me. . . . Your interpretations are shitty food and Steve's cock is a stinking breast," she remarked.

Actually there was relatively little sexual activity between Jackie and George, and most of it was pregenital foreplay. Jackie seemed to derive most of her enjoyment of her affair from going to movies with George and talking about them, sharing reactions to books, and complaining about their respective spouses. Further analysis exposed the fact that one of her major motives for her affair with George was to upset her "ungiving" husband and her "ungiving" analyst. In one dream she arranged to have sex with George in the analyst's office and the analyst was weeping as she and George were enjoying themselves.

She repeatedly acted out the wish to spite her "ungiving" mother by unconsciously trying to arrange for Steve to find out about her affair. After Jackie had been seeing George several times a week for about six months, Steve could no longer defend against his awareness of her affair. One day he arrived home at his usual time and found George and Jackie in bed. Although Jackie was startled, in later analytic sessions she spoke of the incident as her "victory" and talked about her "delicious revenge."

As mentioned earlier in this chapter, individuals who are coping with trust-mistrust conflicts inevitably harbor a great deal of hatred toward their mothers. In Jackie's case she experienced both her male analyst and her husband as insensitive mothers. She wanted their love but could not enjoy it because she felt so much rage toward them, experiencing them as ungiving, narcissistic, unavailable mother figures. Although analyst and husband were emotionally available to her, Jackie could not experience herself as loved, but only as neglected. We learn from Jackie how reality is severely distorted by a person whose childhood frustrations have not been resolved. Perceptions and judgments are contaminated by huge quantities of anger.

Jackie was able to enjoy her lover for several reasons. She was apart from George several hours every day and therefore, unlike her marital relationship, the affair was not reminiscent of her relationship with her mother. Consequently, she could "take in" George's conversation and his tenderness on at least a limited basis. Perhaps more important, she used George as a tool to express her rage and revenge toward Steve and her analyst, both of whom she made into hostile and unempathetic mother figures.

It was not until Jackie could ventilate and understand her hatred toward her mother that she was able to enjoy a close and intimate relationship with any man.

PARADISE REGAINED: THE SYMBIOTIC SPOUSE

Another feature of the oral period is the symbiotic relationship between mother and infant (Mahler, 1968). Although it is appropriate during the first several months of the child's first year of life for mother and infant to feel like Siamese twins, if further maturation is to take place, mother and infant should achieve some distance from each other and begin to feel some autonomy and a sense of separateness. Many mothers feel threatened when their children start to walk on their own instead of wanting to be carried. They resent weaning the child and in their desperation unwittingly engulf the child more and more (A. Freud, 1965). Because the child who is less than two years old is very much a victim of mother's preoccupations and cannot exercise much independence if mother does not provide room for it, he complies with mother's wishes and remains very passive. Furthermore, the desire to be the recipient of mother's indulgence is never given up gracefully.

Although the overprotected child can mature in some ways, most of the time he tends to think that anybody who "really" loves him should be able to anticipate all his needs and be willing to minister to him as his mother did. This "oral character" psychologically wants to devour anybody or anything that appears valuable (Fenichel, 1945). He wants to know all about his loved one and permits the spouse no privacy. He becomes furious if the spouse has loving feelings for others, interests apart from him, and secrets that are not shared. The title of a current popular song captures the sentiments of this person: "You Are My Life and I'll Never Let You Go!" Usually the oral character has little anxiety about his insatiability. He is convinced that it is his right to have what he wants when he wants it (English and Pearson, 1945), and if the spouse is not forthcoming with all of the goodies, he or she is severely admonished for "inconsiderate behavior."

The oral character or symbiotic marital partner usually comes into treatment complaining of feelings of depression. His mate, of course, can never completely satisfy his oral hunger: angry displays do not bring the Garden of Eden into existence, and other forms of manipulation on his part eventually fail as well. By the time this person consults a therapist, he resembles a depressed child who feels severely neglected, if not abandoned, by his mother.

Rudolf Erikson, a 35-year-old high school teacher, sought treatment because he was extremely depressed, constantly experienced insomnia, and found it difficult to work. A few months before seeking psychotherapy, he started drinking a great deal and was worried that he would lose his job because he was missing school. His colleagues noticed his unsteady gait and lack of composure with students.

In the initial consultations with his female analyst, Rudolf spoke of his five-year-old marriage to Helen. He believed himself to be a most considerate husband but could not understand why Helen did not respond to him. "Frequently she lets me go for a walk by myself," he said indignantly. Furthermore, he lamented, "Helen spends more time with the baby than she does with me!" Although he recognized that "an infant needs his mother," he mentioned several times how neglected he felt.

An examination of Rudolf's history revealed that his mother had considered him "the apple of her eye." "She was always interested in me, I could share everything with her and she could tell me anything she wanted," he said proudly. His father was a hard-working mason and although he had a cordial relationship with Rudolf's mother, it was clear that mother and son were very much closer to each other.

The first few months of Rudolf's therapy were like a "honeymoon" (Fine, 1971). Rudolf loved the idea of talking to a warm listener, saying what he felt and thought without censure, and began to experience his therapist like the good mother for whom he was yearning. He gave up his alcoholism, his depression lifted, his work improved, and he felt less resentment toward Helen.

After six months an impasse occurred in Rudolf's therapy. Rudolf began to ask his therapist questions about herself and actively sought her advice about his marriage and his relationship with his child. When the analyst asked Rudolf to examine why he wanted to know, for example, whether she was married, Rudolf did not want to explore his motives. He refused to freely associate to his own thoughts and instead told the therapist that she "refused to believe in friendship" and that she was "a witch" and "a bitch." In his dreams he bit off the analyst's breasts and later likened her to his ungiving wife. "Both of you refuse to accept my love which is free and spontaneous." He felt that his analyst's refusal to give him advice was proof that she hated him.

While Rudolf was involved in a therapeutic impasse with his analyst and was concomitantly feeling a lot of contempt toward his wife, he began an extramarital affair with a waitress. In contrast to his analyst and his wife, he found Geraldine a "giving and nurturing woman." She telephoned him every day to find out how he was feeling, cooked for him, and enjoyed "taking good care" of him. During one analytic session he "confessed" with much embarassment that at times Geraldine read to him. Although Rudolf and Geraldine had occasional sex, it was limited to pregenital foreplay.

While Rudolf felt wonderful about being "petted and stroked" by Geraldine, it became clear that with her he behaved like a regressed baby who constantly had to be fed; the notion of being a sexual man with her frightened him. In one of his dreams about Geraldine she had a vagina that was "as big as a cave and I got lost in it." His associations to the "vaginal cave" helped him recall memories and fantasies from his childhood when he wanted to have sexual intercourse with his mother. As a little boy next to a big mother, Rudolf felt that mother's vagina was a cave—alluring, attractive, but terrifying.

As Rudolf relived some of his boyhood fantasies and began to realize how he both wished but feared to be a little boy in bed with his mother, he was able to acknowledge how he desexualized his wife and to see that by not permitting Helen to be a giving sexual woman, he could avoid confronting his fantasy of being a little boy in a big vaginal cave.

As we have noted, although the unhappy spouse bitterly complains about his marital partner, it frequently emerges in psychoanalytic treatment that the very issue about which the patient complains serves unconsciously as a protection for him. Rudolf appeared to be very angry with Helen for not being sufficiently available to him. However, with Geraldine, a woman who seemed to love him a great deal, he feared sexual intimacy because he unconsciously likened her to the mother of his childhood, whom he wished for but feared.

Very often an extramarital affair can help an individual get emotionally in touch with his fears and stimulate increased self understanding. This happened to Rudolf Erikson. As he became more involved with Geraldine he could see how he basically feared to have sex with a "nurturing" woman.

JUST FRIENDS–AN AFFAIR WITHOUT SEX

We have seen that in the extramarital affairs of Jackie and Rudolf, sexual intercourse was not a major component. Jackie harbored so much hatred toward a maternal figure that the sex she did have was mainly used to express revenge. The closeness of sexual intercourse recapitulated murderous feelings toward her mother. Rudolf had to keep himself in a regressed oral position where he was fed and petted because to be a sexual man with a sexual woman activated wishes and fears of being engulfed. His affair in many ways protected him from being a potent man, which was a very conflictful role for him.

Many people seek escape from the sexual anxieties and other

frustrations of marriage by having a nonsexual extramarital affair. The emotional intimacy inherent in a sexual relationship is very threatening to them because it activates competition with the parent of the same sex, incestuous fantasies, or homosexual desires. Feeding and being fed, talking, seeing movies, and mutually complaining about their spouses—all oral activities— serve as a valuable defense.

Frequently men and women who have nonsexual extramarital relationships rationalize their abstinence on moral grounds, contending that extramarital sex would be destructive to their marriages. They do not consider their emotional commitment to their extramarital partner as destructive to their marriages because it does not create as much anxiety for them as extramarital sex would.

Psychoanalysts have learned that strong platonic relationships usually have a hidden sexual component but the friends fear to express their sexual impulses in the relationship. When two married people have a strong and close extramarital relationship that does not include sex, it can be safely inferred that both of them have stong fears of participating in sexual activity.

Ron Frank, age 37, married for six years, very much resented his reponsibilities toward his wife and two children. When he came home from a day's work, he wanted to relax and read or watch television. He became very angry when his children or wife sought him out to spend time with them. Of course, the more Ron rejected his wife and children, the angrier and more insecure they got and the more they needed reassurance from him. Ron began to spend more and more time away from home with a married woman colleague. They had dinner together, discussed office business, and saw movies. Although they spent a lot of time with each other, except for an occasional hug, sex was completely avoided.

Ron sought therapy not because he wanted help with his marital and family conflicts but because he was not working up to par on his job. A lawyer, he found himself afraid to compete with other professionals and often was tongue-tied when he had to plead a case. Feeling insecure and unsuccessful as an attorney, he had crying jags and had lost interest in sex.

In describing his relationship with his father, Ron talked about how he always felt put down by him. His mother usually joined the father in criticizing Ron for not getting all A's, not hitting enough home runs in baseball, not being a good enough boxer. Rather early in treatment Ron was able to note the parallel between not feeling "up to par" as a lawyer and never pleasing his parents.

It further emerged in Ron's therapy and in his transference relationship with his analyst how much he resented "feeding others." He experienced responding with affection to his wife and children as being exploited, like "feeding my parents' fantasies and producing good grades for them." Ron did not perceive free association in analysis as something that would be beneficial for him. "It's only to feed you," he complained to his analyst.

As Ron got more in tune with how much he resented giving to others, he was able to understand that he viewed sexual relations the same way. "The woman wants my cock and I get nothing from it except anxiety," he said in one therapy session. Once he realized that he saw sex as an experience "where I'm always putting out like I did for my parents," it was not difficult for Ron to appreciate why an extramarital affair without sex was so appealing to him.

A prolonged nonsexual relationship is often not recognized as an extramarital affair but it is nonetheless an escape from marriage and reveals many of the psychodynamics of an affair. Ron experienced marriage, family, and sex with his wife as awesome responsibilities. Consequently, he fled from them by spending a lot of time with a woman talking, eating, and mutually complaining. The woman was his "lover" despite the fact that she did not go to bed with him.

PERCEIVING THE SPOUSE AS OMNIPOTENT

An important feature of the oral stage of development is that the child eventually realizes that he cannot always be "His Majesty the Prince." His narcissism is punctured as he is confronted with weaning and other frustrations. At this point the child transfers to his parents the power he thought he possessed and ascribes omnipotent and omniscient qualities to them. Many adults still harbor the belief that their parents can do anything. One often finds people in their thirties, forties, or even fifties who have strong resentment toward their parents for not meeting their offsprings' needs. These feelings do not abate because the individual maintains the conviction that mother and father could have loved him more if they wanted to. When an individual is emotionally convinced that a parent is omnipotent, he expects the marital partner to be omnipotent too.

But this expectation is always disappointed. Obviously no one is capable of anticipating his spouse's every wish, offering support and advice, and being a fount of wisdom all of the time. Just as the maturing child must eventually accept the reality that his parents are not perfect and all-powerful, every married person must accept with equanimity that the spouse is a human being with vulnerabilities and limitations.

Although the yearning for an omnipotent parent is something that most individuals never completely abandon, persevering in this belief not only leads to disappointment in marriage but results in feelings of weakness. If one believes that the marital partner is omnipotent then one must feel very small next to such a paragon. After a while the individual who ascribes Superman or Wonder Woman qualities to a marital partner becomes full of resentment, because he feels overpowered by these very superiorities.

One of the factors that accounts for the frequent phenomenon of a married couple alternating between periods of loving passion and intense hatred is that they share a common unconscious fantasy. If the husband, for example, ascribes grandiose powers to his wife, he will intensely love his perfect goddess for a while. However, sooner or later he will hate her for not being the goddess she's supposed to be. Exacerbating his disappointment and anger will be the feeling of impotence that evolves when he compares himself to his fantasized "perfect" partner. A common means of coping with disappointment and feelings of weakness is to attack. This temporarily elevates his self-esteem but then frightens him because he needs his "omnipotent mother." He therefore returns to loving her again, only to feel disappointed and weak again. Usually a husband who seeks an omnipotent wife chooses a woman with similar unconscious fantasies. Consequently, both mates are eternally on an emotional seesaw, loving a god and then hating the spouse later for inducing disappointment and feelings of impotence.

When a person believes emotionally that the perfect mate exists, he is going to look for her. Since the spouse always punctures the wish for a perfect mate, the omnipotent partner is sought elsewhere, often in an extramarital affair.

Martha Green, age 41, was married to a physician who was "a devoted husband and father" to her and their ten-year-old-son and nine-year-old-daughter. Although Martha pointed out that in many ways she had "everything a woman could ask for," she had been involved in an affair for over a year and felt very guilty about it. She saw her lover several times a week, loved the praise he always gave her for her clothes, body, good looks, and "even for my mind," but after spending time with him, she felt "dirty inside." She did not want to leave her husband but neither did she want to give up her relationship with Carl. Martha considered herself "greedy" for wanting both a husband and a lover but felt helpless in doing anything about it.

Martha had parents who "I think loved me" but "seemed to care more for my younger sister." As children, Martha and her sister were active competitors and at times their arguments led to physical attacks.

Martha described both parents as "strong" people who expected a lot from her. She worked hard at school and at college to get good grades "so that I could please my parents." Just as she felt intimidated by her parents, Martha was very acquiescent with teachers and tried her best to comply with their demands. Frequently she was successful in sensitizing herself to the requirements of parental figures and often was the teacher's pet.

Martha had few friends as a child or teenager. Most of her extracurricular activities consisted of volunteer work in the community. She had few close relationships with men until she met her husband and was a virgin at marriage. She liked Max for his "brilliance, decisiveness, good looks, professional status, and good family."

Although Martha told her therapist that Max was devoted to

her—he bought her gifts frequently, helped her with household chores, supported her in conflicts with the children—it became clear after several months of therapy how much Martha felt subordinate to Max. She began to describe incidents where Max implied that she used poor judgment. Furthermore, she complained that she was the butt of his jokes and that she had to entertain his professional colleagues even if she did not feel like it.

When her therapist tried to elicit some of her feelings after she had described being criticized by Max, at first Martha was evasive and defended Max as always having her best interests at heart. When the therapist did not agree or disagree but remained neutral, Martha became irritated with him. "I want more support and love from you, but you always make me feel inferior. You know it all and I accept that, but when you don't share your knowledge, I get sore!" Following her angry release, Martha had several dreams that involved the therapist. In one, she was shoving the therapist off a chair that seemed "too high"; in another, she went to another therapist in search of "more compassion." The therapist whom she consulted in the dream was younger than her real therapist and was dressed in more informal clothes than her therapist ususally wore.

Martha's dreams could be interpreted as a wish for a "high and mighty" parental figure, but of more importance was her wish to put him down—to push him off his high chair and get him to be more informal. Similarly, she wanted Max to be an omnipotent parent but then resented him for his power. Martha compared her second dream, involving her seeing another therapist, to her extramarital affair, where things were more informal than at home with Max.

She began to associate Max with the teachers of her past as well as with her parents. After she had discharged a great deal of anger toward "all the big shots that I look for," she was able to get in touch with some of her own dependency wishes. In her fantasies and dreams she arranged to be a little girl and was fondled by her analyst, whom she made very maternal. As she analyzed her wish for a strong and powerful mother, she could begin to feel her rage at Max for "failing her." "I kept my wishes to be taken care of a forbidden secret just like my forbidden and secret affair," she said insightfully.

Many married people feel that an omnipotent parent is somewhere, and that the paradise of the first year of life can be regained in an adult relationship. Like children who fantasize that they are adopted and that their loving natural parents are somewhere to be found, many a married person searches for a "true love" through an affair.

Although there are many factors involved in keeping an extramarital affair a secret, one is that the participants do not want to reveal their symbiotic wishes for the omnipotent parent. These people are embarrassed that they have never been weaned from a mother, and that is why few of them actually end their marital relationships. To separate from the spouse fills the symbiotic husband or wife with terror. When he contemplates the idea of divorce or separation he feels the desperation and loneliness of a young child who is about to be abandoned by his parents.

Complementing those who seek the perfect spouse are the many husbands and wives who like to enact the role of omnipotent parent. When the spouse who wishes to be the all-powerful parent is perceived by the partner more realistically (usually as a result of therapy), he may feel very threatened. Martha, in the previous example, became more maturely assertive and much less masochistic with her husband, at which point Max became very anxious. When she did not cooperate with his wish to dominate her, Max became very sadistic with her. When Martha was unwilling to submit to Max's sadistic attacks, he became more and more depressed. Eventually he sought psychotherapy for himself, which was a very courageous act for a man who needed to appear consistently strong and self-reliant.

When one member of a marital pair makes changes as a result of therapy, this often shakes up a comfortable, albeit neurotic, equilibrium. If the partner who has not been in therapy cannot cope with changes in his mate (either by himself or with therapeutic help), the marriage may dissolve (Ackerman, 1958).

LES MISERABLES: DEFENDING AGAINST SYMBIOSIS

In order to sustain an enjoyable marital relationship, the mates must be able to depend on each other. Mature dependency means that one can support and be supported without engulfment, domination, or submission. It also means that the partners can give to and take from each other and still feel separate and autonomous.

One of the reasons that many married individuals cannot permit much dependency in themselves or their partners is that they experience emotional attachment unconsciously as lack of autonomy and merger. The person who fears attachment rarely is aware of unconscious wishes to merge. All he knows is that too much closeness threatens him and that if he lets down his guard, he fears he will be devoured.

The feeling that one's life is not one's own may lead to marital breakup. If a person with these feelings seeks therapy, it inevitably emerges that he receives unconscious gratification from being sought out constantly by the spouse because this is narcissistically enriching for him. Usually he secretly envies his mate's openness in seeking a closer attachment for he too would like to be open in giving and receiving love. He can't permit this, however, because he fears that he will become a regressed baby.

If the individual fears his own dependency, he may try to protect himself by criticizing his spouse. By acting contemptuously he can feel a sense of power instead of feeling weak and vulnerable. Because he is psychologically an oral child who would love to express and gratify his infantile wishes, he vicariously identifies with the spouse as he or she cries and expresses the wish to be adored, to hug and be hugged. However, when he feels these desires in himself, he fights them with a strong tenacity. He would rather call his spouse a "crybaby" than examine his fears of his own oral desires.

One means of denying the wish for symbiotic dependence is through an extramarital affair. Because the individual feels joined to his partner anatomically, often referring to the partner as his "ball and chain" or "better half," an intermittent extramarital affair provides a less threatening outlet for his wishes for closeness and intimacy.

An extramarital affair is appealing to men and women who fear their symbiotic wishes because it usually does not necessitate the day-to-day mutual dependency that is inherent in most marital relationships. Most extramarital lovers spend only a few hours with each other and then separate for a day or two or more. The separation gives them a feeling of independence and strength and then they are able to like themselves a little more. As one patient put it, "I can sleep and eat well even though I'm not always with Doris. I feel big and strong knowing this." What Tom was unable to admit for a long time was that he needed his wife to sleep and eat with; as long as he had her, he could feel quite independent with Doris.

Dependent people who are involved in extramarital liaisons are able to manipulate their lives so that they do not have to feel the power of their infantile yearnings in any relationship. They can tell themselves that they don't need their spouses too much because they have their lovers available to them; and they can also feel independent with their lovers because they know they can leave them and go home to their spouses.

Psychoanalysts have been able to determine that an extramarital affair is almost always a defensive shield for the symbiotic person. This becomes apparent when the lover wants a more intimate relationship. Then the dependent person becomes acutely anxious and doesn't know which way to turn.

Jerry Gold, age 46, had been married for about twenty years. For most of this marriage he had been unhappy and wanted to separate from his wife. However, each time he thought of leaving Hilda, he found some reason to prevent him from doing so. Jerry had been involved in an affair with a single younger woman for over four years. He sought therapy at this time because Peggy, his lover, was putting pressure on him to leave his wife and marry her.

As Jerry described his relationship with Hilda, it appeared that most of their twenty years were full of almost daily arguments. Hilda would ask for advice, support, or leadership from Jerry, and Jerry would indignantly exclaim that she was too demanding. Hilda then felt hurt and rejected and broke into heavy sobbing. Jerry, threatened by the sobbing, would become even more insulting and admonish Hilda to cut out crying "like a baby." When Hilda was most upset Jerry would leave the house for a day or two. Jerry's leaving the house always distressed Hilda severely so that when he returned she was glad to see him, was full of apologies, and tried to place very few demands on him.

Until Peggy began to want to get married, Jerry very much enjoyed his relationship with her. "I can come and go as I please and don't have to listen to her sob stories," Jerry told his therapist. He was worried, though, that "Peggy might become a pain" if he married her.

Jerry described both of his parents as cold and aloof. Early in life he was taught that he had to take care of himself and be very independent. When he was five years old his parents divorced but they continued their battles. Although Jerry lived with his mother, he tended to identify more with his father, admiring him for his "toughness and callousness." Jerry had no siblings.

Jerry was a poor student and never graduated from high school. He hung out with a gang of boys participating in street fights and some delinquent activity. He had a series of part-time jobs while in high school but fought with his employers as he fought with his high school teachers.

As a businessman, Jerry would do well in various ventures and then get into altercations with associates and would lose the money he invested.

In his treatment with a male therapist, he was extremely guarded and tentative. He frequently questioned his need for treatment and doubted that it could help people resolve their problems. Jerry often cancelled appointments or arrived late. When the therapist interpreted Jerry's fear of closeness to him, Jerry went into a rage. He told the therapist, "I will never get close to you. Being dependent on someone is for sissies. I've always taken care of myself and I won't let you do that." When the therapist did not retalitate for Jerry's expression of hostility, Jerry taunted him for being "scared to fight." During the course of this active opposition to the therapist, Jerry brought in a dream in which he was a father and the therapist was a little boy who was very depressed and Jerry was soothing him. Although Jerry found the dream anxiety-provoking because he caught a glimpse of tender feelings in himself (which he always tried so hard to repudiate), he was able after several sessions to acknowledge the part of him that wanted to give and receive love.

On recognizing his own dependency, Jerry became very depressed. In his sessions he cried as he spoke of his hunger for affection and his need to fight it. It occurred to him that this was why he got so indignant when he observed Hilda crying. "It is my own tears that I hate," Jerry concluded. As Jerry began to accept his own dependency needs more, he became much more tolerant of Hilda and began to see Peggy more sporadically. When this occurred Peggy stopped the relationship. Jerry missed Peggy for a long time but was not too defensive about his own grief. He found occasional subsititutes for her in "one-night-stands," but the more he could accept his own dependency, the more he could relate to Hilda.

THE CHAMPIONING OF AUTONOMY

One of the major themes of the women's liberation movement is an emphasis on autonomy and independence for women. Many women experience this proclamation as a superego mandate and feel uncomfortable if they find themselves experiencing the desire to depend on a man. Frequently, the woman of the 1970s feels less of a person, weak, and "second class" if she wants support or affection from a man. To defend against her own dependent wishes, which seem so unacceptable to her, she may unconsciously arrange to prove that her husband or lover is undependable.

Margaret Hyman, 45, was in her second marriage and expressed a feeling of unhappiness much like the way she felt "when I made a mess of my first marriage. Arthur is kind and considerate, but I treat him like a dog." In addition to her marital conflicts, Margaret had several neurotic symptoms—insomnia, migraine headaches, depression, frigidity, and constant feelings of guilt—because of her affair with Ben, a colleague at the college where Margaret was a professor. A tall, attractive woman, extremely bright and accomplished, Margaret suffered from feelings of low self-esteem. Though she was well liked, she experienced herself as a "social isolate."

Margaret, the youngest of four children, never got along with her three brothers, whom she saw as more accomplished than she. While she maintained a cooperative and conciliatory facade at home and at school, she harbored strong feelings of resentment and envy toward her brothers and classmates. She very much resented her parents because of her belief that they favored her brothers.

Although Margaret was an excellent student she always maintained an emotional distance from her teachers and fellow students. The winner of many awards, she always depreciated her accomplishments. At high school, college, and graduate school, she had few friends and seldom dated. She married shortly before receiving her doctorate but the marriage lasted only a year. She and her husband "fought about everything"— politics, finances, visiting relatives, domestic chores, and recreation. "It was a one-upmanship struggle from day one. If I took a position on something, he took the other and vice-versa."

Margaret had unresolved problems from several stages of the life cycle; however, it was clear that her paramount problem was her strong defense against dependency. In her early sessions with her therapist she constantly championed the idea of never wanting to need anyone "because it makes me feel very vulnerable and I would hate myself for it." Whenever she felt the wish to be taken care of, she fought it doggedly.

Margaret fought closeness with her woman therapist in part by trying to engage the therapist in arguments about the value of psychotherapy, a profession that she claimed was comtemptuous of women. "You keep yourself and your patients weak without knowing it," she remarked. Margaret threatened to quit treatment on many occasions. When the therapist pointed out that Margaret used fighting and arguing as a "helpful" defense against her wish to be helped, Margaret fought harder but with an agitated type of crying. She accused the therapist of trying to "make me dependent on you and I hate you for it." As Margaret discharged a lot of anger and cried a great deal, she did report that her insomnia, headaches, and depression had eased.

With a diminution of her symptoms Margaret began to feel a little more trustful of her analyst. She brought in dreams and fantasies in which she was a little girl sitting on a parent's lap and as soon as she got a little comfortable would run. When the therapist asked her to associate to the feelings and desires she was running away from, Margaret eventually was able to face her strong fears and wishes of oral engulfment. She had fantasies of devouring and being devoured by the analyst, her parents, and lovers. As Margaret could look at her cannibalistic wishes and realized how frightened she was of them, she insightfully remarked, "I see why I'm always on the run in relationships. As soon as I get near someone, I'm afraid of eating him up or being eaten up. So I move away fast."

Individuals with problems on the trust-mistrust level also have conflicts around autonomy versus self doubt, initiative versus guilt, industry versus inferiority, and so on. The analyst addresses those conflicts as they emerge in the treatment, as expressed in the patient's dreams, fantasies, and transference relationship with the therapist. When trust-mistrust problems decline in intensity, the patient is helped to face other issues or may be satisfied with the results of therapy and terminate contact with the analyst.

The extramarital affairs of the patients cited in this chapter were clearly expressions of their trust-mistrust conflicts. Either their appetites were insatiable so that they experienced their spouses as insufficiently gratifying or their fears of dependency were so great that they could not relax in a marital relationship. They were distrustful of their mates and/or wanted too much from them.

In each of these cases, the individuals unconsciously sought mates to prove that their neurotic distortions and childish fantasies were valid. The distrustful person often finds a husband or wife to distrust and the hungry patient can always "see" deprivation. The person who contends that dependency is a weakness will always be able to demonstrate that it cannot be safely expressed in his or her marriage. When trusting and depending on a marital partner are fraught with conflicts, an extramarital affair provides an avenue for revenge and dissipates the hunger for those who are orally insatiable. It also provides a release and a haven for those who cannot rely exclusively on the spouse.

Chapter 5

The Grapes of Wrath:
The Sadomasochistic
Marriage

As we discussed in chapter 2, a task every child has to cope with is toilet training. If the parents are not harsh, angry, punitive, or premature in initiating training but instead empathically help the youngster to gain bladder and sphincter control (and assume other age-appropriate responsibilities), the child will probably grow into an adult who can enjoy autonomy, avoid power struggles, and identify with and like other people. He will not be inclined to perceive a love relationship as "doing duty," losing freedom, or being exploited.

Unfortunately, many children are not trained sensitively and warmly, and as adults they continue to respond to what they perceive as controls, constraints, and responsibilities with anger and the desire for revenge. Many a marital quarrel is reminiscent of the power struggles between parent and child over toilet training. Like the child who feels humiliated and belittled for having to defecate or urinate *for* his parents, many a husband and wife experience doing things for the marital partner as humiliating and belittling. Often dimensions of marital life such as sexual relations, listening to the spouse's complaints and desires, and visiting in-laws are experienced as "being made to shit" for the partner. When a husband or wife feels that he or she is submissively "putting out" for the spouse, sparks can begin to fly.

In chapter 3 we pointed out that when a person has conflicts with power, controls, and dominance, he inevitably finds a marital partner to complement him. The husband and wife argue about how each feels exploited, misunderstood, and unloved in the marriage. Each perceives the other as the controlling, arbitrary, and exacting parent of the past. Psychoanalysts refer to this type of relationship as a sadomasochistic marriage.

Although most people marry because they consciously want to give and receive love, there are probably more sadomasochistic marriages than there are mature loving ones. The "battered wife" syndrome is well known to clinicians, and it has been reported that one fifth of the married women in America beat their husbands (Langley and Levy, 1977). The prizewinning play *Who's Afraid of Virginia Woolf?* is the story of a couple who lived together for over twenty years and gradually destroyed each other. The play was of course written by a master, but perhaps one reason for its popularity was that many of the men and women who saw it could easily identify with the sadism and masochism of Edward Albee's characters.

Partners express unresolved anal problems in their marital relationship in a variety of ways. Those who see love as a duty tend to subordinate their own wishes to those of their spouses and receive gratification from self-sacrifice. This form of masochism, which Anna Freud (1937) termed the "altruistic surrender," frequently does not sustain itself indefinitely. After a while the masochistic husband or wife resents the inferior status (which has been self-created in many ways), switches roles with the spouse who has been dominant, and begins to hurt the partner. One means of hurting a partner, discussed in more detail later in this chapter, is to arrange "accidentally" for the spouse to learn about an affair in which the "misunderstood" husband or wife has been engaged.

What is sometimes overlooked in discussions of the sadomasochistic marriage is the pleasure the couple derives from fighting and suffering. That they are in effect "glad to be unhappy" is soon demonstrated when one or both members visit a therapist. Not only does the therapist learn that the couple has been fighting almost daily for many years, but he also learns early in the therapeutic contact that although there have been many threats of separation and divorce, the couple have never been apart for any substantial length of time.

Even when the sadomasochistic couple does separate or divorce, their deep yearning to fight keeps them in contact with each other. Arguments about alimony, visitation rights, and old injustices keep their battle going even if one or both of them remarry.

A very interesting facet of the sadomasochistic marriage is that the couple has generally had many bitter fights during their courtship. I recall interviewing a young wife who sought marital counseling because her husband was physically beating her almost daily and she felt powerless to do anything about it. In reviewing her history, she told me of the many black eyes and torn ligaments she had received from him during their courtship. She reflected, "I knew he would be a wife beater long before we were married, but I loved him!" What she did not realize until late in her therapy was her own unconscious wish to be beaten. A common finding in studies of battered wives is that during the courtship phase they were physically beaten on many occasions (Langley and Levy, 1977).

Both of the partners in a sadomasochistic marriage suffer from low self-esteem. Consequently they are easily angered and hurt when they are not given a great deal of attention and reassurance. Unaware of their own strong feelings of vulnerability, they are furious at their spouses for "causing" their depression and feelings of low self-worth. One means of acquiring a feeling of strength is by expressing hostility toward the spouse. A husband who attacks his wife feels temporarily potent. However, if the wife continues to suffer, sooner or later the husband feels very guilty and slowly moves into the masochistic position. Guilt and anger are very close to those people—they can't take too much guilt without getting angry and can't feel anger for too long without feeling guilty.

In the hate marriage that we are examining, both of the partners not only suffer from poor self-images and harbor much anger but also have very punitive superegos. Because they cannot permit themselves much pleasure, it becomes very understandable how two self-hating people find each other and sustain each other in their joint misery, sometimes for many years.

When anal conflicts have not been resolved, the child is not able to differentiate emotionally the sexual functions from the eliminative. While adults are, of course, intellectually aware of the differences between eliminative and sexual functions, sadomasochistic people often tend to experience sex as something "dirty" and either avoid it or find someone outside of marriage whom they can use sexually because they feel contempt for the person.

When a child has had a conflictful anal period, he frequently becomes an ambivalent adult—wanting to please and love yet resentful. One means of coping with ambivalence is to have two psychological partners—one to hate and one to love.

OF HUMAN BONDAGE: THE MASOCHISTIC SPOUSE

When parents place excessive demands on a child and withdraw or threaten to withdraw love if the youngster does not produce, the child usually emerges as a hard-working, suffering, self-effacing adult. Rare is the youngster who can say with confidence, "My parents' demands are too arbitrary and insensitive to my needs. I'll take it easy on myself even if they can't!" On the contrary, most if not all children introject their parents' values and make these values part of their "ego ideal," a dimension of the superego that rewards the person when he affirms parental values. Most adults are very much influenced by their "ego ideals" and like themselves more when they are abiding by parental edicts. However, because the masochistic individual's ideals are very perfectionistic, he cannot like himself for very long.

In choosing a marital partner, the masochistic individual is invariably attracted to somebody like his parents—arbitrary, exacting, and sadistic. Recapitulating his childhood in marriage, he works overtime trying to extract love from a demanding parental figure. Usually his exacting superego is projected onto the spouse and he is forever anticipating punishment, scorn, and abuse. It is not only love that the masochistic person wants to extract but enough love to compensate for his feeling of deprivation. However, when he is loved he cannot enjoy it because he feels he does not deserve it.

The psychodynamics of the masochistic spouse are characterized by great amounts of repressed anger. When a child has been subjected to arbitrary rules and regulations for many years, he will harbor much unconscious resentment toward his parents. But, because he has always feared asserting himself with his strict parents, his vengeance goes underground; instead of permitting himself to voice his anger, he feels guilty for even feeling it. He flagellates himself, thinking that if he constantly cries "mea culpa" ("I'm to blame") his punitive spouse will finally appreciate him.

Dr. Theodor Reik (1941) in *Masochism in Modern Man* has shown how the masochistic adult is psychologically an immature child who is willing to undergo all kinds of suffering and deprivation in his quest for love and acceptance. This self-hating person in effect says, "I have a great deal of anger toward my parents for all the humiliation they have made me feel. I would like to hurt them, but if I do, I'll lose their love and feel lost and abandoned. So, I'll repress my anger, submit to my tyrannical superego, and suffer in the hope that some day I will be loved."

> The husband who lets himself be bossed around for years, then one day breaks his shell of "Yes, dears" and kills his hated wife in a moment of intolerable pressure, has hidden his wish to kill under the mask of masochism.
>
> Many masochistic husbands would like a divorce, but their need to suffer will not permit them to get one. In order for a husband who suffers to leave his wife, he must believe he will find someone better. He must have both the incentive to give up the suffering and the vitality to take action. Sometimes a masochistic husband has all he can do just to muster the energy to walk around the house. [Spotnitz and Freeman, 1964, p. 154]

What Spotnitz and Freeman have said about the masochistic husband can, of course, be applied to the masochistic wife. Literature, theatre, and films are full of examples of suffering men and women who have enormous difficulty coping with aggression toward their partners. Phillip in W. Somerset Maugham's (1954) *Of Human Bondage* felt that he couldn't live without his sadistic partner; the more cruelly she behaved, the more she humiliated him, the more attached to her he became. In the film *La Strada*, a carnival man buys an attractive but not very intelligent girl from her parents. He takes her on a tour with him and abuses and tortures her. The more the girl is abused, the happier she becomes. When the man leaves her, she dies.

A character in Eugene O'Neill's play *The Iceman Cometh* is an unfaithful husband who keeps asking for and receiving forgiveness from his wife. But the wife enjoyed making her husband feel guilty and he obviously enjoyed staying with a martyr who inflicted her particular brand of torture on him. This is a very common kind of marriage—the spouses take turns tormenting and being tormented.

Perhaps one of the most poignant and sensitive portrayals of masochism has been presented by Erica Jong in *How to Save Your Own Life* (1977). Isadora gets herself into situation after situation where she makes sure that she'll be hurt. When she is treated lovingly, she flees:

> Every time I had been separated from Bennett in the past, I had worried about him screwing around or finding somebody else or just deciding he didn't want me. This was the first time I was utterly sure of his loyalty to me, his missing me—and now it was just too late. [p. 240]

Masochists always need witnesses to their pain and degradation. They rarely cry alone and most often their main witness is their spouse. The lambskin they wear, however, hides a wolf. Their yielding always includes defiance and their submissiveness always contains some oppostion. Beneath their softness is hardness; behind their obsequiousness, rebellion is concealed. Through their defeated position, they gain a secret victory (Reik, 1941).

How does the masochistic spouse emerge in the clinical situation and what are the factors that motivate him to enter into an extramarital affair?

Saul Hunt, 45, was a capable and succesful business executive but found himself constantly doubting his capacities, feeling inferior to his colleagues and depressed by the fact that "I can never like myself for too long." Saul was also disturbed about his relationship with his wife of 16 years, who "alternates between warmth, indifference, and constantly putting me down." For many years he had had fantasies about getting a divorce, but he found it "very painful to think about what it would be like living without Virginia and the kids." One of the factors precipitating Saul's wish to enter therapy was a growing ambivalence about his two-year affair with Ruth, a married woman in his community whom he was seeing several times a week. Saul was worried that Virginia would find out about the affair and decide to leave him.

Saul described his parents as "strict disciplinarians." If he did not come first in his class, be the outstanding performer on the ball field, or "say the right thing at the right time," he got a tongue lashing. His parents frequently compared him unfavorably with other children whose performance was more to their taste. "Once I got all A's except for one B and my younger sister got all A's and the whole family ridiculed me."

Saul graduated with honors from an Ivy League college and had his choice of several jobs. Women liked him but he was particularly attracted to Virginia "because she had both feet on the ground, seemed to know the rules of the road, and *wouldn't take crap* from anybody."

Rather early in treatment Saul was able to understand how Virginia was an externalization of his "ego ideal," that is, he too would have liked to have been in the position of "not taking crap from anyone." Saul idealized Virginia, who seemed to enjoy her dominant position with her husband—telling him what to do, what not to do, and in general making him toe the line." Virginia was clearly a parental figure for Saul. He craved her approval but rarely felt that he deserved it.

After about four years of marriage, Saul began to feel some resentment toward Virginia for her controlling attitude and behavior. However, when he asserted himself, he would soon become frightened of his aggression and intimidated by his wife's counterarguments.

In his transference relationship with his male analyst, Saul assumed the role of the hard-working son. He conscientiously reported dreams, fantasies, and history; he always accepted his analyst's interpretations, came for his appointments on time, paid his bills promptly, and was very deferential in his attitude. Eventually, however, he began to express his resentment of the analyst for not being more reassuring and supportive. As in his marriage and with his parents, Saul found it difficult to verbalize his anger and was very fearful that the analyst would retaliate. In one of his dreams he was about to yell at a figure that represented the analyst but lost his voice. In another dream, a nightmare that kept him awake for hours afterward, he saw the analyst about to fall off a building and get killed; Saul tried to convince himself in the dream that it was not the analyst who was in danger but some stranger.

Not only did Saul make Virginia his powerful conscience but he experienced pleasure, particularly sexual pleasure, as something "forbidden and to be hidden." His relationship with Ruth could be compared to events of his childhood and adolescence, when he secretly rebelled against his strict parents by "playing hookey" from school, stealing alcohol from his parents' liquor cabinet, "sneaking" into burlesque shows, hiding the evidence that he had masturbated, and professing atheism.

Saul is typical of many masochistic men and women who come for analysis. Initially, they are unaware of the tremendous sadism buried beneath their self-effacing and debasing mien. Psychologically they are children trying to please and extract love from a strict, dominating spouse; when the love they desire is not forthcoming, repressed rage begins to seek expression. Fearful of confronting their spouses, they have to act out their wish to rebel in a "sneaky" way.

An extramarital affair seems to provide much gratification for masochistic husbands and wives. Feeling picked on, they initially feel justified in seeking a lover who will treat them properly. Usually the lover they choose encourages them to voice their complaints about their spouse, and this they enjoy. The idea of going behind mother's or father's back and doing something secret and forbidden makes it appealing to have sex in some hideaway motel or hotel. But the masochistic gratification of the extramarital affair does not sustain itself indefinitely. Guilty over his rebellious activity and uncomfortable about not facing his aggression directly, the masochistic spouse either begins to feel depressed about the affair or arranges unconsciously to get caught.

Married people engaged in affairs often suffer tormenting guilt and anxiety lest the spouse learn about their activity. Several writers (e.g., Ziskin and Ziskin, 1973) have suggested that extramarital relationships should be considered an acceptable part of married life. Inasmuch as monogamous marriage is boring for many and insufficiently gratifying for most, it would appear, on first blush, that if marital partners could accept the affair as another fact of married life, they would feel less unhappiness, resentment, and guilt. Many argue that extramarital affairs are "facts" of married life and should be recognized as such.

While an "open marriage" (O'Neill and O'Neill, 1972) with mutually agreed upon separate vacations and separate evenings out may be helpful to some husbands and wives, it would not appreciably diminish the torment for the masochistic spouse. As we have already noted, the masochistic spouse has strong rebellious wishes for which he needs to be punished. If he cannot express his defiance by taking the route of an extramarital affair, he will try to hurt his spouse in some other way. Furthermore, nothing influences a masochistic spouse more than his tyrannical superego. Even if his partner gave him permission to have an affair, after feeling liberated for a few months, his wish to be punished would assume priority.

Many masochistic marital partners gratify rebellious wishes by acting out defiant fantasies through an affair, but because they feel guilty about it, are actually relieved when they are caught by their spouses. Freud referred to this form of masochism as "crime out of a sense of guilt" (1916). He described the type of patient who arranges to do something immoral or illegal, is consciously unaware of why he feels guilty, gets punished, feels better after he has atoned for his guilt, and then again engages in the very behavior that got him into trouble. Many masochistic marital partners who involve themselves in affairs unconsciously enjoy getting caught and punished. When they are punished by their spouses they can unconsciously atone for a much greater sin—defying their parents—for which they have harbored lifelong guilt.

June Ingersoll, 37, came to treatment in a panic. Her husband, Daniel, had found out about the affair she was having and was threatening to leave her. However, it emerged from her consultation interview with the analyst that this was the fourth time Daniel had "found out" about June's affair with Ross and the fourth time he had threatened divorce. This time, June claimed, Daniel seemed more serious about it.

June was the only daughter of a father whom she described as "a strict minister" and a mother who "felt my father's word was law." As June reviewed her childhood it became quite clear that she derived little pleasure from life and had had to work very hard at school, home, and church to win her parents' approval. As a teenager she began to question her father's moral values and to participate in necking parties. Although the necking was very mild, June always "felt like a whore." Furthermore, this activity usually took place at church parties, so of course her father eventually heard about it, as happened several times during June's adolescence. The pattern was this: June would be caught necking, her father would severely admonish her, sometimes calling her "a whore," she would apologize and atone for her behavior, then go to another necking party, to be caught again.

It was important for June to understand in her analysis that her sexual behavior as a teenager was quite age-appropriate but that she used it to express defiance. It was because she was acting out so much sadism through sex that she felt so guilty about it.

When June realized that basically she was still angry at her parents and perceived her husband as a parental figure, she stopped her affair and began to accept Daniel more as a husband than as a punitive father. When Daniel realized that he derived some gratification from learning of June's affair and punishing her for it, he sought treatment for himself to learn why he felt unentitled to have a woman for himself.

Many people, including some therapists, assume that women are socialized to be somewhat masochistic in any relationship and that the woman's "acceptance of her role, [combined] with her passivity in coitus, impels her to welcome and to value some measure of brutality on the man's part" (Bonaparte, 1953). Anyone who has done intensive psychotherapy is aware that if one experiences a sexual relationship masochistically or sadistically, he or she will be inhibited in giving and receiving in sex and will have few pleasureful feelings of warmth, tenderness, and passion. A woman does not have to experience intercourse passively or masochistically and sharing his penis with a woman in intercourse does not have to be accompanied on the man's part by sadistic fantasies. (Actually, the term "masochism" is derived from the Austrian novelist Leopold van Sacher-Masoch, who lived in the early part of the nineteenth century. Sacher-Mosach enjoyed being whipped, and he married a woman who subjected him to constant humiliations and made him give up writing. Like all masochists he falsely believed that the only way to be loved was to accept being humiliated as part of it.)

PRIDE AND PREJUDICE—THE SADISTIC SPOUSE

Just as masochism has been incorrectly associated with femininity, so sadism has been wrongly considered a "masculine" trait. Sadism is neither masculine nor feminine but is a form of behavior utilized by both sexes to compensate for feelings of vulnerability and low self-worth. The term comes from the Marquis de Sade, a man who spent almost half of his life in prisons and institutions for many sexual offenses, including whipping women until they bled. De Sade was described as "an adorable youth with a soft feminine grace." Like many sadists, he found it difficult to accept his wishes to be a member of the opposite sex and became a proud tyrant instead. (Spotnitz and Freeman, 1964).

Men or women who physically or psychologically beat their spouses hate themselves but cannot acknowledge it. Sadists are forever trying to put their partners in the position they themselves were in as children—overpowered, weak, humiliated, and scorned (Fenichel, 1945). Psychiatrist Charles Socarides (1977) has pointed out that the sadist is a vengeful person who is always trying to get his partner to say, "You are superior, more powerful, and I bow to your judgment and decision."

Otto Fenichel (1945), a contemporary of Freud, posited that the act of elimination can be perceived as destructive and that the sadistic patient is forever attempting to use power to defeat those who he feels are attempting to exert power over him. He has never forgiven his parents for frustrating him and is busy trying to frustrate others in retaliation.

As a child the sadistic person lived in a family where there was little tenderness, concern, or empathy, and little opportunity to develop a sense of autonomy. Interpersonal relationships were heavily contaminated by sadomasochistic elements, by predominant concerns over dominance and submission, and by continual struggles over subjection and subjugation (Meissner, 1978).

Although not many sadistic people seek out therapists, when they do become patients they usually report that they have failed to measure up to the high standards of their parents, who exploited their children to bolster their own low self-esteem. Such patients almost always report that they worked overtime as children to satisfy their parents' exacting demands and insist that they will never again permit themselves to risk feeling defeated and humiliated.

The central theme that governs the sadist's activities is revenge. What happened to him when he was a passive victim he now wants to inflict actively on others. He therefore moves from victim to victor, from passive object of others' hostility and power to director and ruler. In his fantasy life those who have tormented him now are *his* victims. From an impotent child, the sadist, in his mind, becomes a dictator, more powerful than his parents ever were. Through his hostile behavior this basically vulnerable person feels victorious over those who made him feel wretched (Stoller, 1975).

Sadistic spouses almost never yield to their partners; they are extremely stubborn. Invariably they make their partners parental figures and achieve a sense of power over them by not giving the partners what they want. To give warmly, in the sadist's mind, is to lose one's identity and autonomy. Consequently he remains stubborn and enjoys either consciously or unconsciously tormenting others by releasing his rage. "My anger is bubbling to the surface again like boiling mud in a region of volcanos," says Isadora defiantly, in *How to Save Your Own Life* (Jong, 1977, p. 50). (The anal component in stubborness and spite can be noted in the word "mud.")

Flora Joseph, age 32, sought an analyst for support in divorcing her husband, Harvey. Although Flora had her "mind made up," she was worried about hurting Harvey—"he's so vulnerable that he could easily become very depressed when I tell him I want to split." According to Flora, her six-year marriage had been "dull, boring, and very unfullfilling." Flora was nonorgastic sexually with Harvey but was sure that things would be different with another man.

An only child, Flora described her mother as one who "constantly controlled me and never let me go; she watched me all the time." In addition, Flora's training was very harsh and

premature. She was weaned at three months old and toilet training began at seven months. At a year and a half, Flora developed
severe constipation and eventually had to have several operations starting at the age of 3 until 10. Constipation remained a
recurrent symptom as an adult. She described her father as an
extremely passive man "who was Mother's servant much the
way I was. We both took a lot of her shit."

Flora was a shy child, although she did good academic work in
school and later in college. She felt an obligation to tell her
mother about all her activities—occurrences in the classroom,
dates, etc. Interestingly, these conversations often took place in
the bathroom, while Flora was defecating. "I felt like I was showing her my shit in many ways," Flora later remarked in treatment.

Flora was initially attracted to Harvey for his generosity and
ability to make a good living. After just a few months of marriage she began to complain about his lack of imagination and
inarticulateness. The more Flora criticized Harvey, the more he
withdrew. At times she became exasperated with him when he
wouldn't fight back.

It took a long time to involve Flora in treatment. She continually fought the analyst's interpretations and eventually
became quite sadistic with him. In one dream she shoved a rusty
meat hook up his anus and enjoyed seeing his pain. In another
dream she was pleased to discover that his penis was "only a
piece of shit."

Flora frequently threatened to leave treatment because the
analyst was "stupid, unstimulating, and impotent." When the
analyst interpreted Flora's wish to make her husband and
analyst weak and vulnerable, she was outraged. She handled her
anger by missing sessions or coming late and by seeking consultations with other therapists. In addition, she began an affair.

Flora used her affair to prove to the analyst that she could
"make it with men. You and Harvey are jerks but I'm O.K."
When Flora could not get the analyst to argue with her or express jealousy of her lover, Ian, she felt the same exasperation
with him that she felt toward her husband.

In her relationship with Ian, whom she saw once or twice a
week, she spent a good deal of time complaining about her hus-

band and her analyst. When she did have sex with Ian, she did not achieve orgasm and eventually became critical of him for not being able to satisfy her. Flora's affair did help her to become more aware of her sadism toward men. In one session she reported dreaming of defecating all over Ian in bed, urinating over the analyst, and sticking Harvey's face in mud.

Slowly Flora began to realize that she was doing with men what her mother did with her. Her relationships with men were motivated by a wish to be sadistically triumphant over them. Similar to the way she was overpowered as a child, Flora delighted in turning men into "pieces of shit."

Inasmuch as the sadist is not capable of loving consistently, his marriage and affairs eventually deteriorate into fights. For the sadistic person, loving someone means losing power. Consequently, he defends against loving feelings by trying to overpower the partner. When the sadist is loved, he feels contemptuous toward the person who is loving. As Flora stated it, "Anybody who loves is confessing weakness. How can you respect that kind of an individual?"

For the sadistic person, an affair provides only limited solace. Inasmuch as he can't tolerate being loved for long, the affair degenerates into a series of feuds or open battles. When Ian showed affection toward Flora, she considered him a weakling.

One way of understanding the sadistic person is to see what characteristics he projects onto the other person. It almost always turns out that the sadist hates in others what he is trying to protect in himself. Hitler could not stand vulnerable people, particularly Jews, and had to exterminate them. Yet, it is well known that Hitler had to work overtime to deny his own identification with Jews. The late Senator Joseph P. McCarthy hated homosexuals; yet, many who followed his personal and political career were convinced that he had strong homosexual leanings (Wertham, 1969).

Because sadistic and masochistic responses are in effect neurotic reactions to faulty training, we frequently, if not always, find both features in the same person. The masochist feels so humiliated by his loss of power that he resorts occasionally to sadistic behavior. When the sadist recognizes how unlovable he is, he may for a time become submissive and apologetic. Even Hitler had to atone for some of his guilt feelings by being whipped by a woman friend (Wertham, 1969).

Sadism and masochism seem to be two sides of the same coin. That is why we frequently use the term "sadomasochistic," referring to behavior that alternates between striving for power and then becoming powerless.

DR. JEKYLL AND MR. HYDE—THE AMBIVALENT SPOUSE

As we pointed out earlier, many adults equate sexual discharge with anal or urinary discharge and consequently tend to regard sexual activity as something "dirty." It is as if they are urinating or defecating in or on their partners or as if that is what is being done to them. A popular British play dealing with the sexual lives of members of Parliament was entitled *Dirty Linen*, a double pun referring to the idiom for guilty secrets and the British term for underwear. When analytic patients resist describing their sexual fantasies and sexual activities, they frequently say, "I don't want to wash my dirty linen in public."

Psychoanalysis has demonstrated that many individuals perceive sexuality as if it were a bathroom affair only. A male patient referred to visiting a prostitute as "paying money to drop a load in the toilet." A woman in analysis described expressions of pleasure during sex as "grunts and groans that sound like farts." Many men who try to withhold having an orgasm as long as possible show in analysis that what they are doing with their sperm they had previously done with their feces (Fenichel, 1945). These men are of course different from those who delay their orgasm out of consideration for their partners. Men who unconsciously equate sperm with feces cannot enjoy the stimulating tensions in orgastic delay because they feel too guilty about their hostile wish "to shit" on the mate.

When a sexual relationship is perceived as a bathroom ritual, the person frequently feels some reluctance to participate in it with a loved one. One means of resolving the conflict is to "love and honor" the spouse with little or no sexual relationship and to discharge the "dirty stuff" with someone outside the marriage. Usually the conflict becomes extended so that everything that is pleasureful (and therefore dirty) is gratified away from the partner and everything nonpleasureful remains within the marital relationship. This neurotic problem explains why many men and women have enjoyable sex with their partners before marriage and then become disinterested in sex when their partners become their spouses.

Inasmuch as many people unconsciously ascribe parental qualities to their partners, the idea of "shitting and pissing on mother or father" becomes unbearable; it can only be done elsewhere. Therefore, many a husband or wife behaves like Dr. Jekyll and Mr. Hyde—as a tender, dutiful "child" with the marital partner and as a child having fun in the dirt with a lover.

Carmine King told the therapist in his first consultation that he felt very depressed "for no accountable reason"; he suffered from migraine headaches and colitis, was frequently afraid to assert himself, and derived "little pleasure out of living."

Carmine described his wife, Ida, as "a good woman," a devoted mother and wife who "took her responsibilities very seriously" and always kept a "stiff upper lip." While Carmine had a great deal of respect, admiration, and even some awe for Ida, there was little spontaneity in their relationship and almost a complete absence of physical demonstrations of affection.

It took Carmine several months before he could discuss his sex life in his therapy. It turned out that sexual relations were very infrequent—once or twice a month—and accompanied by a ritual that both Carmine and Ida were compelled to enact. Each would take a long bath before sex "to make sure our private parts were clean" and then after sexual relations each would take another bath "to get rid of the dirty stuff on our private parts." Evidently both of them experienced intercourse as a soiling experience and therefore had to take many precautions. In treatment Carmine once exclaimed, "How can I soil such a fine woman?"

Carmine's history was typical of patients with anal problems. Both parents were described as compulsive people whose living room wall actually displayed the embroidered motto "Cleanliness is next to godliness." As a boy Carmine had to wear clean, white, starched shirts and "never get dirty."

After about a year of treatment during which the analyst tried to help Carmine diminish the power of his superego, Carmine began to loosen some of his resistance to pleasure. He joined a bowling group, tried some clay modeling, and started to go to the movies. As he permitted himself to have some fun he started to feel increased sexual yearnings and began an extramarital affair. With Effie, Carmine found that he enjoyed cursing. He delighted in taking her to porno films where they had sex on occasion, "and instead of being so uptight I wear dungarees when I'm with her."

As Carmine's analysis moved on, he began to get in touch with his strong anal eroticism. In one of his dreams, he and Effie were children playing in the mud. In another dream he had anal intercourse with her and "when she came she shit all over me and it was fun."

Although Carmine was in many ways very free with Effie, he continued to be a "clean boy" with Ida. It took him a long time to realize how he made Ida a virgin mother who had to be protected from his dirt. Only when he could begin to accept some of his boyish wishes "to shit on my mother" could he begin to relax and enjoy himself with Ida.

As we have observed in several case illustrations, when the husband or wife ascribes parental qualities to the marital partner, sex with the spouse decreases in enjoyment. While this form of behavior has oedipal and incestuous implications, which we will discuss in the next chapter, when sex with the spouse is experienced as a bathroom affair with a parental figure, then the person has to worry about soiling or being soiled upon. The soiling, as we saw in Carmine King's case, usually can be enjoyed only extramaritally. However, in this day and age, when many nonmarried couples live together, analysts have noted a slight modification in how the soiling conflict is handled.

Some cohabiting couples resist marriage so that they can have pleasure with a partner who is not experienced as a parental figure. Like rebellious adolescents, these couples are defying convention by playing in the mud. While this kind of arrangement can be gratifying and fulfilling in many ways, many patients voice a longing for a more tender, nonerotic companionship. They sometimes find what they are looking for in a nonsexual relationship where companionship, talking, studying, and going to the theatre together become the major activities.

In sum, the person who has not resolved the major conflicts and tasks of the anal period is usually plagued by self-doubt and ambivalence (Erikson, 1950). Unable to feel or act autonomously because he experienced parents as arbitrary, punitive, and ambivalent, he has many masochistic and sadistic desires. The masochistic spouse may eventually tire of suffering and find an extramarital affair a respite for a while. However, the affair is not enjoyable for long because he must be punished for it. The sadistic person can express hatred through an affair but eventually gets irritated with the lover if he or she offers warmth and respect—a sign of weaknesss. Sometimes the Jekyll-Hyde personality can maintain two relationships indefinitely, provided that he can cope with an enormously complicated life. He stays in his marriage because of his need for punishment. Although he initially seeks an affair because he wants to find tenderness and acceptance his spouse cannot (or is not permitted to) express, it eventually becomes an arena in which he acts out his suppressed sadistic impulses.

Chapter 6

Oedipus: The Royal Road to the Extramarital Affair

By naming the central conflict of childhood after an ancient Greek trilogy, Freud was emphasizing the venerability and universality of the Oedipus complex. In the bible, little David slew big Goliath; orphaned Esther seduced the king and drove away his wife; and young Joseph not only surpassed his father but emerged as far wiser and more capable than his older brothers.

For generations, fairy tales have delighted the imaginations and gratified the wishes of children (Marasse and Hart, 1975). Brave Jack chopped down the beanstalk, killed the giant, and lived with his mother happily ever after. Both Cinderella and Snow White were able to compete successfully with their stepmothers and marry handsome princes. Most children memorize a nursery song that combines oedipal wishes and punishment for them:

> *Three blind mice,* *
> *Three blind mice,*
> *See how they run!*
> *See how they run!*
> *They all ran after the farmer's wife*
> *Who cut off their tails with a carving knife.*
> *Did you ever see such a sight in your life*
> *As three blind mice?*

In the play *Tea and Sympathy*, a young man is seduced by a mother figure and triumphs over her husband, his football coach

---

*In Sophocles' *Oedipus Trilogy*, young Oedipus is punished for seducing his mother and killing his father by being blinded.

and a father figure to him. James Thurber, in *The Secret Life of Walter Mitty,"* has illustrated that many people have fantasies of being a conquering hero or heroine. A song that has been popular for decades is "I Want a Girl Just like the Girl That Married Dear Old Dad."

Not only are popular media replete with examples of "oedipal winners" but "oedipal losers" have also captured the interest of many people. Herman Wouk's *Marjorie Morningstar* (1955) and *The Caine Mutiny* (1955) reveal the tremendous animosity that children can have toward the oedipal rival; yet the offspring, these works show, must finally submit to the parental figure or feel tremendous anguish and guilt. In many ways this defeated position is *Portnoy's Complaint* (Roth, 1969).

When Freud first observed the oedipal conflict in his patients, he did not fully understand its dynamics. Listening to women patients who suffered from hysterical symptoms (e.g., phobias, paralyses, pervasive anxiety), he at first gave credence to his analysands' reports that they had been seduced by their fathers and attributed their neuroses to this event. Eventually Freud realized that his patients had not been physically seduced but did experience sexual desires toward their fathers. Because the patients were unable to accept their sexual fantasies, they repressed them, and this led to their neurotic symptomotology (Freud, 1954).

No child escapes the Oedipus conflict; the "family romance" influences the love life of every adult in every society (Malinowski, 1963). As we have implied in previous chapters, virtually every married person ascribes some parental qualities to the partner. When the partner is unconsciously experienced as a parent of the opposite sex, sexual intimacy may be perceived as incest. As ubiquitous as oedipal wishes are, the incest taboo also appears to be a close-to-universal phenomenon. In all 250 societies studied by anthropologist George Murdock (1949a) and in all 200 of the societies examined by the anthropologists Ford and Beach (1951) sexual intercourse and marriage are forbidden between parents and children.

From a psychoanalytic perspective, one of the reasons a marital relationship can be trying is that the husband or wife secretly desires an incestuous relationship with the marital partner and at the same time dreads it. One means of trying to resolve this dilemma is for the married person to permit only tender feelings toward the spouse and only lustful feelings toward the extramarital partner.

Says Isadora of one of her two lovers in *How to Save Your Own Life* (Jong, 1977), "When Jeffrey makes love to me, I relax entirely—maybe because I have never felt the slightest stirring of romantic love for him and therefore feel wholly safe" (p. 83). Later she says very insightfully about her two men, "One I loved but couldn't fuck. The other I couldn't love but loved to fuck" (p. 87). We will discuss this phenomenon in more detail later in this chapter.

Men and women who have not resolved oedipal conflicts are usually anxious people who are constantly fearing punishment for their competitive and incestuous fantasies. Inasmuch as their fantasies are unconscious, they do not relate their fears of impending doom, abandonment, death, or mutilation to anything specific, but are always ready for something to go wrong.

Belle Arlington, 25, came to treatment because she felt entitled to nothing. An underachiever at school and at work and a self-confessed failure in all her relationships with men, Belle was always ready for a disaster.

It took her well over two years of therapy to realize that her conviction that disaster would inevitably befall her was related to her strong competitive wishes toward her mother, for which she felt very guilty. Every time Belle was involved with a man or trying to achieve something for herself, she unconsciously fantasized that she was at war with her mother for father, and then expected "the axe to fall."

Adults who have unresolved oedipal conflicts are usually in a state of high excitement. Although they are unaware of it, they are in strong pursuit of the parent of the opposite sex. Because these people frequently experience "high anxiety" and guilt, they spend much of their time trying to diminish their torment by placating others and trying to become lovable. Many "oedipal warriors," therefore, develop considerable charm, imagination, feeling, and sensitivity. Their expansive fantasy life serves as a refuge and a substitute for unpleasant reality and gives color to their conversations and actions (Austin, 1958). Their many real strengths and abilities, combined with a defensive capacity to simulate more adequacy than they feel, often enable them to conceal their feelings of inadequacy (Abraham, 1927).

What is often deceptive about the husbands and wives who have oedipal conflicts is that they present their marital problems to the therapist in terms of differences and incompatibilities in all areas of living other than the sexual and usually insist that it is the other partner who is at fault.

Pamela Bornstein, 30, told her therapist that she wanted to divorce her husband because they could not agree on how to raise the chldren and how to manage the budget. She also said that she had lost interest in her husband because he had had a violent temper tantrum several years before and threw a chair at her.

It was not until Pamela's sixth month of treatment that she could talk about her sexual problems. As it turned out, she had strong yearnings for her father, who was in and out of the home when she was a child, and felt very guilty about these wishes. Pamela's oedipal guilt was compounded by hearing her mother frequently belittling her father. This made Pamela feel very fearful about losing her mother's love if she got close to her father.

The life history of the husbands and wives under discussion usually reveals that they were very anxious children—afraid to go to school, afraid to be away from mother, afraid of the dark, and afraid of new experiences. Wives frequently speak of themselves as "good little girls, too afraid to be anything else." They were frequently depressed and moody, and toys and pets often became substitute friends. Husbands present themselves as having been onlookers rather than participants in sports and frail in physical build, at least in their own comparison to their fathers. They were mothers' boys, not just in the passive, effeminate sense, but "mother's little man" with good manners and consideration for the mother's friends (Austin, 1958).

Both men and women in this group show a difficult adolescence. Menstruation for women and pubescence for men were fearful experiences. During their teenage years both sexes were shy, had marked feelings of inferiority, and had problems in dating. The girls had crushes on women teachers and other older women and had more girlfriends than boyfriends. Frequently they dated only the man whom they subsequently married and often he was an older man. Often the husband is described as "gentle, understanding, and not sexual."

The men show a tendency to separate sexual and tender feelings in their discussions of premarital relationships. Often, they married women who were sexually inhibited.

In many instances these husbands and wives stay in touch with their parents and after marriage many live near them or even with them for a period. From early childhood the relationship to the parent of the same sex is characterized by hostile competition, with an accompanying overdevotion to the parent of the opposite sex. Often the behavior is rationalized. For example, one woman in analysis said "No one liked my mother and everyone liked my father."

In chapter 1 it was pointed out that after the honeymoon is over, marriage can become monotonous and unstimulating for many people; men and women feel unfulfilled and ask, "Is that all there is?" One of the forces contributing to boredom in marriage is the repression of oedipal fantasies. This can induce the dissatisfied spouse to look for the mate of his dreams outside of the marriage.

SONS AND LOVERS

Orgasm is not a panacea for all marital woe. Rather, psychoanalysts have learned that sex can cause as much trouble when intercourse is physiologically successful as when it is unsuccessful. Paradoxically, successful sex can sometimes be the beginning of difficulty in marriage. States Kubie:

> There are individuals who bring into marriage such deep-seated feelings of sexual guilt that they can tolerate sex only as long as it is unsuccessful and consequently react to orgasm with guilt or panic. I have more than once treated a man who was on the verge of leaving his wife, with whom he was physically happy, because each orgasm threw him into a panic and from panic into rage and from rage into depression. I have dealt with women for whom an episode of happy

and successful love-making always terminated in depression, followed by a subtle undercurrent of resentment that would express itself on entirely unrelated matters in the subsequent days. [1956, p. 26].

Usually sexual guilt in marriage is caused by incestuous fantasies. One male patient said of his wife as she began to be more sexually responsive to him, "The better she screws the more I feel like a mother-fucker and that isn't a good feeling!" Frequently a man loses his potency with the woman he loves and is able to be potent with one he scorns.

Lionel Zane, 32, sought treatment because he was dissatisfied with his poor job performance as a stockbroker, was depressed, had difficulty in most relationships, where he would get involved in power struggles, and had several psychosomatic complaints, including insomnia and occasional impotence.

Lionel described his wife as warm, pleasant, kind, good to the children, but unexciting. He felt that marriage was like "having a noose tied around my neck" and he had to break out of it. He blamed his sexual impotence with his wife on her lack of responsiveness. He also found her statements of love to him "abominable" — "she sounds like my mother who wants to envelop me." To prove that his impotence was his wife's problem, Lionel boasted of his big erections and sustained potency with his lover, who was "exciting," "stimulating," and who "never controls [him]."

As treatment moved on, Lionel's oedipal conflicts became clearer. In one of his dreams he shoved a suspicious-looking man out of the way and went into a bedroom to rescue a woman from him. Although he felt angry and competitive toward the man in the dream, as soon as he got near the bed where the woman was, he fell down and hurt himself. In another dream, Lionel took the analyst's seat, had the analyst lie on the couch, and instructed him on sexual techniques. Like his dreams, Lionel's fantasies involved fights and arguments with father figures in which he would be pursuing their women. As he was about to rescue the woman from the man (mother from father), he would either fall down or become hurt (become impotent or castrated).

While Lionel was analyzing his oedipal conflicts as they became recapitulated in his treatment, particularly in the transference relationship with the analyst, he took his lover, Rhoda, on a vacation to a motel in the country. Part of the arrangement at the motel was that Rhoda would cook and assume other traditional chores of a wife. While the first day or two of the vacation were described as blissful, Lionel, to his surprise, humiliation, and indignation, became impotent with Rhoda. Analysis revealed that as Rhoda assumed domestic responsibilities such as cooking and cleaning, Lionel fantasied her as his mother, and as in his experience with his wife, perceived sex as incest.

Freud (1916) referred to a personality type he often met in analysis who "splits the woman in two"—one woman in his life, usually his wife, becomes a virgin mother in his mind and the other, usually a lover, is assigned the role of a whore. This splitting process helps the patient to deny his erotic feelings toward his mother—she becomes a virgin while the whore is the disguised representative of the sexual part of the mother that is repressed. Such a man may frequently fantasize and dream, as did Lionel in the above case, of rescuing a woman from another man, i.e., rescuing mother from father. A man with a strong incestuous conflict can live indefinitely with a "virgin mother-wife" and have limited or no sex with her, while he has an affair with an erotic, non-maternal woman. Danger arises, however, if the wife begins to appear more sexual or the lover becomes maternal.

Dr. Sandor Feldman (1964), in a paper on "The Attraction of 'The Other Woman'" (which could also read "the other man"), points out that "the other woman" seems to be the woman for whom the man has been secretly waiting all his life; he sees her as beautiful, subtle, exciting, and sexually ideal. Yet, he loves his wife and has no intention of divorcing her. The psychological background in such cases, points out Feldman, is monotonously the same: the mother was beautiful, sensitive, cultured, romantically minded and unhappy with her simple-minded husband, who was interested mainly in being successful in his profession. The boy pictured himself as understanding his mother's feelings and needs; he made silent vows to make up to her for her frustrations when he grew up. Both the wife and the other woman are idealized aspects of the mother: The wife is that aspect of the mother that is interested in the happiness of her family; the mistress is that aspect of the mother that is hungry for romance and for the complete love of a "real man." The fantasies the little boy had of taking father's place, or of some day perfectly loving a woman like his mother, seem to be coming true; the rebellious, regressive self, denying reality, acts out the old impossible daydreams. Yet no lover thinks of it this way—the love he feels seems to him a response to the real person herself and to his need for her. But the man does little or nothing to make their relationship permanent and at some level of awareness acts as if he knew that she was not for him.

Patients in psychoanalysis who are involved in extramarital affairs frequently acknowledge after a great deal of reflection that the extramarital partner is neither more charming nor more exciting than the spouse. But the lover always has one distinct asset: he or she fulfills the fantasy that "sex equals the forbidden" (Bergler, 1963).

Kubie reports:

> I had a patient who had had a happy affair with a woman for many years, during which his wife was hopelessly ill. He married his mistress eagerly after his wife's death, only to become impotent with her on their wedding night and thereafter. Comparable reactions occur in women as well; in anyone, in fact, in whom the incest taboo on sex is so deep-seated that it can be shared only extralegally or in the gutter. [1956, p. 28]

WIVES AND LOVERS

Unresolved tasks from more than one stage of development may contribute to marital and other interpersonal conflicts. Unresolved oedipal, anal, and oral problems may all appear in day-to-day interaction with the spouse. For example, a man or woman may have incestuous fantasies toward the partner, defend against sexuality in the marriage by having little or no sex, and move toward an extramarital affair. The same person may also have unresolved problems with anality and experience everything pleasureful as "dirty." He may refrain from exposing his "dirty linen" in the marriage because of fear of "contaminating" the spouse who invariably is experienced as a parental figure. Furthermore, the same person might also have to defend against symbiotic wishes by denying his dependency wishes when with the spouse. When conflicts evolve from many unresolved maturational tasks (which analysts refer to as an "overdetermination" of problems), anxiety is powerful, marital conflict is pervasive, and the prognosis for resolution is not always hopeful. Such "overdetermined" marital conflict may lead to seeking an extramarital partner.

Sandy Young, 38, was referred by her physician for analysis. She had many psychosomatic complaints—headaches, frequent nausea, constipation, and insomnia. In addition, she had difficulty getting along with her aged mother and was conflicted about how much time she should devote to her; she had identity problems and felt insecure at work, feeling that her job as a librarian was "over my head." Sandy also had a lot of resentment toward her husband, Arthur, whom she said acted "like a know-it-all," "considers me beneath him" and "screws like a naive boy." Rarely orgastic, Sandy felt that if Arthur were not so "controlled," she could have more pleasure.

Sandy described her physician father as a "charming, seductive man who knew how to make women feel good." Early in her treatment she recalled how he frequently walked around the house in the nude and that she was "turned on" by it. Although Sandy felt her sexual fantasies toward her father were taboo and therefore did not discuss them with anybody, she mentioned that from age 6 to about 11, she got pains in her legs at night and her father would join her in bed and rub her legs until she fell asleep.

Sandy described her mother as a conscientious housekeeper and attentive to her children's needs but somewhat cold and distant. Sandy did say several times that she often felt sorry for her mother, who was neglected by her father. He worked many evenings and liked "wine, women, and song."

Although Sandy was a good student, she never felt competent and, despite the fact that she had many dates as a teenager, she never "got turned on to anybody." She married Arthur because he seemed "the loyal and devoted type."

After maintaining a lot of distance from her male analyst for the first few months of treatment, Sandy developed what she called "a crush" on him. She liked the fact that he always listened to her, seemed to care about her welfare, and was "empathetic." Sandy could easily talk about her love for the analyst, but, she insisted, "I'll never have any sexual feelings for you! That would be horrendous!" Further exploration of Sandy's resistance to feeling sexual toward the analyst led to associations that the analyst would be corrupted if he responded sexually to her: "I want to keep you as a virgin father!"

While Sandy was expressing her deep love for her analyst but defending against the sexual component of the transferrence, she began an affair with her garbage man. Like Lady Chatterley, Sandy contrasted him with her husband because "he's not uptight and controlled. He really likes to fuck!" In contrast to her sexual responses in her marriage, Sandy was very orgastic with him.

Sandy spent several weeks telling her analyst every detail of her erotic life with her lover, Tony. It was not until she had a dream in which she made Tony her analyst that she was able to begin to face some of her incestuous fantasies in the transference relationship. However, as Sandy began to have sexual fantasies toward the analyst and desires to take him away from his wife, she pointed out that sex was better with Tony than it could be with the analyst. Tony and Sandy had a great deal of anal sex, cursed a lot while doing so, wrestled and "hurt each other" from time to time, and enjoyed a ritual of urinating on each other in the shower.

Analysis of Sandy's split of the father figure showed that when she was a little girl she had fantasies of showering with her father and wanted to urinate on him. Slowly Sandy could acknowledge some of these wishes in the transference. However, on recognizing some of her anal masochistic fantasies, she regressed and began wanting to have an oral symbiosis with the analyst; that is, she had fantasies of spending several hours a day with him, living with him, etc. She acted out some of these wishes with Tony and began to spend more time with him sailing, going to the movies, talking more about her feelings, etc. Tony's love toward Sandy increased as she became more psychologically intimate, and this gradually alienated Sandy. She "turned off" sexually, began to argue with Tony, resented his dependency on her, and started to think of him as less masculine.

Sandy eventually saw that, like Jong's Isadora, she could love a man only if sex was absent and she could enjoy sex only with a man she didn't love.

Sandy and Lionel needed their marriages. Like young children, they wanted the ministrations of parental figures but could not tolerate sex with their spouses. Sexuality with their spouses was experienced as overwhelming, controlling, and debilitating—much as children would experience sex if they particiapted in it with parents.

Both Sandy and Lionel experienced extramarital partners as love objects whom they could enjoy only so long as they did not have to live with them on a sustained basis. As soon as the relationship moved in this direction, their incestuous wishes became activated and the bliss of their extramarital affair deteriorated.

One of the reasons that some people choose "open marriage" or not to marry at all is to avoid the anxiety that is stimulated by a dependent, incestuous attachment which they crave but fear.

THE RIVALS

For close to a century, millions of sports fans have identified with world boxing champions, baseball pennant winners, and tennis tournament victors. Political rivalries exhilarate countless numbers of people and in debates the audience is often disappointed if the opponents "do not go for the jugular." The Rose Bowl game in football is often referred to as "The War of Roses."

Psychoanalysts have been able to demonstrate that the thrill of a battle, physical or intellectual, is often an expression of unresolved oedipal conflicts. Many adult men and women are still seeking revenge for feeling smaller and less powerful than their parents. As they identify with the victorious boxer or tennis player, they feel the momentary thrill of vanquishing and humiliating their parents and becoming the one in the driver's seat. Many patients in psychoanalysis have dreams in which they are wearing their mother's or father's shoes while their parents are in bare feet. These dreams reveal the strong wish to be "in mother's or father's shoes"—i.e., in the superior position—while the parents are subordinate. All children love to play house, physically getting into their parents' shoes and acting out mommy or daddy.

When the wish to vie with a competitor is strong, one victory is usually not enough. Many a businessman is motivated not only to amass a fortune but to "make a killing" as well. Few boxers retire as champions because they savor the taste of repeated victories. One boxer reported how he felt after a victory. "I'm *cock-sure* of myself for only a few days. I have to fight soon again!"

The persistent yearning to vanquish father or mother certainly enters into marital conflicts and extramarital affairs. Many men and women choose as their marital partners people who were lovers or even spouses of fantasized and real rivals. However, winning one prize is not enough for them; after a while they are compelled to compete again with a new rival. One of the motives for new and different extramarital affairs is a desire to compete in a new and different "tournament." Dr. Mary Ann Bartusis (1978) writes of a patient who saw each woman's response to him as a "goal." He was an aging ex-football player who felt he was still out on the field "scoring."

Many individuals are attracted unconsciously to a lover, not so much because the lover has characteristics that are appealing, but because his spouse seems like a formidable opponent. If the partner in an affair is reluctant to leave his spouse, the competitive battle becomes very exciting inasmuch as the drama seems so reminiscent of the oedipal duel of childhood. For example, if a woman is involved with a man whose wife does not want to divorce him, the pursuing woman can experience his wife as the mother of her past with whom she relishes battling. In her extramarital affair she may be a passionate lover, yet analysis will probably reveal that the chief source of her excitement is competing with her symbolic maternal rival.

Psychoanalysts have seen many people who derived great

satisfaction from an affair with a married person who was firmly committed to his or her marriage. These individuals continued to feel the stimulation of the seduction and competition only if the battle endured. If their lover ever said that he or she was ready to divorce the spouse and marry them, these patients frequently became depressed and in almost every case were not ready to marry the lovers they courted. To these men and women the competitive battle was always exciting—not the possibilities of a love-and-be-loved relationship.

Terry Wolfe, 37, sought treatment because he was "in a panic." Married for fifteen years to a woman whom he regarded as warm, considerate, and pleasant, Terry came to an analyst because his lover of three years had just announced that she was ready to leave her husband and marry him. Terry lamented, "Now that she's ready, the idea repels me."

Soon after Terry began therapy, he contrasted his wife, Jane, with Arlene, his extramarital partner. "Jane is so warm, so pleasant, so sexually responsive, you'd think I'd be satisfied. But no, I've been going with that bitch for years," he remarked with much agitation. As Terry's relationship with Arlene unfolded in his analysis, it turned out that Arlene's husband reminded him of a rival at college with whom he had competed in debates and student elections. That Terry was more interested in winning a battle than in a loving relationship with a woman came through in several of his dreams. In one of them he was in bed with Arlene but interrupted sex with her to turn on the radio and listen to the Mohammed Ali-Spinks fight. In another dream he won a bowling tournament and selected a cup as a prize rather than ten lessons at a dance studio.

Terry's compulsive need to beat a rival became clearer when he described his courtship of his wife. At the time of the courtship, Jane was engaged to Sam, another man in Terry's profession. Terry described how excited he felt competing with Sam and winning Jane away from him. Similar to his reaction when Arlene said that she was ready to marry him, when Jane told him that she was ready to get married, Terry had "a let-down feeling and was disappointed that the battle was over."

Analysis revealed that Terry's strong competitive urges started in his childhood. He had a father who competed with him; much of their relationship involved his pushing Terry to excel and then proudly showing himself off and saying, "I can do anything better than you can." As a child and teenager, Terry enjoyed showing up his father and older brother in arguments. "I always wanted to be the best and could never accept back seat to any man."

In his relationship with his analyst, Terry was extremely competitive. His desire to surpass the analyst was so strong that at one point he seriously considered giving up his successful accounting career to become a psychoanalyst. He fantasized that he would be "twice as rich and three times as competent as you are." At another point in the analysis, Terry had several fantasies and dreams in which he was seducing the analyst's wife or women patients.

As Terry's treatment moved on, he was more and more able to see that close, warm relationships with women really disinterested him. He painfully realized that he used women to prove his virility to himself and to surpass other men.

A COMEDY OF ERRORS

Just as there are people who passionately desire to be "the one and only" at all times, there are others who must always lose. These "wreckers of success" (Freud, 1916) feel so guilty about surpassing anybody, particularly parental figures of the same sex, that they unconsciously arrange to be defeated; any form of achievement is experienced as a hostile victory for which they must be severely punished. Despite the fact that these losers consciously mourn their unhappy fates, analysis demonstrates that they love to battle and also love to lose.

Although the person predisposed to lose is a very competitive individual with strong oedipal desires, he needs to be defeated to protect himself from the discovery that he secretly harbors many rivalrous and resentful fantasies. What better way to defend against his wish to compete and defeat than to constantly lick his wounds and demonstrate how unsuccessful he is?

The need to lose is a defense that is frequently utilized and often extolled. A "booby prize" is sometimes awarded to people who come in last in tournaments. At West Point, the cadet who ranks the lowest is cheered at a special ceremony. "Star Dust," a song that has been popular for over three decades, poignantly captures the sentiments of the loser—"Sometimes I wonder why I spend the lonely night dreaming of a song. The melody haunts my reverie and I am once again with you. Though I dream in vain. . . " High on the list of current popular songs is "I Can Dream Can't I?" The rejected lover sings, "I can see you don't belong to me, but I can dream can't I?"

The wish to lose enters, of course, into marital and extramarital relationships. When a man or woman experiences a love relationship in oedipal terms, he or she will tend to perceive being loved by a member of the opposite sex as a victory over a parent for which punishment is necessary. Many unattached people who consciously desire a mate have to arrange unconsciously to drive their lovers away just when the relationship appears about to be formalized. Many individuals break engagements because the idea of marriage fills them with so much guilt. Similarly, there are those who can enjoy cohabitation but resist the idea of marital commitment because it would be experienced as a hostile triumph, which is unacceptable to them. Finally, there are individuals who do marry but feel unentitled to a spouse of their own. Because they have unconsciously defied their superego and married a mother or father figure, they must turn the marriage into a prison.

The "prisoner of love" is very frequently an individual who feels intense fondness and sexual passion for his mate but is tormented by his imaginary evil deeds. Because he feels so insecure, he needs constant reassurance that the partner appreciates him. However, reassurance usually does not sustain a guilt-ridden person for long, and after a while he arranges to be rejected or becomes convinced that he is rejected. It is not uncommon for a man or woman to be very successful in nine or ten relationships but to fasten on the one person who rejects him as the one who "really knows what I'm like." As a woman patient stated it, "Ten guys can love me, but if the eleventh doesn't, I know he knows the score about me. I have to be 'The Goodbye Girl,' always getting dumped."

The oedipal loser is an extremely jealous person. As sociologists Clanton and Smith have pointed out: "It is not easy to study jealousy. We cannot reliably observe jealousy because its expressions take many diverse forms, because it is often displayed only in private, and because individuals often repress or deny it" (Clanton and Smith, 1977, p. x). Sokoloff, in his book *Jealousy: A Psychiatric Study*, has noted:

> . . . Jealousy is an emotion of which a great majority of us are somewhat ashamed and which we are ready to conceal as completely as possible. . . . Not only is it the most common human emotion but the most concealed and disguised. It is present when no one suspects its presence, demonstrating itself in the most bizarre ways. [1947, p. 13]

Psychoanalysts have been able to demonstrate that the jealous person has many angry fantasies. One of the main reasons for his anger is that he cannot tolerate his parents' love for each other. He conceals his anger and wish to kill and can only feel his self-hatred and wish to be destroyed. In the novel *Love in Greenwich Village* (Dell, 1926) the main character is a man who describes the conscious pain of jealousy, the self-hatred that he experiences, and the denial of murderous wishes.

> . . . I didn't know that anybody could hurt so much and live. I suppose it's jealousy. I didn't know it was like this. I thought jealousy was an idea. It isn't. It's a pain. But I don't feel as they do in Broadway melodrama. *I don't want to kill anybody.* I just want to die. [p. 231].

Many writers such as Norman Lobsenz (1975) have suggested that jealousy is becoming outdated as we move into an era of "liberated relationships" between men and women. However, Lobsenz's case examples demonstrate that the "liberated" are frequently troubled by "unexpected jealous feelings" which are all the more painful because they have convinced themselves that they should not feel jealous.

In the previous chapter we described the masochist who is guilt-ridden because he has "dirty" anal thoughts and has to punish himself for them. Similarly, many people cannot liberate themselves from the need to be punished for oedipal victories. No matter how much reassurance they receive, they must be losers and suffer masochistically.

Hermine Vine, 23, came for psychoanalytic help because she felt she was "always chasing rainbows." Within the previous year her marriage and two affairs had terminated, and she was feeling depressed and unloved.

In her early interviews with a woman analyst, Hermine brought out that she had always been popular with men in high school and college but ended up feeling miserable. "I must do something to drive men away but I'm not aware of what I do. I devote myself to them but they get to hate me."

The reasons for Hermine's conflicts became apparent when she reviewed her childhood history and explored her transference relationship with her analyst. Hermine described her relationship with her father as very loving and enjoyable and her interaction with her mother as "mutually cold and distant." As treatment went on, Hermine recalled how much she envied her parents' relationship and remembered with bitterness how she could "talk for hours with Daddy in his study and then Mother would always yell out, 'It's time to go to bed.' I hated the idea of them going to bed together. But I was only a daughter."

All Hermine's dreams and fantasies contained themes of oedipal victories. However, each time she related them to her analyst, she also had fantasies that the analyst would hurt, maim, criticize, or even kill her. When the analyst showed Hermine that she was inviting punishment for her oedipal wishes, Hermine responded, "You are just being permissive because that's your job. I am a monster and you should hate me."

It was not until Hermine could acknowledge how much she wanted to fight and lose that the pattern of her love life changed.

The oedipal conflict is a complex one. Not only does the child want to possess the parent of the opposite sex, but he or she also wants to be a bigger and better man or woman than the parent of the same sex. These are tall orders and wishes that are difficult to tame.

When adults cannot identify clearly with members of their own sex, it usually turns out that when they were children their parents conveyed to them directly or indirectly that the expression of sexual drives was prohibited. As a result, they feel guilty about their own sexual wishes and immobilized by their competitive fantasies.

Oedipal fantasies in children sometimes threaten parents who may respond by depriving their children. This emotional deprivation is of a particular kind. It is not that the child is not loved, but that the parents cannot love him to the extent of accepting the fact that he has sexual and competitive strivings (Perry, 1958). The parents' deprivation may cause the child to withdraw from resolving the conflict, to feel guilty about his own behavior, and to blame the parents in an exaggerated manner for the situation.

When people with an oedipal conflict marry, they cannot enjoy their spouses. Guilty about incestuous and murderous fantasies, they desexualize their marital partners. If they become involved in an extramarital affair, they may derive sexual pleasure from the nonparental figure. Should the extramarital partner want a closer relationship, they become very threatened because intimacy inevitably conjures up oedipal fantasies.

Further oedipal conflicts emerge during the latency period and in adolescence. In the next two chapters we will discuss how unresolved maturational problems that emanate from the latency and adolescent years emerge in marital conflicts and manifest themselves in extramarital affairs.

Chapter 7

"Latent Heterosexuals": Their Marriages and Affairs

As noted in chapter 2, Freud referred to the ages from 6 to 10 as the "latency" period because the child's sexual impulses are rarely expressed directly. To ward off the possibility that their sadistic, competitive, and other sexual and aggressive drives will erupt, latency children utilize a variety of defense mechanisms to cope with their instinctual impulses. One means of defense is the development of rituals; latency children avoid cracks in sidewalks, count fenceposts, and reward and punish themselves for "good" and "bad" thoughts and deeds. In A. A. Milne's *When We Were Very Young*, a latency child says:

> *They try to pretend that nobody cares*
> *Whether you walk on the lines or squares*
> *But only the sillies believe their talk*
> *It's ever so 'portant how you walk*

A common defense used by most latency children, it will be recalled, is the "inverted" or "negative" Oedipus complex. Inasmuch as most children need and love the parent with whom they compete, their battle with this parent becomes too threatening to them. Rather than continue to fight with the one whom they admire, love, and need, they submit. The boy, instead of trying to surpass and vanquish his father, idealizes him and makes him, in his fantasies, into a lover; the girl does the same thing with her mother. Submitting to the parent of the same sex and identifying

116

with the parent of the opposite sex is known as the negative or inverted Oedipal complex.

The negative Oedipus complex, Freudian psychoanalysts allege, is the major etiological factor in homosexuality (Freud, 1905). The female homosexual identifies and competes with men and chooses companions who remind her of herself when she was a child. The more passive member of this liaison experiences the active partner as somebody she would like to be. A similar phenomenon occurs in male homosexuality.

The negative Oedipus complex is frequently enacted and enlarged upon during the latency years and manifests itself in the battle of the sexes. Boys and girls not only keep pretty much to same-sex groups but are often unfriendly or actively antagonistic toward each other. Because both boys and girls feel unsure of their sexual identity, they accentuate their virility and femininity—boys boast about their athletic feats and "superman" accomplishments and girls brag about their capacity to give birth to many babies and other "Wonder Woman" abilities. It is usually not obvious how much each sex envies the other. Motivated by their unconscious inverted oedipal wishes, boys want to be girls in many ways and girls secretly admire many of the boys' traditional roles.

Freud stated that the superego was the heir to the Oedipus complex. By this he meant that when the child sees that the parent of the opposite sex can't be possessed he or she internalizes the incest taboo and makes it part of the self. The hostility that is experienced as a consequence of the frustration of incestuous impulses explains the harshness of the superego. Instead of angrily proclaiming, "I want mother (father) and I must destroy father (mother)," the child converts his anger into an internal voice that says, "You are a bad person if you have incestuous or murderous thoughts! Stop them!"

Many of the dynamics of conflicted interpersonal relationships between the sexes as well as some of the problems and motivations of marital partners can be better understood if we take the inverted Oedipus complex and the superego into account.

An example of the inverted Oedipus complex in operation is the adult man who must have many sexual conquests so that he can brag to his male confreres about them. The gratification he derives from his relationships with women is usually far less than the excitement he feels when he describes his adventures to other men.

Many latency and preadolescent boys and girls form informal groups with peers of their own sex and gratify their homosexual wishes by endlessly discussing their dates and other encounters with members of the opposite sex even though the "date" may have been a five-minute exchange in the school corridor. Although psychoanalysts refer to this kind of gratification as a manifestation of latent homosexuality, "latent heterosexuality" is probably a more apt term to describe a phenomenon in which males and females are overtly involved in heterosexual activity but derive most of their pleasure from contact with peers of their own sex.

Edward Thomas, 27, was in analysis because he could feel only limited emotional and sexual pleasure with his wife. Yet he spent countless hours with his male analyst describing his sexual adventures with other women and went into every detail of how he wooed and seduced them. For a few months Edward was very euphoric and praised his analyst constantly, because "I have never felt better in my whole life." However, when the analyst continued to listen to his tales without praise or condemnation, Edward eventually became depressed and wanted to leave treatment. Exploring his wish to leave the analyst, he said angrily, "I can't turn *you* on! You don't seem impressed with me. Are you some kind of uptight fag? I thought we'd have a buddy-buddy relationship and exchange stories."

Edward's boasting of his sexual exploits was an unconscious attempt to arouse the analyst sexually. When his dreams were analyzed, Edward's homosexual interests became even clearer. For example, in one dream he was having sex with a woman while the analyst watched. As the sex became more intense, the analyst got an erection and then ejaculated over Edward.

When men and women who are involved in group sex, swinging, or switching become psychoanalytic patients, their dreams, fantasies, and transference relationship with the analyst usually reveal that they are unconsciously motivated by homosexual wishes. As a husband, for example, watches how another man behaves sexually with his wife, he often identifies with his wife and unconsciously experiences the wife's lover as having sex with him.

Married people who openly advocate extramarital relationships also derive a great deal of homosexual pleasure as they identify with their spouse and unconsciously have sex with the spouse's lover. Because this is an unconscious process, most couples who sanction extramarital activity deny their homosexual involvement and justify their stance on the basis of "free expression."

Very often when a husband or wife is painfully obsessing about a marital partner's lover, there is an unconscious homosexual attraction to the lover. Reports Isadora in Jong's *How to Save Your Own Life* (1977), after hearing about her husband's affair with her friend Penny, "We fucked with more passion than we had in years" and "from then on, we had a third person living with us in our house. I went to sleep with Penny at night, and woke up with her in the morning. I dreamed about Penny night after night. I remembered things I hadn't thought of in years: Penny's stretch bikini underpants hanging on the towel rack in the bleak bathroom of her bleak army apartment, pushing the thin strands of copper hair away from her freckled forehead. . . ." (p. 47)

When a husband or wife "fucks with more passion" after hearing about a spouse's affair, from a psychoanalytic perspective there is always a homosexual attraction to the marital partner's lover. While it is a terrible blow to self-esteem to be displaced sexually, when a husband or wife painfully obsesses about the lover night after night and day after day as Isadora did, the enormous expenditure of energy and thought almost always means that behind the preoccupation is homosexual interest.

The inverted Oedipus complex (or latent homosexuality) seems to be the dominant motif in such projects as *The Harrod Experiment* (Rimmer, 1966). In this experiment two couples with their children join in a corporate marriage and pool all their resources—sexual, emotional, and economic. Psychologist Joel Block (1978) refers to this alternative to traditional marriage as "a kind of double-the-pleasure togetherness."

In chapter 3, we noted that many people choose a marital partner because they are attracted to the partner's parents. Analysts have learned from men patients who go into business with their fathers-in-law that these men are unconsciously motivated by a strong homosexual wish to get close to a father figure. One male patient who argued daily with his father-in-law would dream at night that the two of them were showering and masturbating together.

Psychoanalysts have also observed that many women are unconsciously attracted to their mates because they experience their husband's mother as warm and supportive. One woman patient, for example, first felt a desire to divorce her husband shortly after her mother-in-law's death. "There's nothing here that is exciting for me any more," she complained.

People with latent homosexual problems are frequently attracted to each other and marry. The man who suffers from a great deal of castration anxiety and has unconscious wishes to be a woman often finds a woman with phallic strivings to his liking. As one male analysand said of his wife, "She has the strength I lack." If such a wife unconsciously fantasizes herself as a man, she may complain about her husband's lack of assertiveness, but unconsciously she relishes it. Sooner or later, however, the husband begins to resent his inferior position and his wife eventually feels guilty about her aggression and dissatisfied with the burden of "taking over" all the time. A frequent escape from this tempestuous relationship is an extramarital affair in which the spouse who is unsure about his or her sexuality can prove that he is a "real" man or "real" woman. We will examine this type of marital relationship in further detail later in this chapter and show how an affair for one or both of these spouses can be protective and anxiety-reducing, at least for a while.

As we have mentioned, one of the features of the latency period is the development of the superego. If the internal voices of the superego are relatively benign, the child will like himself and experience the world as a comfortable place. If, however, superego mandates are harsh, the child will feel guilty, dislike himself, and experience teachers, parents, and other figures of authority as punitive. Psychoanalysts have learned that most individuals project the voices of their superego onto others. For example, the child who feels that his aggressive fantasies and sexual desires are "bad" will feel intimidated by others and worry that at any moment a "bogey man" or witch may appear on the scene and punish him. He fears that his teacher, a policeman, or some supernatural figure is watching, and he cannot relax and enjoy himself because danger is always imminent.

The rebellious child or adult often has a very strict conscience. He projects his own powerful superego onto institutions such as the school, church, or government and believes, "They are out to get me!" When figures of authority assert that they wish to be fair, the rebellious person does not believe them. He is convinced that others are determined to hurt him and is unaware that he unconsciously needs enemies to punish him for his "evil" fantasies.

The superego is as strong or as weak as the id wishes. When, for example, incestuous or sadistic desires are intense, the superego has to work overtime to subdue these wishes. An example of a person with strong id wishes and a powerful superego is the vice crusader. While he rails against pornographic films and literature, nudity, curse words, and so on, in his crusades against vice, he spends hours every day carefully examining the porno films, nude pictures, and erotic literature that he consciously seeks to eradicate.

To appreciate the psychodynamics of interpersonal relationships, particularly attitudes toward marriage, it is important to keep in mind that the superego is an independent agency—the internal punitive voices speak out even if the parents or other authorities whose edicts are the content of the superego are thousands of miles away or even dead. Joan Baez, portraying a guilt-ridden girl making love, sings, "Don't Speak too Loud or You'll Wake up my Mother!" Psychoanalysts observe daily that people who repudiate pleasure are their own worst enemies—the voice of their own superego beats them more severely than any other person could or would. While individuals with punitive superegos like to feel that they are victims of sadistic exploiters, examination of their dreams and fantasies always demonstrates that they unconsciously seek punishment.

Like the child who projects his own primitive superego onto the school and feels victimized by the arbitrariness and unfairness of every school official and teacher, the adult with a primitive superego repudiates marriage because he must avoid being trapped and controlled by an arbitrary and unfair spouse. Many young people who allege that marriage is "an unnecessary and undesirable relic of a Puritan past and an outmoded and dysfunctional attempt on the part of society to limit the freedom and dictate the life of the individual" (Bowman, 1974) are in a battle with their own superegos. Conceiving of a love relationship in which *their own* superego mandates compel them to "honor and obey," they want no part of a committed relationship. A popular song that reflects their sentiments is, "Release Me, Let Me Go."

The self-punitive adult experiences the institution of marriage in the same way that the self-punitive child perceives school—as something that exploits, demands, and ruins. As one young patient quoting Groucho Marx averred, "Marriage is a very fine institution if you like to live in an institution."

The operations of the superego affect not only an individual's attitudes toward the institution of marriage but also his attitudes toward extramarital affairs. Just as the decision to have an affair may be made for neurotic reasons, so may the refusal of an affair.

As we suggested in the Prologue, psychoanalysts have long contended that behavior in and of itself cannot be fully understood unless the individual's unconscious wishes, history, superego admonitions, defenses, fantasies, dreams, and the like are taken into account. Many people avoid an affair to placate a punitive superego. Very often a husband or wife assigns to the marital partner the role of his or her superego. Like a child who feels his parents are always present even when they are far away, many a husband or wife cannot believe (because of a wish not to do so) that he or she can do anything without the partner's knowing about it. Thus they avoid an affair, not because of an absence of lustful wishes or fantasies, but because they need to feel like innocent children in front of their superego-spouses. They refuse to have an affair simply becasue they are fearful of not being "good children" (Block, 1978). A psychoanalyst would not regard this type of fidelity as mature because the decision to be faithful is not based on rational concerns but on a need to submit to a punitive superego.

One of the reasons that many people cannot permit themselves to remarry after the death of a spouse also relates to the superego and its activities. Like children who bring the image of a restrictive parent with them wherever they go, many widows and widowers do the same thing with their deceased spouses. Said a widower in his fifties, "I can't even consider remarriage. My wife is always watching me, and if I have a date with a woman I feel I'm two-timing my wife." The dead spouse as the superego who always watches and punishes is the theme of Neil Simon's play *Chapter Two*. The protagonist, although very much in love with his second wife, is so tormented by guilt for defying the image of his dead wife that he has to shorten his honeymoon, leave his second wife, and "return" to his deceased wife.

The interference of allegiance to the dead spouse with the widower's remarriage is also the theme of Noel Coward's *Blithe Spirit* and of the famous Thurber cartoon in which the first wife is perched on top of a bookcase (whether in spirit or in effigy has never been clear).

Because husbands and wives project their punitive consciences onto their mates, psychoanalysts and others have frequently noted that a divorced or widowed person often seeks a second spouse who is quite similar to the first mate. If people unconsciously need to be controlled or punished, they will find others to do it for them, and a spouse often seems to be the best candidate.

Inasmuch as the spouse is so frequently assigned the role of superego, many married people feel very constricted and confined in their marriages. Although they resent the marital partner's power and control, much as children resent parents' or teachers' controls, their feelings of obligation to the spouse stem from their own wish to "love, honor, and obey." When the role of superego is ascribed to the husband or wife, he or she is experienced as "uptight" and "stuffy."

One of the ways to express resentment toward an uptight and stuffy marital partner and feel more autonomous is to have an extramarital affair. However, as we have observed in earlier chapters, a guilt-ridden person needs to be punished, for real or imagined misdeeds. Consequently, the spouse with a punitive superego who has an affair usually leaves evidence of it around so that the partner can find out about it and administer punishment.

Psychiatrist, Mary Ann Bartusis, in *Every Other Man* (1978), relates that one of her woman patients came to her after she found condoms that her husband had stored in the glove compartment of the family car. He had never used the condoms with his wife. Bartusis points out that even if the husband did not realize it consciously, the fact that he left the evidence lying around indicated that he probably wanted to get the problem out into the open.

Morton Hunt (1969) refers to the extramarital escapade of a hus-

band or wife with a punitive superego as the "affair of rebellion."
A frequent characteristic of such affairs is the considerable ambivalence the married participant feels toward the lover.

> . . . He wishes to love but would like to stop; he defies his own
> superego yet would prefer to obey it; he loves but also dislikes or
> disapproves of his beloved; he enjoys staying up all night, talking,
> drinking, and making love, but also wants to get some sleep, carry
> out his duties properly the next day, and hold on to his marriage,
> home, business, and friendships. Even in the flourishing phase,
> therefore, such love affairs are rarely even-going and continuous, but
> turbulent and intermittent, being driven by inner and outer struggles,
> fights and flights, reunions and rejoicings, alternations between star-
> chy self-control and surrender to impulse. Time and again the lover
> struggles to deny his own desires and then abandons himself to them
> and to the clouded future they portend. [Hunt, 1969, pp. 181–182]

The unhappy husband or wife, who feels very controlled by a
superego spouse and wants to defy but feels guilty when he or she
does so, is far from a rarity. We will discuss this unhappy spouse
in greater detail later in this chapter.

A TALE OF TWO SEXES

Psychoanalysis has demonstrated that all people have active and
passive desires to be members of both sexes (Fenichel, 1945; Freud,
1905). When a person is unconsciously conflicted about whether to
be male or female, this dilemma seriously interferes with the individual's marital relationship. Inasmuch as men and women who
have uncertainties about their sexual identites are unconsciously
attracted to each other and often marry, when the honeymoon is
over both members of the dyad may find themselves in the position of having to protect themselves from anxiety. They experience
continual tension because in their marital relationship the conscious expectation that they will be exclusively "masculine" or
"feminine" interferes with their unconscious wish to be a member
of the other sex. Many married men who suffer from castration
anxiety and cannot tolerate their passive wishes protect their feeling of vulnerability in the marriage through promiscuous extramarital activity. Similarly, a woman who is dominated by

phallic strivings and the wish to castrate and compete with her husband may try to prove her "femininity" by outside sexual activity.

One of the psychological functions of an extramarital affair is that urges to be a member of both sexes can be gratified without gratification appearing obvious to anybody. For example, the passive man who has unconscious wishes to be dominated can remain in his unhappy marriage and complain about it to his more passive mistress. Similarly, a wife can derive satisfaction from complaining about her weak husband to her more potent lover.

Many married people "need" ongoing relationships with two members of the opposite sex. One part of themselves is gratified in their marriage and the other part is gratified by their affair. It may be noted that unconscious homosexuality is probably at the base of the practice of a ménage à trois—one man and two women or one woman and two men sharing a household or, more usually, a bed. All participants are probably gratifying their homosexual orientations under the guise of "enrichment," "excitement," and "stimulation."

Julie Singer, 36, sought treatment for help with her six-year-old son, whom she described as "very effeminate and passive." As she elaborated on Andy's difficulties, one could easily see that Julie derived considerable pleasure from constantly referring to him as weak. Exploration of Julie's marriage revealed that she had formed a similar relationship with her husband, Morris. With scorn and contempt, she described Morris as "fragile" and less adept than she at mechanical and athletic pursuits. She smiled when she remarked that Morris was very sensitive to her criticism.

Julie's phallic competition with her husband and son came out in her dreams. In one dream, Morris and Andy were at the toilet bowl but were unable to urinate. Julie grabbed their penises from them, attached them to her body and then demonstrated how to urinate properly.

Julie's relationship to her son and husband was similar to the one she formed with her male analyst. For long periods in the analysis, she was critical of his interpretations, speech, clothes, analytic credentials, and office furniture. She found it difficult to take any responsibility for her competition with men and constantly insisted that she was a very feminine person caught in a web with a sissified son, castrated husband and incompetent analyst.

As Julie continued to flail away at the men in her life, her dreams began to reveal her sexual conflicts with more clarity. In one dream she turned the analyst into a woman and became the male analyst. She was able to associate the dream to her strong competitive relationships with her brother and father, whom she admired for their strength and "masculinity," but could not stand "feeling so small next to them." She described her mother "as even looking smaller next to Daddy than my brother and I did."

When Julie started to become aware of some of her wishes to be a man, she began an affair with Tim. Tim was an older married man who was "truly masculine, adept in athletics and mechanics and a great lover." Although she had a few fantasies of marrying Tim, in one session Julie said, "I get much security out of my marriage. My husband and son are always there. They both accept my craziness but Tim does make me feel like a woman. I need both."

Julie's conflicted sexual identity was clear. At home with Morris and Andy, she could be the phallic, aggressive woman. However, she experienced a great deal of discomfort in seeing herself exclusively in this role despite the fact that it permitted her to rationalize her contempt for her husband and son. Although Julie constantly compared herself to Morris and Andy and talked a great deal in her therapy about her superior strength and wisdom, she never utilized her assets to bolster them.

While Julie enjoyed her superior position to the men in her family she could not rest comfortably in it. She also needed a relationship in which she could "feel like a woman." Her affair with Tim provided this for her. Whenever she seriously considered leaving her family and marrying Tim, she concluded that "feeling like a woman with Tim was not enough." She needed *both* Morris and Tim—one to dominate and the other to admire.

Psychoanalysts have learned from their work with patients that homosexual fantasies are the root causes of many extramarital affairs. When homosexual desires are well analyzed, the patient often gives up the affair because he no longer has to defend himself from the anxiety that homosexual wishes usually create.

Warren Roberts, a 39-year-old salesman, was in treatment because of poor job performance; phobic reactions to cars, subways, and airplanes; psychosomatic problems; and general depression. He felt intimidated by his wife but rather than assert his own wishes, he often submitted to her commands. "Sexually," Warren reported, "my wife calls the shots as well as the positions. She's usually on top." Warren also mentioned that his wife, Elaine, did not want to have sexual relations often.

Warren acknowledged in his early interviews with his analyst that "to compensate for my feeling of low self-worth with Elaine," he had become involved in an affair with a younger married woman who had many sexual difficulites. In contrast to his passive position with his wife, Warren enjoyed educating his lover to sex. He felt "very much the man" as he dominated her and was admired by her. Early in his treatment Warren pointed out that he did not wish to marry his lover because "Elaine is wonderful even though she's asexual." He further said, jokingly, "It's good to have two women. It makes for a fuller life. With one you are the boss and with the other you're a servant."

When Warren's histroy was reviewed, he described a very conflicted relationship with both parents. "Father was a very bright and tough guy—I always obeyed him. Although I had a lot of anger toward him, I never expressed it. I was afraid he'd beat the shit out of me if I did. So I was a good boy who did what he was told. I guess you'd say I licked his ass." About his mother Warren said, "She was an attractive and nice lady who was my father's handmaiden. She worshipped him and thought he was God. I couldn't talk to her very much because she was always worried about what to do next for my father."

Warren described himself as a "loner" in school and in the community who always yearned for some wise and older person to guide and love him. His wife seemed to fill the bill, and for a number of years he enjoyed his relationship with her. "She took over and I could always depend on her. When she told me to do something I always thought she had my best interests at heart."

After ten years of marriage, Warren began to resent his wife. "She never complimented me and it gradually became uncomfortable. When I met Janet, who constantly said nice things to me and wanted me sexually, I couldn't resist." However, after three years with Janet, Warren began to feel conflicted about his double life. He still longed for "one good woman," and he was getting tired of all the lies he had to tell.

In Warren's relationship with his analyst, he was very deferential and laudatory. He enjoyed being listened to and looked forward to his analytic hours. Enthusiastically he examined his dreams, fantasies, history, and transference relationship with the analyst. After about eight or nine months of treatment, he began to have strong homosexual fantasies about the analyst. In his dreams he would have anal intercourse with the analyst or else would make himself a woman and then have sex with the analyst. In one dream the analyst impregnated him and Warren gave birth to "a lovely little Warren."

As Warren's homosexual wishes were made conscious and as he became less needful of a father, his self-esteem improved. He became more assertive with Elaine and eventually more tender with her. At first Elaine reacted with fright to Warren's more mature behavior, but he was not put off by it and continued to be more of an adult and less of a docile boy with her. When Elaine went into therapy, Warren gave up his affair. Though he missed Janet for a number of months, because he began to enjoy Elaine much more, his grief eventually subsided.

CRIME AND PUNISHMENT

As we have stated several times, many people bring residues of childhood attachments into their marital relationships. Most husbands and wives ascribe parental qualities to their partners and then try to please them, in much the same way that children try to ingratiate themselves with parents. Marital partners, in effect, become embodiments of each other's superego and their approval becomes very much desired.

When an individual has a tyrannical superego, he will inevitably experience the marital partner as punitive and severe. A neutral comment is perceived as a rejection and a realistic complaint becomes a devastating rebuke. Like the constricted child with a punitive conscience who feels that all authorities are out to get him, the married person who projects his superego commands onto the spouse is convinced that he is unloved and no amount of reassurance will persuade him to the contrary. The only way such an individual can alter his perceptions of other people is to become aware of the sadistic wishes that helped create the strong superego in the first place.

In chapter 3 we discussed some of the dynamics of guilt-ridden individuals who unconsciously choose a mate who will be very critical of them. These people are usually unaware of how much they want to be squelched for their forbidden sexual and aggressive wishes. Like children who develop defensive rituals to contain their id impulses, married individuals with strict consciences develop marital rituals. They find themselves compulsively reporting all their activities to their partners and are driven by a need to confess all of their vulnerabilities; usually, they provoke criticism.

After a while spouses who are busy honoring and obeying their partners begin to hate themselves because they feel so small, powerless, and dependent. To cope with the unpleasant feeling of vulnerability, they start to resist listening to their nagging spouse—not realizing, of course, that they helped to create this ogre. Feeling like victims of abusive power, unappreciated as mature men and women, and defiant because their autonomy is challenged, they retaliate against their partners and do what they can to dethrone them from the lofty positions in which they had placed them.

Having an extramarital affair is a way of fighting the "superego spouse." The married individual who feels abused may put distance between himself and the partner and find a lover. Usually he finds a lover who will join him in verbally attacking the abusing spouse.

For married individuals with severely punitive superegos, having an affair is usually an act of spite. Often, they arrange to hurt their marital partners by "accidentally" letting them learn of their affairs. I recall a male patient who reported that during a marital argument his wife said in anger, "What would you say if I told you I'm having an affair with your best friend?" The patient, in a caustic tone, replied, "I'd say you were a lesbian," implying, of course, that his "best friend" was his mistress.

In the foregoing example, both spouses were unconsciously encouraging their partner's affair. When a husband or wife persistently refuses to acknowledge that the partner is involved extramaritally, it is frequently the case that he or she is enmeshed in an affair as well and feels very guilty about it.

Although the individual with a punitive superego enjoys spiting the partner, his pleasure in doing so diminishes rapidly because he feels guilty about his "crimes." Inevitably, he will seek punishment, often by unconsciously arranging for his partner to find out about his affair.

Bonnie Levit, 40, had been married to a prominent minister for over fifteen years when she sought treatment. Very early in her therapy, she discussed her resentment toward her husband, who "always stands for propriety. He is always helping people, never hurting others, and is another Jesus." Bonnie objected to these qualities in her husband because "after all, Jesus never liked sex!"

As the analysis proceeded, it emerged that Al, Bonnie's husband, enjoyed sex and often wished that Bonnie were less inhibited and more spontaneous. However, she remained convinced that having sex with Al was "dirtying" him. With some light banter that covered her own real conviction, Bonnie reflected, "Cleanliness is next to godliness. When I'm next to Al, I should be clean and keep Al clean." Cleanliness to Bonnie meant being asexual because in her unconscious mind, sex was dirty.

Bonnie came into treatment because of increasing conflict about her two-year affair with Rick, who, according to Bonnie, was also married to an "uptight, non-sexual person." Although she was enjoying her relationship with Rick very much "because we both get a chance to be rebels," she was feeling increasing guilt about it. She loved going for walks with Rick in the woods and having sex there," shacking up in illicit motels," and going to porno films, but after every meeting with him, she would fantasy asking Al for forgiveness. So strong were Bonnie's superego admonitions and so completely had she projected them onto Al that even when he was thousands of miles away, in her fantasies he would be barging through the motel door and grabbing her by the neck in anger. In one of her dreams she arranged for Al to find her in bed with Rick and then whip her for her transgressions.

In Bonnie's transference relationship, she made her female analyst into a punitive superego figure. For example, she was sure the analyst thought very little of her because she not only was having an affair but, in addition, harbored a lot of resentment toward her husband. Bonnie was able to see how guilt-ridden she was after she associated to a dream in which her analyst rebuked her for having an affair and then called Al to tell him about it.

As Bonnie began to feel intense resentment toward her husband and analyst for "always standing over me as if [they were] the ten commandments," she recalled a similar relationship with her parents, "who were always controlling [her] life." When she began to examine her relationships with her parents, she saw how intimidated she felt by them. "They were against all pleasure, particularly sexual pleasure," she reported.

After several months of treatment Bonnie acknowledged how essentially inhibited she was sexually. The only place she could enjoy sex was at "illicit places where I can rebel." "It's dirty with someone you love," she pointed out many times. When she began to realize how dirty she felt sex was, she could begin to see why she needed to feel that she had a lily-white husband who would keep her pure. She also began to understand why every time she had sex with Rick, she would have a fantasy in which she was seeking Al's forgiveness.

Bonnie is typical of many people engaged in an extramarital affair. Projecting their own superego commands on to their marital partners, these men and women experience their partners as stopping them from enjoying sex and other pleasures. Actually they are very inhibited and repressed people who experience the expression of instinctual impulses as criminal acts for which they must be punished. When their therapy helps them to resolve their distortions about libidinal pleasure, they do not need to maintain so rigid a superego. They then feel less threatened by their partners, who begin to emerge as more human to them. With the spouse perceived as more human, rebellion is less necessary, and then they do not need an affair so much.

Josh North, a 35-year-old lawyer, sought treatment because he was depressed, had various gastric disorders and other psychosomatic complaints, insomnia, and unexplained temper tantrums. He was married to Sylvia, a woman three years older than himself, whom he consciously revered for her warmth, kindness, and competence in mothering their children. Easily intimidated by Sylvia, Josh would hide when he smoked because he feared her criticism; yet, he would frequently be "caught" smoking by her and would be rebuked by her. Josh liked cursing and did so in front of Sylvia, although she would criticize him for this as well. Although Sylvia was not much interested in sex, Josh handled her resistance by protesting very mildly to her.

In his initial interviews with the therapist, Josh saw himself as a "good boy" with Sylvia, who, in his mind, "stood for law and order." Although he could defy her by cursing and smoking, basically he was compliant. Every day he dutifully reported his business activities to her and listened to her advice on how to conduct himself with others. She decided who their friends would be, which political candidates they would vote for, and what movies and plays they would see.

At the time Josh came into analysis, he was involved in an extramarital affair with Paula, a married woman who loved Josh's cursing, rebelliousness, and seeming self-confident worldliness. In contrast to his wife, Paula wanted to be educated to sex because her husband was "too moralistic" and not sufficiently exciting. Josh dutifully became her mentor and educated her to the ways of the world, particularly to sexual techniques.

Although Josh very much enjoyed the first several months of his affair, he had begun to feel guilty and depressed about it. "Initially," Josh pointed out, " I felt very powerful and extremely happy with Paula in my life. After a while I felt like a crook. I was cheating on Sylvia and hurting Paula's husband. Even if he and Sylvia didn't know what we were doing, I always felt they did. I thought that at any time and at any place, they'd appear on the scene and put us in jail."

A review of Josh's history revealed that throughout most of his childhood and adolescence, he felt dominated by both parents. "My parents' word was law and I always obeyed." One of his dreams pointed to the fact that he experienced his parents as the supreme law of the land. In the dream he had successfully argued a case before the Supreme Court, which declared Josh the winner. However, later in the dream his parents vetoed the Court's decision and Josh was compelled to comply with his parents' point of view.

Josh also experienced his analyst as someone to be feared. He was convinced that the analyst felt very rejecting of him because of his extramarital affair. Furthermore, Josh had several fantasies in which the analyst was "tattling" on him to Sylvia.

When Josh's wish to be punished was interpreted to him, he recalled many episodes from his childhood in which he sought punishment for what he experienced as crimes. For example, when he was a boy his parents observed the dietary laws of orthodox Judaism and each time he violated them, he felt compelled to confess his "transgressions" to them. Josh also recalled that as a teenager he had prayed to God to forgive him for masturbating. Once, on the Day of Atonement, he fasted longer than the required 24 hours because he felt so guilty for masturbating, having sex play with girls, and feeling resentment toward his parents.

The recognition of his feelings that pleasure of almost any kind was something forbidden was an important insight for Josh. He could soon turn to an examination of how and why he expressed his defiance through pleasureful activity. He learned, for example, that as a boy he was not merely enjoying the taste of bacon but also was telling his parents to go to hell. Similarly, when he masturbated or had sex play with girlfriends, the pleasureful activity was accompanied by hostile fantasies toward his parents, and it was for those defiant and hostile fantasies that he had to be punished.

After about two years of analysis, Josh began to realize that he was expressing hostility to Sylvia by having an affair. Experiencing her as the forbidding mother to whom he had to submit, Josh could only defy her secretly. Yet he ascribed so much power to her that he believed she knew about his activities wherever he was. Slowly he began to recognize how he was keeping himself a little boy in relation to Sylvia, his analyst, and most other people. As long as he felt he was a little boy, he was angry because he felt so insignificant next to adults. To cope with his feelings of insignificance, he had to rebel. However, like a child rebelling against parents whose love he wanted, he had to be punished.

As Josh began to experience Sylvia more as a woman and less as a punitive mother-figure, he could be more amorous with her. At first she tried to ward off Josh's expressions of sexuality and tenderness, but because Josh was no longer feeling defiant when he was feeling sexual, he did not respond to her complaints like a guilt-ridden child but instead tried to empathize with her anxiety.

Josh's more mature attitude toward sex helped Sylvia a great deal. At first she reacted to his assertiveness with anger and depression. However, when she saw that Josh was not intimidated but concerned about her discomfort, she was able to seek therapy for herself. As she began to feel more comfortable with her sexual feelings and could express them more in her marriage, Josh and Sylvia could enjoy themselves more and more with each other. As Josh derived more gratification from his marital relationship, he needed Paula less.

The conflicts that provoked Josh's seeking an extramarital affair were similar to Bonnie's. Both Josh and Bonnie projected their own powerful superego commands onto their marital partners. Feeling resentful of their domination, they fought their controls. Through their affairs, they expressed a great deal of defiance, but they were always anticipating punishment. It was not until they became aware of their wishes to be controlled that they could begin to enjoy warmth, intimacy, and sexuality. In the past this was almost impossible with their partners because they felt so resentful of them.

LOOK HOMEWARD

A conflict that emanates from the latency years manifests itself in a marriage where one or both of the spouses feel that being married means being estranged from their parents. Like children who feel very uncomfortable about going to school because they miss the comforts of home and parental support, these married individuals begin to resent their spouses and want to go home again.

Although there are many married people who sustain strong dependent relationships with their parents, the desire for "Home Sweet Home" is not always expressed directly. Sometimes the parents of the married person are not physically accessible; sometimes they are dead. More often the married adult feels too uncomfortable to confront his wish to regress and be with his parents. Although he believes that "there's no place like home," the idea creates too much anxiety and he looks for a substitute. An extramarital affair may serve the purpose of being with somebody who reminds the unhappily married person of mother, father, sister, or brother.

Libby Olsen, 24, sought treatment because she was very depressed, had migraine headaches and other psychosomatic ailments, could not concentrate at work, and was very unhappy in her marriage. Although Libby found it difficult to point out anything specific about her husband that bothered her, she felt that he was a stranger to her after two years of marriage.

Libby had previously been engaged to John, a young man from her small hometown in the midwest. The engagement was broken when her fiancé was transferred to a job in Europe and Libby was too fearful to join him there. John experienced Libby's unwillingness to join him as a powerful rejection and, in anger, broke the engagement, vowing never to see Libby again.

While trying to forget John, Libby met Henry, a man who had struggled hard and overcome many adversities. Libby responded to his warm concern, kindness, and courage in the face of hardships. A few months after they met, Libby and Henry married, and Libby moved to a large Eastern city where Henry was principal of a junior high school.

Early in her therapy, while talking about how much she hated the city and missed home, Libby began an affair. It did not take long to realize that her lover, Jim, reminded her of John, for whom she still yearned. As she began to really mourn John for the first time, she had many associations to her father and realized that John was in many ways a father figure for her.

Examining her transference responses to her male analyst, Libby began to realize that her relationship with Jim was an acting out of repressed wishes to be close to her father, John, and her analyst. By marrying Henry, she was trying to deny her incestuous wishes toward her father, for Henry, a black, appeared very different from her "white Anglo-Saxon, Protestant, Republican father." Libby also realized that in many ways she had married to spite her father, since Henry was not someone of whom her father would ever approve.

When Libby became aware of her incestuous fantasies, she abruptly broke up her relationship with Jim and tried to get more emotionally involved with her husband. However, this did not last very long. Henry still seemed very much a stranger to Libby.

After unsuccessfully trying to effect a reconciliation with Henry, Libby became very depressed and agitated. She blamed the analyst for not helping her and discharged a great deal of anger toward him and "all the other men I know who are so emotionally unavailable." Libby then formed an erotic transference with the analyst. As her fantasies were analyzed, she was able eventually to experience her powerful oedipal conflict. She recalled many occasions in which she and her father were very seductive with each other. Slowly she began to see how a close relationship with any man stimulated urges to return to "my favorite—Daddy."

Libby's story not only demonstrates how unresolved oedipal conflicts prevent a harmonious interaction in a love relationship, but her spiteful marital choice was a residue of a conflict from the latency period. Just as many latency children defy the mandates of their superego by defying parental edicts, many people choose a mate from a different race, socioeconomic class, or country to rebel against superego mandates. Of course, not every interracial or interdemoninational marriage consists of one or more rebels, but such a marriage is frequently entered into to gratify spiteful wishes.

Although the latency period is regarded as a stage of development when expressions of the child's instinctual impulses are quiet, there are nonetheless hurdles to overcome and tasks to master. If oedipal conflicts are not resolved, the latency child expresses them in such forms as latent homosexuality, a strict superego, and the inability to feel separate from the parents.

When married men or women have to protect themselves

against the eruption of homosexual fantasies, they often choose the route of an extramarital affair. With their lovers, they affirm their sexual identities; with their spouses, they unconsciously gratify their homosexual desires.

Many married people project their own punitive superegos onto their spouses. When this occurs, they feel controlled and squelched by their spouses and need to rebel against the restraints that they feel are imposed on them. One means of expressing their rebellious wishes is through an affair. However, because these people are very guilt ridden, they unconsciously arrange for their spouses to become aware of their affair and then receive the punishment that they feel they deserve.

Chapter 8

Midsummer Night's Dream: Adult Adolescents and Their Extramarital Affairs

I apologized like a madman, because the band was starting a fast one. She started jitterbugging with me—but just very nice and easy, not corny. She was really good. All you had to do was touch her. And when she turned around, her pretty little butt twitched so nice and all. She knocked me out. I mean it. I was about half in love with her by the time we sat down. That's the thing about girls. Every time they do something pretty, even if they're sort of stupid, you fall half in love with them, and then you never know where the hell you are. [Salinger, 1945, p. 95]

In this passage from *Catcher in the Rye*, Salinger reveals the turmoil of teenagers—their jumpiness, excitement, and doubts—attributes that are common to adolescents virtually everywhere (Muensterberger, 1961). Regardless of culture, adolescents more often than not present problems to themselves and to those around them (Kiell, 1964). Consequently, literary portrayals of adolescence have abounded. *Romeo and Juliet* depicts the romantic ardor of teenage passion. Shakespeare's version of Prince Hal's transition to King Henry V is an excellent example of an older adolescent responding to a developmental crisis and having difficulty with identity formation. In our own century, James Joyce, Thomas Mann, Carson McCullers, and countless others have continued this literary tradition of describing the turmoil of adolescence (Esman, 1975).

The scientific study of adolescence is a product of the twentieth century and coincides with the growth of psychoanalysis as a theoretical system. Prior to the publication of *Three Essays on the Theory of Sexuality* (Freud, 1905), adolescence was considered to be the beginning of an individual's sexual life. After Freud's monumental discovery of infantile sexuality, the status of adolescence was reduced to that of a period of final transformation, a bridge between diffuse infantile sexuality and genitally centered adult sexuality. In 1922, Freud's colleague Ernest Jones, in a paper on "Some Problems of Adolescence," pointed out that "adolescence recapitulates infancy, and that the precise way in which a given person will pass through the necessary stages of development in adolescence is to a very great extent determined by the form of his infantile development. . . . The individual recapitulates and expands in the second decennium of life the development he passed through during the first five years" (pp. 398-399).

In the 1940s and 1950s Anna Freud was able to document that the "Sturm und Drang" of adolescence are to be expected. She showed how oedipal and other childish fantasies are revived in adolescence and therefore the teenager has a desire to regress. This wish to regress, to be a young child again, conflicts with the desire to be independent and emancipated from parents (A. Freud, 1937). The emotional seesaw that the teenager experiences—very much wanting cuddling, hugging, and dependent gratification versus wanting to take care of himself—accounts for his moodiness. The adolescent can go from the height of elation to the depth of despair in a single hour. He can be enthusiastic one day and hopeless the next. Frequently feeling oppressed by parents, the young person, to establish an identity, loudly exclaims, "I rebel, therefore I am!" (Blos, 1967; Erikson, 1956; Esman, 1975).

In a parable, the philosopher Schopenhauer describes a company of porcupines who crowded together on a cold winter's day so that they could profit from one another's warmth and avoid being frozen to death. Soon they felt one another's quills, which made them separate from each other. When the need for warmth brought them close again, they once again felt the pain of the quills. They were driven backward and forward until they were able to discover a mean distance at which they could most tolerably exist. This parable describes in many ways the typical teenager's dilemma. There is no end to the ingenious devices by which adolescents engage with and disengage from their families and others. They want warmth yet repudiate it. They want advice but shun it. They love praise but often repel it.

What makes physical and sexual expressions of warmth and love so anxiety-provoking for the adolescent is that, in the unconscious mind, hugging, touching, hand holding, etc., arouse memories of where and when these activities took place for the first thirteen or fourteen years of life—with mother, father, grandparents, and occasionally siblings. Much of the young person's self-consciousness surrounding bodily contact is due to his concern that he may be a baby again and is being too infantile. Particularly among boys, verbal and physical expressions of affection are often considered sissified.

It is important to remember that the more teenagers fight for power, the more they act like angry rebels, the more they are defiant, then the more vulnerable they feel, the more dependency they are trying to deny, the more insecure they are about their own identity. Erik Erikson (1950), a leading authority on the social and psychological dynamics of adolescence, has used the term "negative identity" to describe how the teenager, by taking on roles that are the antithesis of his mentors, defines himself. If parents are academically and intellectually oriented, the adolescent champions anti-intellectualism and materialism; if the parents are religious, atheism becomes a modus vivendi; if the parents are free thinkers, the young person may become an orthodox religionist.

During adolescence the teenager regresses to older forms of behavior. His reactivated orality appears in the habit of hoarding food or abstaining from it. Anal-sadistic activities are frequently observed in the use of "foul" language and in disregard of, or excessive preoccupation with, clothes and cleanliness. Phallic and oedipal interests are embodied in crushes on rock heroes, sports figures, or television stars.

As has been demonstrated in previous chapters, when maturational tasks of childhood are not mastered, an unhappy marriage will result. Because "adolescence recapitulates infancy" (Jones, 1922) and adolescent conflicts are in many ways unresolved struggles from previous developmental periods, expressed in intensified form, the marital and extramarital problems that we will discuss in this chapter will show much similarity to those in earlier chapters—i.e., problems with dependency wishes, sadism, masochism, incest, aggression, and homosexuality. However, the unique problems of the teenager—identity conflicts, sexual anxieties, strong wishes to regress and rebel—emerge in certain types of conflicted marriages, as we will see in the case illustrations.

One means of coping with the anxiety that increased responsibilities bring is to regress. Many teeangers who resent work, whether at home or school, become infants and insist that it is the responsibility of others to make them happy. Some spouses expect their partners to minister to their every need. When they are not indulged, they get angry and either threaten divorce or actually do get divorced. Usually there is little evidence that they have tried to share the responsibility of preserving the marriage before seeking the divorce route. In some instances they have sought marriage counseling, but soon abandoned that approach because it did not result in a change in their partner's behavior (Josselyn, 1971). Wanting what they want when they want it, these husbands and wives demonstrate their wish to be indulged through their extramarital affairs. The blissful feeling that the affair creates reinforces their belief that an omnipotent parent is available. However, sooner or later the lover becomes a disappointment because he or she is unable to fulfill all the requirements of the role of "perfect parent."

As we have already indicated, teenagers frequently feel that they have to fight their dependency feelings and to convince themselves and others that they are independent adults. Their need for nurturant parents causes them tremendous anxiety. When the conflict between dependence and independence is not mastered, it inevitably expresses itself in marriage. A situation that confronts many therapists is the young person who expresses the wish for independence by getting married but then finds the partner's desire for closeness too reminiscent of the parent's wish to foster a dependent relationship. To fight the uncomfortable feelings of intimacy that marriage creates, the young person rebels by becoming involved in an extramarital affair. While the affair can reduce anxiety for a while, sooner or later the issue of divided loyalties has to be confronted.

Some teenagers cope with burgeoning sexual impulses that cause them anxiety by "bribing the superego" (Alexander, 1952); that is, they vow not to "go all the way." They "pet above the waist but not below"; they "do not neck on the first date," and they do not have sex until there is an agreement to go steady. These compromises appease the superego and assuage guilt feelings.

Although defenses against the expression of sexuality weaken as the young person matures physically, if sexual conflicts are not resolved, they will, of course, appear in marriage. Usually the inhibited husband or wife rationalizes the distance that he or she has created from the marital partner and becomes convinced that it is the partner who does not want the good life. Feeling embittered, this spouse tries an extramarital affair. However, like the teenager with a tyrannical superego, such a person often limits sexual activity in the affair to "petting above the waist" and "not going all the way."

Clinicians who have worked with teenagers have frequently observed the resurgence of the oedipal conflict during adolescence. When the conflict is not mastered, the young person is never wholly comfortable with his or her sexual identity. As we have discussed in previous chapters, when the family romance is not relinquished, homosexual and bisexual wishes emerge. To deny their impact the young person may become sexually promiscuous. If the problem continues into marriage, he or she will seek extramarital affairs to alleviate the anxiety created by homosexual and bisexual wishes.

BABES IN ARMS

In a culture that stimulates much excitement and urges to regress, many husbands and wives, like many adolescents, find the responsibilities of an adult relationship irritating and taxing. Washing the dishes, listening to the details of the spouse's day, and resolving conflicts among the children are boring and unpleasant tasks compared with the garden of delights that seems within reach. It is not easy to consistently exercise high-level judgment, tolerate frustration, use mature reality testing, and defer gratification—essential responsibilities if a marital relationship is going to endure.

Like adolescents who fear the increased responsibilities of school, work, and love relationships and regress to infantile behavior, many frightened spouses cope with their marital anxieties by regressing to the position of a megalomanic child. Instead of offering support, they want to be continually supported; instead of listening, they want to do most of the talking; instead of empathically relating to their mate's dissatisfactions, they want to be the sole complainer in the dyad; instead of consoling, they want constant sympathy and indulgence. The regressed spouse, like the regressed teenager, resorts to verbal or even physical assaults when frustrated. He wants what he wants when he wants it and is ready to kill when he does not get it.

In order to function well in a marriage, one must have resolved the wish to be a parasitic baby and be able to derive satisfaction from being a nurturing adult. Many husbands and wives are unable to assume a nurturing role because they did not witness their own parents pleasurably nurturing each other. Often, these husbands and wives themselves received inconsistent parental nurturance. On entering marriage, they are unconsciously prepared for power struggles and show a readiness to be neglected and ungratified.

When husbands or wives experience their childhood pasts as depriving, they are usually psychologically hungry, but fight against recognizing this fact. Instead, they project their own hunger onto their mates and accuse *them* of wanting too much. Not only do they criticize their partners for *their* parasitic behavior, but blame them for all of their frustrations. I remember a patient who had to stop smoking because of a heart condition. He resisted the realization that his enemy was his coronary disease; instead, he experienced his wife as a hostile foe because she refused to buy him cigarettes. Like an immature teenager, he wanted to see people, particularly his wife, as depriving him rather than confront his own limitations.

If a married person regresses to the narcissistic and omnipotent position of an adolescent, he will become very angry at his marital partner when his strong oral-dependent desires go ungratified. Feeling gypped and misunderstood, he may think an extramarital affair is a good way to fulfill himself.

Lloyd Pearson, age 35, sought analytic help because he was very depressed. Married for more than ten years, Lloyd described his wife, Susan, as a devoted mother and wife who kept a good home, was very responsible, entertained nicely, and did all of her jobs efficiently. When other dimensions of Lloyd's married life were explored, he acknowledged that there was something missing. While he and Susan were "loyal" to each other, their sex life was "routine" and "not very exciting." There was little laughter between Lloyd and Susan, although occasionally they could have fun on picnics with their son and daughter, aged 8 and 7, respectively.

Although Lloyd found his job as an accountant "all right," he was unable to feel enthusiastic about anything on the job. He spoke the same way about friends, family, and other associations.

After about six sessions of therapy, Lloyd brought out a great deal of resentment toward Susan. "She shows no passion, rarely gets excited, and is a stick-in-the-mud." He told his analyst, a woman, that Susan needed treatment more than he did so that she could learn to enjoy life. When the analyst did not immediately gratify Lloyd's request that she treat Susan but tried to explore its meaning further, Lloyd became enraged. He accused the analyst of being a "cold potato" who was not interested in being his ally but was "more interested in being a shrink and going through your rituals."

When the analyst confronted Lloyd with her observation that he seemed to experience her in the same way that he perceived Susan—"cold, stiff, and going through rituals"—Lloyd at first rejected the interpretation and then, after a few sessions, associated to his mother. He recalled that when he was a teenager his mother frequently wanted to dance with him and often asked him for the details of his dates with girlfriends. Concomitant with his mother's increased interest in him, she became quite distant from his father, who traveled a great deal at that time.

As Lloyd began to experience strong incestuous fantasies in his therapy, he became very frightened. Just as he had desexualized his relationship with his mother when he became frightened of his sexuality, he did the same thing with his analyst. He began to call her "a stupid looking nun" and an "intellectual snob." As in his past when he coped with oedipal wishes by regressing to orality and asking his mother to bake for him, to do his homework for him, and to shop for him, he asked his analyst to indulge him. He wanted advice on how to make Susan "more appetizing" and he also demanded that the fee for his analytic sessions be reduced. When the analyst did not respond to Lloyd's demands but instead tried to get him to free-associate to them, Lloyd again became very angry. He threatened to leave treatment and also began arguing a great deal with his wife, whom he also threatened to leave.

While in the throes of a negative transference toward the analyst and Susan, Lloyd began an affair with a married woman, Nina. Although there was some sex between Lloyd and Nina, what pleased Lloyd most was the tremendous oral gratification he received from the relationship. "She brings me cakes, buys me books, gets me shirts and ties, and really takes care of me!" Lloyd exulted.

For the first six months of Lloyd's affair, he seemed unconflicted about it. Not only did he enjoy Nina's consistent devotion, but the excitement and increased self-esteem he derived from the relationship made it easier for him to cope with Susan and his domestic and work responsibilities. However, as time went on, Lloyd began to feel depressed again. After some time, it became clear that Lloyd was angry at Nina. She didn't call him every time he wanted her to do so, she didn't always have a gift for him, and Lloyd did not like hearing from time to time that Nina felt guilty about neglecting her husband and children.

When the analyst asked him what he felt toward Nina's husband and children, Lloyd was eventually able to face his unresolved oedipal conflicts. As he began to associate to Nina's husband, he experienced rivalrous feelings toward his own father and toward his analyst's husband. The more he could acknowledge and feel his competition with these men, the more he could begin to see how he had been spending a lot of time and energy to avoid feeling sexual toward his wife, his mother, and even Nina.

Because Lloyd had many incestuous fantasies that frightened him, he regressed to an oral position. Nina, his lover, was made the feeding mother who could help him maintain his regressed position. Lloyd shunned the responsibilities of marriage because if he assumed them he would feel like an oedipal victor, and this was much too anxiety-provoking for him.

Lloyd, and men and women like him, may be compared to Peter Pan (Barrie, 1950), a childlike figure whose sexual identity is not yet firmly established (Jacobs, 1978) and whose sexual anxieties are very strong. Peter ran away because he heard his father and mother talking about what he was to be when he became a man. Said Peter, "I want always to be a little boy and have fun." He escaped to a magical world called Neverland where all things are possible, all one's wishes can be granted, and one never grows old.

For some men and women the realities of marriage are experienced as so burdensome that they have to escape to a Neverland—the blissful land of an extramarital affair.

REBEL WITHOUT A CAUSE

When teenagers are caught in the tormenting conflict between dependence and independence, they may attempt to resolve the dilemma by denying their dependency and rebelliously adopting a facade of exaggerated self-sufficiency. Not infrequently such young people become involved with and often fanatical in adherence to causes, beliefs, leaders, ideologies—anything that provides a sense of stability and direction for their fragile identities (Meissner, 1978a) and that also is counter-cultural (i.e., rebellious).

Erikson (1950) and other writers (Bettleheim, 1971; Meissner, 1978) have pointed out that the stance of rebellion reflects a defective identity just as much as a compliant stance does. The rebel defines his shaky identity in terms of opposition to someone else and takes his stand only after the other person has made his position known. In fact, the rebel has no greater autonomy than a submissive person, despite his apparent independence. As a married adult, his affair, which he almost always announces to his spouse, is an expression of contempt that bolsters his shaky identity.

Just as rebellious teenagers focus blame for their intrapsychic problems on parents, teachers, and society in general, rebellious spouses are convinced that their marital woes are provoked by their mates. They love to use their marital partners as scapegoats so that they can obscure the real unconscious roots of their own suffering. Frequently, rebellious spouses blame their marital conflicts on the institution of marriage. I remember asking a patient who was about to begin psychoanalytic treatment why she was considering divorcing her husband. She responded, "Everybody who is married should get divorced. Marriage is an antiquated institution and I'll be damned if I want to comply with something that was all right in the Dark Ages." I also recall a male patient who said at his first consultation interview, "Anyone who says monogamy is a valid form of living is a liar or a hypocrite. It's endorsed by the church and government and that's enough to make it a ridiculous way to run one's life. The smart set knows better."

Forbidden Fruit

Many people can enjoy sex only if it is forbidden. As we discussed in chapter 2, children often have the misconception that everything sexual is mysterious and therefore sex acquires a connotation of danger and of the forbidden. Sex in marriage never lives up to these infantile conceptions and then becomes worthless for many people (Bergler, 1960). Relating to this theme, an analysand remarked in a session, "Can you refute the fact that many people drank during Prohibition *because* drinking was legally forbidden? And isn't that why many teenagers smoke? I think sex is enjoyed for the same reason. If it's not forbidden, it's not fun."

One of the reasons extramarital affairs are so popular is that sex in marriage is legally and morally sanctioned. Psychoanalysts frequently observe in their practices people who find marital sex boring but feel very excited when involved in a "forbidden" or "illicit" extramarital affair. As we saw in previous chapters, if their extramarital partners suggest marriage, the affair becomes dull for them because the forbidden dimension is missing.

Long before Freud, the poet Henrich Heine suspected the connection between sex and the forbidden. In his book on the philosopher Ludwig Boerne, Heine wrote:

> . . . We, Boerne and I, also visited Bornheim. . . . There were beautiful girls . . . Boerne's eyes twinkled. In this mysterious twinkle, in this insecure lewd blinking, afraid of the inner voice, the whole difference in our feelings was enclosed. Boerne was, though not in his thoughts, but therefore more in his feelings, a slave of . . .abstinence. As usual with all people of that sort, who accept sensual abstinence as the highest virtue, but are incapable of living up to that ideal, he dared only in the secretive twinkling and blushing, like a gluttonous boy, to taste of Eve's forbidden apples. I know not whether the enjoyment of these people is more intense than with us who miss the allurement of the secret absconding and moral contraband. On the other hand, it is said that Mohammed forbade wine to his Turks for that purpose: that it should taste sweeter to them. . . . [Bergler, 1960, pp. 38–39]

Injustice Collecting

One form of adolescent rebellion is injustice collecting. Because teenagers often fear sexual pleasure, are guilty about sadistic fantasies, and are gluttons for punishment, they unconsciously receive gratification from defeat, humiliation, and failure. Millions of adults also constantly bring about situations in which they will be unjustly treated. On the surface they appear to be innocent victims of a heartless environment, but in fact they are constantly provoking rejection and defeat and then pity themselves (Bergler, 1960). Inasmuch as they can document all the unfair treatment they have received, they feel quite justified in pursuing an extramarital affair. They are completely unaware of their masochism and of their overweaning unconscious goal—to prove that someone has been unjust to them (Reik, 1941).

Louise Nelson, 24, sought therapy because she could not decide whether to divorce Barry, her husband of two years. She had many complaints about Barry—he never praised her, frequently criticized her, was rarely warm or romantic, did not make enough money, and was insufficiently decisive.

In therapy it became quite clear that Louise had an impoverished identity and had never really developed values or convictions of her own. As a teenager she vascillated from celibacy to promiscuousness, from endorsing communism to championing capitalism, from being a devout religionist to an infidel. The only child of wealthy parents who indulged her, Louise constantly incorporated strengths that she could find in other people. She never thought for herself and emerged as a person with a character disorder described by the psychoanalyst Helene Deutsch (1965) as an "as-if personality"—a person who has no identity of his own and copies the behavior of others.

In treatment Louise tried to ascertain the analyst's values on marriage, divorce, child-rearing, and work. When he pointed out that she was not too sure of her own ideas on these areas and that her mixed feelings could be profitably explored in treatment, she became furious. Similar to her complaints of Barry, Louise, during her third month of treatment, complained to her analyst: "You never praise me, you never support me, you never give me a human response. All you want are things from me!" As in her marriage, she wanted to "fire" the analyst but couldn't be sure it was the right thing to do.

When Louise could not elicit the analyst's opinions on the issues about which she was uncertain, she began to feel and act very rebelliously. She came late for appointments, cancelled several, delayed paying her analyst's bill, and constantly criticized him. Her negativism also appeared in her dreams. In one dream she went to the library and read a book written by the analyst in which he endorsed masturbation. Louise thereupon vowed that she would never masturbate again. In another dream, Barry tried to praise her and she told him to stop. In still another dream she found out that the analyst was Jewish and then decided to enter a convent.

During this period of negative tirades toward her husband and analyst, Louise started an affair. She selected a man "as unlike Barry as [she] could find" and in an openly defiant manner made sure that everybody in her immediate vicinity knew about her "project." She took particular pains to make Barry aware of her affair by going with her lover to a motel on the same street as Barry's office.

When Barry confronted her with the fact of her affair, Louise responded with complaints about *his* behavior. Barry's reaction to her tirade was to suggest divorce. Louise reacted to this with enormous anxiety and within a few days promised to end her affair.

When Louise stopped seeing her lover, she realized that the affair had served to protect her against experiencing her strong dependency wishes. She began to have dreams that suggested that unconsciously she harbored strong symbiotic wishes. In one of her dreams she was walking down the street with the analyst's arm tied around her with a rope. In another, she was a baby inside her mother's stomach.

As Louise resolved some of her symbiotic wishes, she became more individuated and less dependent on others for opinions, ideas, and values. As her self-esteem improved, so did her relationship with Barry.

Bruno Bettelheim (1971) has contended that the "adolescent revolt" occurs because society keeps the next generation in a state of dependence much too long. He has further suggested that if the young person does not experience enough independent achievements, he will emerge as an angry and rebellious adult. Bettelheim's hypothesis seems quite applicable to people like Louise, who are indulged and kept dependent as children and adolescents. Feeling uncomfortable and insecure in their roles as husbands or wives, they rebel by having an affair and provocatively bringing it to everybody's attention.

A Taste of Honey

> *Friar Barnardine*: Thou hast committed. . . .
> *Barabas*: Fornication. But that was in another country.
> > Christopher Marlowe

Barabas, the "Jew of Malta," when accused of "committing fornication," excused himself because the sex act occurred in another country. The poet Christopher Marlowe was able to recognize that in a foreign land many people can free themselves from superego commands and experience a type of freedom that they lack in their own environs. Psychoanalysts have frequently seen patients who need to go outside of their home town or state to have sexual relations. There have also been cases reported of patients who could enjoy sexual relations only in a foreign land (Birner, 1971).

Over 650,000 teenagers run away from home each year because they cannot tolerate living with their parents' restrictions. Their superego admonitions are projected onto the home and school, and to fight what appear to be arbitrary controls, they run away. In another city or state they can gratify sexual and aggressive impulses that they feel would be forbidden in their own community.

Similarly, many married people experience their homes as oppressive places where sex and other pleasures cannot be enjoyed. When pleasures are taboo in one's home, this is because the adult, like the teenager, is unconsciously arranging for his spouse to be a restrictive and punitive superego.

The notion that sex and other pleasures can be enjoyed only in a place other than one's home is embodied in the biblical tale of Adam and Eve, the story of the human's first sexual experience and first sin. According to the Bible, Adam and Eve were placed by God in the Garden of Eden and admonished not to sample the fruits of the Tree of Knowledge. When they broke this rule, they became guiltily aware of their nakedness and their sexual desires. God punished them by chasing them out of the Garden. In psychoanalytic terms it could be said that their own guilt forced them out. Like teenagers dominated by the voices of their superegos, Adam and Eve could have sex only if it took place away from Eden, their home. Only the land outside Eden was free of the sexual taboo (Birner, 1971).

As we have discussed in previous chapters, a punitive superego protects the person from experiencing his id wishes. One of the main reasons the home seems restrictive to so many married people is that their marital partners are experienced as parental figures. Pleasure with the partner, particularly sexual pleasure, becomes associated with incest, and incestuous pleasure is taboo. When the marital partner is perceived as an incestuous object, the husband or wife seeks sex elsewhere.

Percy Olsen, 36, sought therapy because he was "tired of the life I'm leading." Married for over ten years to a woman he described as warm but asexual, Percy had had three prolonged affairs during the previous seven years. In addition to feeling guilty for "cheating" on his wife, Gloria, Percy was beginning to find it very expensive and inconvenient to have a lover 300 miles from his home. "Not only does it cost me a fortune traveling to see my friend and calling her long distance, but I have trouble finding excuses to tell Gloria why I'm away from home so often."

When Percy's history was reviewed, he mentioned that he had had a very close and intimate relationship with his mother, whom he described as a very seductive woman who frequently dressed and undressed in front of him, often told him "dirty jokes," and subtly criticized her husband in front of Percy.

Percy's fantasies and dreams demonstrated that he had strong incestuous fantasies toward his mother but felt very guilty about them. In one of his dreams, Percy went to an alumni reunion of his college, started to dance with a professor's wife, and, when she became very seductive, left the dance to visit a prostitute in another town, where nobody knew him. Other dreams demonstrated that Percy could not enjoy sex or have any other pleasures at his home because he experienced much guilt while doing so. The only type of sexual relationship that was acceptable to him was one that was some distance from home and with a woman who was very different from his mother.

In Percy's transference relationship with a woman analyst, he was alternately distant, seductive, and defiant. In one of his dreams, he made the analyst a prostitute. He complained that paying for treatment was "like paying a whore for some love." To the analyst's question, "What comes to mind about bought love?" Percy replied that paying for the love he received from the analyst made her unlike his mother, who "freely seduced me and made me uncomfortable."

An interesting part of Percy's history was that as an adolescent he divided his girlfriends into two groups—those who were interested in sex and responsive to him sexually and those who were not. The girls who were not sexually responsive to Percy lived in his neighborhood while those with whom he was sexually freer lived in a neighborhood several miles away.

When Percy was able to see that enjoying sex only if it transpired in "foreign lands" with "foreign women" was an old problem that went back to his adolescence, he began to realize that his having extramarital affairs far away from home was more than a coincidence. As Percy said after 18 months of therapy, "It's too close for comfort to have sex in your own house. If I'm in a place far away from my house, I'm much safer. I don't feel so much like a dirty mother fucker!"

As we mentioned earlier, another means of coping with superego admonitions is to bribe the superego. Guilt is reduced if one does not "go all the way" sexually. Many an adolescent can live with himself or herself if sex is only partially enjoyed.

The ambivalence toward sexual pleasure that so many teenagers exhibit is also found among adults who equate sexuality with forbidden pleasures—incest, oedipal victory, sadism, masochism, oral mergers, etc. For these people, their spouses can be only asexual companions. After a while marriage becomes very boring because libidinal pleasure is being renounced. Inasmuch as the bored spouse rarely takes any responsibility for his monotonous marriage, he feels justified in seeking an extramarital affair. However, in the affair, he behaves like a guilty teenager. To assure himself nothing wrong is being done, only limited sex takes place.

Rose Temple, 40, sought therapy because she felt very bored with her marriage of 15 years to a "stable, kind, and reliable man." She complained of feeling unstimulated "in and out of bed." Because Oscar, her husband, was "an interesting conversationalist" who was also devoted to her and to their children, Rose felt very guilty about the fact that she had been involved in an affair for over two years.

Although Rose saw her lover, Willie, almost every day, they had sexual intercourse on only one occasion. They spent many hours conversing about politics, philosophy, marriage, and the family; for the most part, sex was confined to occasional kissing and hugging.

In Rose's transference relationship with her analyst, she constantly avoided a close relationship with him. When her intellectualized approach to the analytic relationship was interpreted to her, she was enraged. She accused the analyst of being "much too seductive" and "a dirty old man." He reminded her of her father who used to walk around "bare-chested with his balls hanging out of his underwear."

As Rose discussed her contempt for her analyst and her father, she began to look more carefully at her relationship with her husband. Slowly she began to realize how much she needed to experience him as asexual. "Otherwise," she remarked, "I'd be having sex with my father." A little later Rose made the same connection when examining her relationship with Willie. "I seek out asexual guys and then blame them for their lack of sexual intimacy. In many ways it's my fault," she insightfully reported.

Compulsion

Like the oedipal youngster who finds the rivalry with the parent of the same sex too intense and gives up the battle by passively submitting to that parent, the adolescent often goes through a transitory phase of homosexuality. Friendship usually disguises the homosexual element, but it is not uncommon for youths between 12 and 15 to sexually experiment with each other. Often, the inverted oedipal position can take the form of a real attachment to an older person of the same sex, such as a teacher. Many of these relationships are free from any overt sexual response and the love is a desexualized one.

When the teenager continues to feel a strong attraction toward members of his or her own sex, this often creates enormous anxiety. To compensate for the discomfort homosexual fantasies induce, teenagers may become very promiscuous. If this conflict around homosexuality is not resolved, it, of course, enters into the individual's marital relationship. As we discussed in chapter 7, a married person with latent homosexual desires has unconscious wishes to make the marital partner a member of his or her own sex. Feeling a vague discomfort in the marital relationship but not knowing what the tension is about, the husband or wife with unconscious homosexual desires negates them by having an extramarital affair to prove that he or she is heterosexual.

Harvey Ungar, 29, sought therapy so that he could better understand why he was "always running away from my marriage." In the four years of his marriage, he had had eight extramarital affairs, each with a single woman who was "very hot and had lots of experience with men."

Contrasting his wife, Linda, with his girlfriends, Harvey described Linda as warm and affectionate but "not sexy." While devoted to him and "very attractive in clothes," according to Harvey, Linda didn't "have what it takes."

Harvey was in treatment no more than a couple of months when he began to see that his compulsive extramarital activity was related to his homosexual wishes. He realized that in contrast to his lovers, Linda had no sexual experience with other men. This realization helped him to start exploring what appealed to him about women who had considerable sexual experience. Analysis revealed that Harvey was very much interested in the other male partners of his lovers and had many sexual fantasies about them.

In Harvey's dreams he had orgies with men present, and in his transference relationship with his male analyst, he constantly fantasied having fellatio and anal intercourse with him. All of these fantasies represented a powerful yearning for a father figure who would "be with me all of the time and whose strength I could depend on."

As Harvey examined his homosexual fantasies and became less compulsive about proving his potency, his marriage improved.

Adolescence recapitulates all phases of development. When tasks of the oral, anal, phallic-oedipal, or latency periods are not mastered well, residues of these conflicts will emerge during adolescence.

Although adolescent conflicts are in many ways unresolved struggles from previous developmental periods expressed in intensified form, the teenager is particularly prone to identity conflicts, anxiety about sexual wishes—heterosexual and homosexual—and ambivalence about dependency. To protect himself against his strong dependent yearnings, the teenager may act very independently; to ward off sexual doubt he may become promiscuous; to feel some sense of identity he may become a rebel.

The married person who has not resolved adolescent tasks often starts an extramarital affair. An affair can bolster a shaky sexual identity, provide rebellious satisfaction for one who is fighting a tyrannical superego, deny dependency on the spouse, and remove the person from a forbidden incestuous object. Eventually, however, the voices of the superego assert themselves and the individual begins to experience mixed feelings toward the extramarital partner. It is then that he or she often seeks therapy.

Part III

Responses
of the
"Injured Party"

Chapter 9

After the Fall: The Spouse's Reactions

How do husbands and wives respond when they become aware of their partners' extramarital affairs? Reactions seem to be as varied and complex as are the motives that spark an affair. They can range from murderous or suicidal feelings, deep depression, revengeful fantasies, and cold indifference to curiosity, fascination, and even exultation. Even those spouses who have secret liaisons of their own may react with shock, anger, jealousy, and dejection; others feel relieved because their guilt can now be shared (Block, 1978).

Nearly three quarters of the married men and women interviewed by Morton Hunt (1969) who found out about their partners' affairs experienced negative emotions ranging from "paralyzing fright to fulminating rage, including jealousy, humiliation, and overwhelming depression. Their behavior ran the gamut from total passivity to violent action, depending on how easy or difficult it was for them to express anger, how much they blamed themselves for the affair and how alarming the thought of divorce seemed to them. Some men smashed furniture, beat their wives, and threatened to kill their wives' lovers; women sometimes did similar things, though more often they threw tantrums, wept hysterically, or threatened to kill themselves." (p. 221).

The reaction to a partner's affair can change even over a short period of time. For example, Joe Arlington told his therapist that he was "not too disturbed" when he first learned about his wife's

159

affair. He reflected, "She's a good wife, a good mother, and a good bed partner. I usually get what I want, so why should I feel unhappy about her affair? It doesn't take anything away from me!" Only ten days later Joe complained, "I can't take it any longer. I feel like a patsy. I feel I'm second best and I keep seeing my wife in bed with that lousy bastard! I can't concentrate on anything! Please, please help me!"

On hearing that her husband was involved in an affair, Stella Brightman broke chairs, smashed mirrors, threatened murder, and hired a lawyer to "wipe out the son of a bitch." Only a month later she reported, "I feel a sense of liberation that I can't explain. Sometimes I think that the thing I dreaded the most has happened and I'm still alive. One thing I've realized is that I'm not going to punish my husband or me any longer."

Husbands and wives are frequently amazed when they evaluate their own reactions to a spouse's affair. Many who had professed to believe in "open marriage" are shocked to find that they are feeling depressed or murderous. On the other hand, some who regard themselves as very conservative are surprised to find that they respond with compassion and understanding.

A good example of an individual who prescribes one form of marital behavior but behaves in the opposite manner can be found in the life and work of the late psychiatrist, Wilhelm Reich. Reich insisted in his writings that strictly monogamous relationships are contrary to the sexual needs and emotional health of human beings. Yet he himself admitted that he was continually plagued by feelings of sexual jealousy (Stolorow and Atwood, 1979).

Reich's widow, Ilse Ollendorff Reich, observed:

> Always, in times of stress, one of Reich's very human failings came to the foreground, and that was his violent jealousy. He would always emphatically deny that he was jealous, but there is no getting away from the fact that he would accuse [me] of infidelity with any man who came to his mind as a possible rival, whether colleague, friend, local shopkeeper, or casual aquaintance. It was one of those strange contradictions in Reich's makeup, and one that must have been founded on some basic unresolved feelings of insecurity, because there were in fact no reasons for these jealousies [I. O. Reich, 1970, p. 71]

Whether the reaction is short-lived or of long endurance, there is almost always a strong emotional response to the marital partner's affair, usually expressive of pain and discomfort. Psychologist Joel Block, who may be regarded as a "middle of the road" commentator on the extramarital affair, has written: "The noninvolved mate rarely can be reassured quickly or easily. A shattered emotional reaction of five, ten, twenty or more years' duration is not easily repaired. It may be months or years before trust and a sense of security are established. (1978, p. 87).

Even advocates of the extramarital affair have acknowledged that when the extramarital acitivities of one's spouse have become known, the other partner is

> . . . cast in the role of a victim. Where the husband has been the victim he is commonly the object of ridicule, as exemplified by the term "cuckold.". . . . He has, according to the existing standards, failed in that most critical psychological matter, his masculinity. . . . The wife whose husband strays has also been considered a victim, but usually more a tragic figure to be pitied rather than ridiculed. [Ziskin and Ziskin, 1973, pp. 216–217]

In *The Wandering Husband*, a book written to help wives of straying husbands better understand their own role in the extramarital affair, Spotnitz and Freeman write, "It is safe to say that every wife feels hurt if she learns her husband is unfaithful. Even when she has told him she wishes he would have an affair, that she doesn't care if he sleeps with other women, she will feel his infidelity as an indignity" (1964, p. 121).

SAY IT ISN'T SO

Husbands and wives usually work hard to fight their intuitive feeling that the partner is involved extramaritally. If a spouse really wants to find out about a partner's affair, there are generally many opportunities to do so. However, the deceived spouse frequently refuses to notice or to believe the clues before him. He rationalizes the meaning of slips of the tongue, unexplained phone calls, unusual travel plans, bites and bruises on the face or other parts of the body, and lipstick smudges. Even when a spouse has face-to-face encounters with the partner's lover, he represses the fact that this could be a person with whom his partner is involved. Many a married couple frequently socializes with the husband's or wife's long-term lover (and his or her spouse) without ever suspecting the existence of the affair. In many of these situations, the errant husband or wife is so careless in displaying evidence of the affair that it is obvious that the marital partner is making a supreme effort to overlook it. Even when mates openly flaunt infidelity to provoke their partners, many partners refuse to believe what is right in front of them.

As the case examples in this chapter will demonstrate, one of the reasons that an extramarital affair can endure for many years is that the betrayed spouse unconsciously cooperates to sustain it. In addition to the unconscious gratification the deceived spouse receives from abetting the affair, the facade of fidelity is usually quite important to maintain despite one's suspicions.

Outraged and extremely hurt when her husband told her about his affair, Erica Jong's (1977) Isadora reflected: "Bennett's affair with Penny had begun (I now realize) the previous fall, and he had become more and more rejecting toward me. Even though I didn't 'know' about Penny, I *knew*. My antennae were too good for me not to know." (p. 109)

Reports Morton Hunt:

> The same wife who will quietly live with suspicions for years may be either crushed or enraged if her husband openly admits his infidelities, and the wife who does know about and tolerate discreet infidelity may sue for all she can if her husband grows careless. Which is why one veteran adulterer said, concerning the confrontation scene, "Deny! Lie! Say anything. She'll believe you because she wants to!" and another said, "Never admit a thing, but if you have to, tell him the least you possibly can. Resist the temptation to make a clean breast of it." [1969, pp. 155–156]

Bishop Pike in *You and the New Morality* (1967) argues that when two lovers have decided to embark on an affair, they have a responsibility to lie about it for the sake of their mates. He contends that once a primary, ethical decision has been made in a particular way, more often than not secondary ethical responsibilities are entailed.

Most husbands and wives are so reluctant to confront the truth of their partner's affairs that they have to be virtually forced to recognize it. My research and that of others (Bartusis, 1978; Hunt, 1969) reveals that many, if not most, spouses involved in an affair consciously or unconsciously want to incriminate themselves. Guilty about their liaisons, they "accidentally" arrange for a letter, picture, or phone call from the lover to be seen or heard by the mate. Even open confessions are common. Of Hunt's respondents (1969), roughly one third of those spouses knew about their affairs and said that they themselves had told them.

Psychoanalysts and other therapists are often asked how a husband or wife "should" respond if confronted with the fact that the partner is having an affair. There is no answer to this question. As has been demonstrated throughout this book, an individual's response to any external event is the result of a complex array of many variables—unconscious wishes, defenses, superego admonitions, personal history, and a host of other factors. Regardless of how a husband or wife consciously plans to react to the mate's affair, these unconscious factors will play a major role.

Many husbands and wives whose mates have wandered have reported to therapists that they resisted acknowledging the fact that the partner was involved in an affair because there was no cultural norm available to them that clearly indicated the appropriate next step. That adultery has persisted so long as the primary, and, in some places, the sole, legal ground for divorce suggests a societal attitude that divorce *should* be the result. Yet many people resist the idea of divorce. Regardless of what the grounds for the divorce are, ending a marital relationship is almost always painful and disruptive for both partners and for their children. If only to protect their children, most parents will tolerate a good deal of misery in their marriage before seeking to dissolve it.

From a sociological perspective it is probably still true that women stand to lose a great deal more in a divorce than men do, and often women have to be more concerned about the effects divorce will have on the children. For many women in our society, divorce, with its potential economic and social losses, may be a more threatening prospect than the loss of self-esteem that usually results from living with a spouse one knows to be adulterous.

There are always social and economic factors that contribute to the extramarital affair and to the way it is handled by the wandering spouse and eventually by the offended mate. From a psychoanalytic point of view, the husband or wife of a spouse who is engaged in an affair has been a willing, albeit unconscious, accomplice. He has chosen a partner to complement his neurotic anxiety about being loved in a sexually monogamous marriage.

There are some husbands and wives who cannot permit themselves to be the recipients of monogamous love because to do so signifies to them that they are robbers—oedipal victors who should be punished for their misdeeds. Other spouses cannot tolerate being loved by their mates because to them that connotes that they are weaklings. As we noted in chapter 5, sadomasochistic men and women often feel that if they express or receive warmth and affection they are losing a battle and have been tricked into something that is humiliating to them. Finally, husbands and wives with strong unconscious dependency wishes must ward off a loving relationship lest their oral cravings erupt. These men and women feel uncomfortable if they are loved consistently by one mate and unconsciously arrange to feel and be deprived.

In attempting to more fully understand a spouse's response to his partner's affair, we should bear in mind once again that every time a spouse complains about his partner, he is gratifying a wish; what he consciously abhors about the partner is very often unconsciously desired. Therefore, when a married person comes to a psychoanalyst to complain about the partner's involvement in an extramarital affair, analyst and patient will eventually explore how the analysand has unconsciously aided the mate in initiating and sustaining the affair.

Psychoanalysts maintain that every individual has the capacity to understand important dimensions of the unconscious mind of another person. Consequently, it never is a surprise to an analyst when he observes that two unhappy people have unconsciously sought and found each other—thus, the deceiving person attracts one who unconsciously wants to be deceived. According to psychoanalytic theory, when a person feels abandoned and rejected, there are more basic reasons for these feelings than are apparent in the current situation. He or she is probably responding to childhood hurts—e.g., neglect by a mother, an absent father.

Let us now look at some men and women who were in analytic therapy when they became aware of their spouses' affairs and see what we can learn from them.

I REMEMBER MAMA

A maturational task of childhood is to wean oneself from a dependent relationship on one's parents and move toward autonomy. When this task is not resolved, the person continues to cling to parental figures and inevitably will marry someone whom he experiences as a mother or father. As we discussed in chapter 4, the dependent person forms a symbiotic marital relationship and wants to know all about the loved one's thoughts, feelings, and activities—permitting the mate no privacy. The dependent spouse becomes furious if his partner has loving feelings for others, is hurt if the mate has interests apart from him, and is particularly intolerant if secrets are not shared. Symbiotic mates are convinced that in order to survive they need to possess their marital partners completely. If the partner shows interest in or expresses affection toward somebody else, it seems like the end of the world, and murderous and suicidal fantasies then become common reactions.

When Sigmund Freud heard that his fiancée, Martha, was encouraging Fritz Wahle to express his affections for her although she was engaged to Freud, he wrote in one of his 900 letters to her:

> When the memory of your letter to Fritz . . . comes back to me I lose all control of myself, and had I the power to destroy the whole world . . . I would do so without hesitation. [Jones, 1953, pp. 114–115]

The symbiotic partner, whose emotional attachment to the spouse may be compared to an infant's clinging to the mother, responds to the mate's interest in someone else much as the infant reacts to the birth of a sibling. Thus Freud's analysis of the child's response to a sibling in *The New Introductory Lectures* (1932) is also an excellent description of how a symbiotic spouse reacts to his partner's sexual involvement with another:

> . . . what the child grudges the unwanted intruder and rival is not only the suckling but all the other signs of maternal care. *It feels that it has been dethroned, despoiled, prejudiced in its rights;* it casts a *jealous hatred* upon the new baby and develops a grievance against the *faithless* mother. . . . We rarely form a correct idea of the

strength of these jealous impulses, of the tenacity with which they persist and of the magnitude of their influence on later development. [p. 123]

Inasmuch as the symbiotic spouse wants psychologically to merge with the marital partner, he always feels deprived. Such a spouse makes incessant demands on the partner, always complaining of his or her selfishness. Eventually the partner becomes exasperated and wants distance. Through an extramarital affair, the partner expresses this hostility and achieves distance from the nagging spouse.

David Cramer, 37, married for eight years, sought therapy because he had recently learned of his wife's affair and was extremely depressed, with many suicidal fantasies. "The thing is driving me crazy. I can't think of anything else but how dejected and miserable I feel. She couldn't have done anything worse. I'd rather be dead. I'm not eating or sleeping. I've lost 15 pounds."

David described his wife, Jo, as a very strong and intelligent woman. "I always liked to please her and share my life with her. But she's a private person. Sometimes she doesn't want to tell me about the books she reads, the people she talks with, or the dreams and fantasies she has. In the last year or two she's called me a pest for prying into her 'affairs.' She never saw that as her problem. She is scared of closeness but has called me a pest!"

David reported that he had had a close relationship with his late parents. "I remember Mama as someone who lived for me. She often said that it was so important for me to feel loved that she resolved after I was born not to have any more children." He described his father as "a quiet man who let Mama be the leader. But he was nice too, and would give me the shirt off his back."

As a child David hardly ever heard the word "no" and, consequently, developed poor frustration tolerance and weak impulse control. He did not have much to do with his peers "because they didn't give me enough attention."

"Mama" was an elementary school teacher at the school David attended. When David entered high school, his mother was able to get transferred there. Tied to his parents, David never went to camp or participated in anything that would separate him from his mother and father. He lived at home when he went to college, where he majored in education (like his mother).

During their courtship, Jo and David "were very close and confided everything to each other." In the first few years of their marriage, "we were like twins. We bathed together, walked together, and it was great! We didn't need children because we had each other."

David was threatened very much by Jo's attempts to become more autonomous. When Jo suggested after six years of marriage that she and David should be more independent of each other, David became furious and called her "despicable and disloyal." The more David fought Jo, the more stubborn she became. She began to spend more and more time away from home, which, of course, further infuriated David. He cursed her, called her a whore, and punished her by not talking to her for days at a time. Sometimes he would have crying jags and beg Jo to be more caring and loving. She reacted to David's pleas with indifference and hostility and eventually moved into an affair with an older married man.

David reported to his analyst that on many occasions he had had inklings that Jo was involved in an affair but he always resisted the idea. He recalled that one day he saw a man's name and phone number on a piece of paper on the kitchen table. "Although it was the same guy I had met at a party with Jo, I told myself it was a parent of one of the kids Jo taught." On another occasion David actually saw Jo and her lover walk out of a library together, but again he denied the possiblility that she was involved with another man. He told himself that "the guy was just some other teacher."

David could not do much work in his analysis for a long time. His associations alternated between angry tirades and suicidal fantasies, but in no way would he take responsibility for any of his marital woes. Eventually he became irriatated with the analyst for "not doing more." He wanted the analyst to "ball out" Jo, help him kill her or plan his suicide. When the analyst did not gratify any of David's requests but instead tried to help him explore their meaning, David became very critical and told the analyst he was disloyal and uncaring.

After about eight months of treatment David could begin to see that his complaints about the analyst were very similar to those he had about his wife. Slowly he realized how much he wanted to be a "mama's boy," always nurtured and never frustrated. As he recalled how indulgent his mother was, he was able to realize that he was trying to make Jo into her replica.

In one of David's dreams, Jo and her lover took him to a restaurant as their guest. In his associations to the dream, David recalled how much he enjoyed being fondled and fed by both of his parents. Much later in treatment David was able to see that one of the unconscious gratifications he derived from Jo's affair was that she and her lover served as parental surrogates for him and in many ways he delighted in being their symbolic son.

As already suggested, a husband or wife who has strong symbiotic yearnings experiences the marital partner's affair as a devastating blow. It is as if the forsaken spouse has lost a needed organ such as a heart or lung. Feeling mutilated, he cannot eat or sleep because the necessary bodily equipment does not seem to be available.

The British psychoanalyst John Bowlby (1973) has done a great deal of research on infants who have been physically or psychologically abandoned by their mothers; his findings appear to be applicable to the symbiotic spouse's reactions to the mate's affair. According to Bowlby, the child who is abandoned or feels abandoned by the mother passes through a sequence of reactions from protest to despair to apathy—possibly even death. The symbiotic spouse, on becoming aware of the marital partner's affair, behaves much like an abandoned child. At first he protests, then becomes desperate, losing his appetite and the ability to sleep, and finally may become suicidal.

Husbands and wives who cannot tolerate any separation from their mates are like immature children who believe their parents are omnipotent. Those who deify their marital partners depend almost exclusively on their partners' love to buttress their own very low self-esteem (Rank, 1926). Consequently, what they perceive as a withdrawal of the partner's love can activate fantasies of suicide.

Although relatively few husbands and wives do kill themselves when they hear about their mate's affair, suicidal gestures are common. In threatening suicide, scorned spouses gratify many unconscious desires: they satisfy their wish for revenge by making their spouses feel guilty and humiliated, they receive sympathy and concern from their spouses and others when they dramatically exhibit their pain, and they usually receive some form of reparation from their partners when they appear very helpless and hopeless. Frequently, wounded partners who threaten suicide cannot think of anything else to do that is sufficiently dramatic to express their sufferings.

The suicidal spouse is usually a masochistic person who has been an extremely devoted and self-sacrificing partner. He enjoys suffering as Don Quixote enjoyed his defeats—for his lady's sake (Reik, 1941).

DENYING JEALOUSY

For many spouses, to attach themselves is extremely frightening because this may lead to disappointment and rejection. Although the desire for closeness is alive in these people's unconscious minds, whenever the wish is stimulated, they repudiate it. When these individuals marry, they expend considerable energy maintaining emotional distance from the partner. Sex and other forms of intimacy are threatening and therefore avoided. If the partner complains about distance in the marital relationship, this spouse tells him to "get lost" or find another mate. If the partner does move away and have an affair, the "independent" spouse responds with characteristic coolness and restraint. While the facade of autonomy may be maintained for a long time, it eventually breaks down.

Ellen Dale, 37, came to therapy because she had many psychosomatic ills, including frequent bouts of acute migraine headaches, insomnia, heart palpitations, dizziness, and nausea. In addition, Ellen described a feeling of depression that "has lasted most of my life." Although married for ten years to Gerald, she felt their relationship was "meaningless." "We go our separate ways," Ellen said, "and don't talk to each other very much." Sex was virtually absent from their relationship, and what conversation they had was on routine matters. While Ellen felt that both she and Gerald cared a good deal for their six-year-old daughter, they rarely discussed her with each other.

In reviewing her history, it became quite clear that Ellen's relationship with her parents was similar to the one she had with Gerald. "Although they seemed to try to be good parents," Ellen reflected, "they never knew how I felt." She hardly ever communicated feelings of joy or sadness to her parents "because they never seemed interested."

As a student, Ellen had had few friends and spent a good part of her time reading books. Her socially isolated pattern had continued in her marriage. Ellen met Gerald when they were graduate students. She liked him for his "quietness, coolness, and scholarly manner." During their courtship they displayed very little affection toward each other, and "after we got married, except for two or three times, we didn't have sex until we wanted to have a child."

Ellen was emotionally detached in her analytic sessions and warded off warm feelings toward her male analyst. When her fear of intimacy was interpreted to her, Ellen accused the analyst of trying to gratify his own needs for closeness, accusing him of being "a dirty old man," "a pimp" and "an incompetent." She likened the analyst to both of her parents, whom she described as very narcissistic.

After spending weeks castigating her analyst, Ellen reported a dream in which she was in a library with the analyst and he was asking for some information about a book. In her dream, Ellen's first response was to give the analyst the correct information, but she soon grew suspicious of him and withdrew. When the analyst interpreted the dream and told Ellen that her reluctance to reveal information to him was because she was not sure what he would do with it, Ellen began to talk of her suspicions about Gerald. She said that he was staying away from home a great deal and was becoming more and more withdrawn; she wondered whether he was having a relationship with another woman. When the analyst asked Ellen how she would feel about Gerald's having an affair, Ellen replied, "It would be an interesting thing!" and refused to pursue the matter further.

A month later Ellen had a dream in which Gerald was with another woman and Ellen sneered at them. When the analyst mentioned that the sneering in the dream meant that Ellen was not indifferent about the possibility of Gerald having an affair, she denied feeling anything. To prove the analyst wrong, she told Gerald that she suspected he was having an affair but it didn't bother her because she had no interest in sex. After a few defensive remarks, Gerald acknowledged that he was indeed involved with another woman. Ellen again claimed that it did not bother her.

Concomitant with Ellen's persistent denial of feelings about Gerald's affair, she had a repetitive dream. In the dream she would come into the analyst's office, take off her shoes, and then her feet would become icicles. Associations to the dream revealed that Ellen wanted some closeness with the analyst but had to freeze her warm feelings. On discussing her fear of warm feelings toward the analyst, Ellen began bitterly to recall many childhood deprivations. While she was discharging her anger and exposing some of her yearnings for parental affection, Ellen's psychosomatic symptoms diminished. Recognizing that she was feeling better, she hesitantly expressed gratitude to the analyst.

Feeling more capable of warmth, Ellen moved a little closer toward Gerald and then started to experience some anger about his affair. Although she moved back and forth between "caring" and "not caring," she finally summoned enough courage to tell Gerald that she would like him to end the affair. On hearing and feeling her concern, Gerald "gave me the biggest hug he ever did. I enjoyed it a little."

Husbands and wives like Ellen, who have developed a lifelong facade of indifference and coldness to protect themselves against their frightening dependency feelings, respond to the partner's extramarital affair with their characteristic defense—an "I don't care" attitude. However, indifference frequently conceals powerful jealousy and anger. Ellen was concerned about Gerald's liaison but she had to deny the pain that was smoldering beneath her apparent detachment.

Spotnitz and Freeman (1964) comment on the indifference that some wives demonstrate on learning about their husbands' affairs and point out that whether or not the wife thinks she doesn't want him sexually, if he actually confronts her with his unfaithfulness, she believes he should have remained true to her, no matter what. Dr. William Silverberg (1952) in *The Childhood Experience and Personal Destiny* says that the spouse who seems calm on hearing about his or her partner's extramarital affair is merely burying rage.

WAR AND PEACE

It should by now be clear that husbands and wives utilize their lifelong characteristic means of coping when they react to their partners' extramarital affairs. The dependent spouse feels like an abandoned waif and becomes despondent; the emotionally isolated spouse clings to the defense of denial. It should not surprise us, therefore, to learn that the sadomasochistic spouse will deal with the marital partner's affair by alternately attacking and submitting to the mate.

In our earlier discussion of sadomasochistic husbands and wives (chapter 5) we pointed out that these individuals are reliving an old power struggle. Still resenting the power their parents had over them, they act out their rage by displacing it on to their marital partners. However, just as these sadistic husbands and wives needed their parents' love when they were children, they also need and want their marital partners' love. Consequently, after periods of derogating their partners, they apologize and behave—temporarily—in a subservient and masochistic manner. As we have also demonstrated in previous chapters, sadomasochistic individuals are narcissistically attracted to each other and often marry. However, their marriages usually consist of constant fracases and frequent threats of divorce. They rarely do divorce because unconsciously they love the battle and also need each other.

After finding out about his wife's affair, Sam Ein sought a therapist to help him "figure out the best way to divorce Roberta." Sam described his five-year marriage as "a neverending battle." "We argue about everything—politics, clothes, the house, sex—we can't agree on anything." Sam tearfully went on to say, "Now I want a divorce because I just heard that she's shacking up with this stupid jerk and this has to be the end."

Although Sam seemed adamant about getting a divorce, in subsequent interviews with his therapist, he began to express ambivalence. "As much as she has hurt me, I think she still needs me and if I leave her, that will crush her too much," Sam reasoned. When the therapist asked Sam to elaborate on how he thought Roberta would be "crushed," he had fantasies of maiming and eventually destroying her. Although he could admit deriving some pleasure from these fantasies, they were followed by expressions of guilt and anxiety with self-attacking statements such as, "I guess I deserved this. I often cursed her and told her what a dope she was. I often said that she was lousy in bed and that any other guy would know it."

Sam's alternating sadistic and masochistic fantasies were also acted out in reality. Within the same hour he would tell Roberta that she was a "no-good slut for screwing somebody else" and then apologize for having provoked her into an affair. In his masochistic mood, he would ask Roberta to "just tell me what you want and I'll do it"; when he felt sadistic, he would demand that Roberta make a "supreme sacrifice" to atone for her affair and give *him* constant attention, affection, and admiration.

Sam's transference relationship to his therapist was quite similar to his way of relating to Roberta. In one analytic session he would berate the therapist for not making him feel better and then in the next session apologize for being an uncooperative patient. When his sadomasochistic patterns with his wife and therapist were pointed out to him, Sam recalled some childhood memories. He voiced much resentment toward his mother for always insisting that he be "a clean boy" and recalled episodes from his childhood when he would purposely dirty his room and then seek his mother's forgiveness. While reliving battles with his mother, he had a dream of defecating on the analyst's couch and spending hours cleaning it up. His wish to spite another person and then undo it, he began to realize, entered into almost all of his interpersonal transactions.

THAT CHAMPIONSHIP SEASON

As we saw in chapter 6, when husbands or wives have not resolved their competitiveness with the parent of the same sex, their
marriages are not enjoyable. They feel guilty for having a mate all
to themselves. In their unconscious minds, marriage means that
they have won a murderous victory, and their marital partners are
experienced as stolen property.

One way in which the "oedipal spouse" can cope with the guilt
and anxiety caused by his or her imaginary victory is by provoking
the mate to seek out other sexual partners. Because "oedipal
spouses" love to compete, they do not surrender their mates to
their competitors—they fight for them as they did in fantasy, when
they were fighting for the parent of the opposite sex. By always
participating in a competitive battle, they see to it that their marriage is never dull. In John Updike's *Too Far to Go* (1979), Richard
Maple accuses his wife, Joan, of having a lover. Aware of her husband's dynamics, Joan answers, "I have no lover. Stop trying to
make me more interesting than I am."

Barbara Fuld told her therapist that she constantly felt like a
failure. Although she was successful in her job as a social
worker, she obsessed a great deal about what she was *not* doing
for her clients. Her feeling of being a failure also extended to
other areas of living. She felt that she was a poor conversationalist, unattractive physically, and intellectually dull. She
also felt that she was an inadequate wife and feared that, if she
did not improve, her husband would leave her. When asked to
elaborate on what she considered inadequate about herself as a
wife, Barbara responded, "Everything! I'm a lousy cook, I'm
unresponsive sexually, and I'm easily hurt. I don't discuss Jerry's
work with him very much, but he has to listen to *me*. I'm very
selfish."

Discussing her history, Barbara spoke adoringly of her father.
She said, "He was the apple of every woman's eye. *We* all had
the hots for him." Barbara's mother was described as "a devoted
wife who was not as fun-loving as Daddy but a hard worker and
a good mother."

As a child and teenager, Barbara was a good student but always felt shy and inhibited in interpersonal situations. "Although I've always been ambitious," Barbara noted, "I was scared to compete actively." If another girl was interested in a boy she liked, she "gave up the battle very quickly."

While a graduate student, Barbara met Jerry, who was completing his internship as a physician (the same profession as her father). She was very flattered by Jerry's interest in her but she couldn't figure out what he saw in her. "There were better women around." After a six-month courtship, Jerry proposed marriage. Barbara persisted in asking him, "Don't you want to think some more about whether you can do better?" When Jerry became furious with Barbara for constantly questioning his love, she stopped pestering him and they did get married.

When Barbara started therapy, she and Jerry had been married for three years. Although the first year of marriage was "blissful," the last two years were "uncomfortable." She constantly doubted Jerry's love and had fantasies that he would leave her and that he was off with other women. She needed constant reassurance from Jerry, but the reassurance that he did provide did not help her feel secure for long.

Barbara related to her female analyst in a subservient manner. Comparing herself to her analyst, Barbara spoke about her fantasies of the analyst, "You are a bright woman, a successful professional, and a good sexual partner. I'm none of these." Asked to look at why she had to put herself down constantly, particularly in relation to other women, Barbara began to speak of her competition with her peers at school, her father's women patients, and her mother. "I always would have liked to win," Barbara acknowledged, "but I was afraid of coming on strong."

While Barbara was examining her fear of her own aggression, she started to look at her marriage more closely and realized that Jerry's rejecting behavior complemented her own self-image. Barbara reflected, "I don't think much of myself, and he's away from the house so much. Jerry gives me what I deserve." As Barbara talked more about being neglected by Jerry, she was finally able to tell him that she wanted him to be with her more often. When he reacted with one rationalization after another, she began to suspect that he was having an affair. She finally had Jerry followed until she could prove that he was involved with another woman.

From a seemingly noncompetitive, taciturn woman, Barbara became very combative. She went to Jerry's lover's home and physically ripped the house apart, told the woman's husband and children of her extramartial involvement, and vowed to "destroy" her. Although Barbara felt some anger and hurt toward Jerry, most of her aggression was directed against his lover.

In many ways Barbara showed more interest in Jerry after hearing about his affair. In one of her dreams, she was in a boxing ring with Jerry's lover fighting for a prize, which was Jerry. In another dream, Barbara was in a bowling tournament and the winner got a free trip to the Caribbean with Jerry.

As Barbara further examined her reactions to Jerry's affair, she was able to get in touch with the strong rivalrous feelings she had as a child. She spoke of her envy of her mother, who shared a bedroom with her adored father, her competition with her father's women patients, who "undressed in front of him and got all of his attention," and her ambivalence toward girlfriends who seemed "like the top dogs."

Barbara's analysis revealed that she experienced her husband as a father figure. As in her relationship with her father, Barbara loved Jerry but felt that she wasn't entitled to him. Consequently, she acted like an insecure little girl with him and in many ways provoked him to seek distance.

The oedipal spouse loves competition. Thus, Barbara became very much enlivened when she could compete actively for her husband. His lover's existence provided a rationale for her to take up arms, and she could enjoy a battle that she felt was provoked by her competitor.

The more an oedipal spouse can battle for his or her mate, the more interesting the mate becomes. Conversely, when such a spouse wins the battle, he or she often loses interest in the partner. Competing seems to be more interesting than loving (Eisenstein, 1956).

THE LATENT HETEROSEXUAL'S RESPONSE TO THE SPOUSE'S AFFAIR

There is no such thing as an innocent victim of an extramarital affair. For every deceiving husband or wife, there is a spouse who unconsciously wants to be deceived. Sometimes extramarital affairs are actively thrust upon one spouse by the other. This is particularly true of impotent or latent homosexual men, who drop hints to their wives and sometimes even urge them openly to have affairs, and of frigid or latent homosexual women, who sometimes tell their husbands to enjoy sex with other partners.

Although husbands and wives with latent homosexual problems frequently provoke their mates to have affairs, when they learn about the affair, their reactions vary considerably, because such individuals cope with their homosexuality in very different ways. There are those who can consciously accept their homosexual fantasies and even derive gratification from them. On the other hand, many men and women feel only repugnance for their homosexual wishes. I recall one woman patient who had a strong homosexual orientation and very much enjoyed identifying with men. On hearing about her husband's affair, she felt ecstatic; she constantly pictured herself having sex with her husband's lover and was very excited by it. I also remember a male patient who after learning about his wife's affair suffered for a long time. He had a recurring fantasy of his wife's lover in the nude (the homosexual wish) but then would feel acute panic. On one occasion, he fantasied having fellatio with his wife's lover and then vomited for three hours.

When the homosexual impulse causes little or no anxiety, a husband or wife frequently welcomes hearing about the mate's affair and may even encourage it. This is what happens in "swapping." Under the guise of "liberalism" and "freedom," spouses encourage each other to have extramarital sex in order to gratify their own unconscious homosexual fantasies.

In my clinical work I have observed that while most heterosexual men and women have difficulty acknowledging their homosexual fantasies, men seem to find it harder to face their desires to make love with another man. I have observed many men with a latent homosexual orientation go virtually berserk when they learned of their wife's affair. What they found so painful to face was their unconscious attraction to their wife's lover and their unconscious envy of their wife's sexual and emotional position with him.

It should not be overlooked that there is still wide acceptance of the double standard—husbands are "allowed" extramarital sex but wives are not. Many male patients who have themselves been involved in extramarital affairs nonetheless are outraged by the suggestion that their wives might be doing the same thing. Said one male patient, with his wife partially agreeing, "Stepping out is for married men only."

Although women's liberation, psychoanalysis, and other institutions are helping to puncture the fantasy, women are still viewed unconsciously by many men as chattels, as their husband's property. Consequently, while women are inclined to feel betrayed when they learn of their husbands' affairs, men are more likely to feel that they have been robbed.

Many men are convinced that they own their wives. It has been frequently observed that married men in particular demand exclusive sexual rights to their lovers, even though they themselves are living with and having sex with another woman.

Don Goll, 31, was referred for psychotherapy by his physician. Although he himself was involved in an extramarital relationship, Don had just heard of his wife's affair and was feeling desparate. He was not sleeping, eating, or working and could do nothing else but "picture the two of them in bed with that guy having a ball. I'm miserable thinking about it."

Reviewing his childhood, Don spoke of a very seductive mother and a withdrawn father. When his father was away on a trip, Don recalled, his mother would "grab me and bite me. Sometimes she would hug me so hard it would hurt." Don recalled how guilty he felt whenever he was with his father because "I *did* want him out of the way. When he was on trips I'd wish he'd never come back."

When Don was 12, his father died suddenly of a heart attack. Don remembered that he did not cry at the funeral and was "sort of numb." However, he did enjoy having other father figures such as his uncle feel sorry for him. While reconstructing the trauma of his father's death, Don recalled how frightening it was for him to be alone with his mother. He also remembered having fantasies during most of his teenage years of being reunited with father. "Sometimes we would hug and kiss but more often I'd fantasize that I was begging him to return to life," Don tearfully remarked.

As Don used his therapy to discuss his strong yearning for a father, he began to feel some loving feelings toward his analyst and expressed the fantasy that the analyst would adopt him as a son. In a dream, Don was having a meal with the analyst and the analyst's wife. It was not too difficult for Don then to move to a discussion of how he wanted his wife and her lover to be parents and adopt him. However, as he began to discuss this wish, he became very anxious and found the idea of getting close to Jack very repulsive. His strong homosexual fantasies toward Jack were creating the anxiety. With the analyst's help, Don was eventually able to understand that his wife's affair had stimulated strong homosexual fantasies toward Jack, who was the father figure he really wanted.

The idea of the partner's having an extramarital affair is painful for most husbands and wives but may be particularly distressing to those who must defend against homosexual fantasies. It is therefore naive and even irresponsible to advise such a husband or wife to "try hard to remember that time has a way of healing even the deepest wounds. These are difficult days for you. But time will pass, and so will much of the anger's pain. No matter what happens today, the sun will rise tomorrow" (Bartusis, 1978, pp. 25–26). Although time may attenuate the intensity of these feelings, anger and pain will not pass until the "victimized" husband or wife gets in touch with what is angering and paining him or her. When it is homosexuality that is repressed, only psychotherapy will heal the pain and anger—not just time.

As we indicated earlier, some husbands and wives who are accepting of their own homosexual fantasies, if not excited by them, will tend to be tolerant of their spouse's affair. They may even be stimulated by fantasizing themselves in bed with the mate's lover.

Patricia Holt, 24, came to treatment because she could not find
a job that pleased her. Over a period of three years she had been
a teacher, a computer analyst, a social service aide, and a group
leader. "No matter what I do," Patricia said, "it always works
out the same way. I get interested at first and then my interest
"fizzles out." Patricia recognized that her behavior with men
was the same as it was on jobs. Before her marriage to Harold,
she had many boyfriends. As soon as they wanted her to commit
herself to a more permanent relationship, Patricia "fizzled out."
Although she had been married for only two years, she had
already had three extramarital affairs, each one lasting three to
four months.

Reviewing her childhood, Patricia referred to herself as a
"tomboy" and described how she identified and competed with
boys, including her two older brothers, and was very disparaging
of girls. "Mother never let me feel that there was anything good
about being a girl and I got that message from Father, too.
Father would rather see me throw a football or swim than play
with a doll or dance with a boy," said Patricia with a snicker.

Describing her marriage to Harold, Patricia spoke of their
strong rivalry with each other. "We spend so much time criticizing each other that we don't have time to do too much else," she
said with a laugh. In their arguments, Patricia often boasted that
she could seduce any man she desired and challenged Harold to
"beat that record" with women.

When Patricia found out about Harold's affair, for several
weeks thereafter each session with her therapist was devoted to
details of her sex life with Harold, which had now become
"tremendous." At first Patricia could not understand what it was
about Harold's affair that drew her closer to him; a little later,
her dreams informed her of her motives. In one dream she was in
bed with Harold and his lover, and while Harold was having intercourse with his friend, he was also fondling Patricia's breasts.
In another dream, Patricia had Harold's penis between her legs
and was having intercourse with his lover.

Patricia began to realize how attracted she was to women and
how she wanted to have sex with them "like Harold does." Her
wish to be a man derived from her competition with her brothers
and her wish to please her parents, who valued only boys. Pro-

voking Harold to have an affair was one way she could get close to a woman, and when she had sex with Harold she could fantasize herself having sex with his lover.

Patricia's reaction to Harold's affair was very similar to the response of Jong's Isadora to Bennett's affair, to which we referred in chapter 7. Isadora, after hearing of Bennett's affair, reported: "We fucked with more passion than we had in years. . . . From then on, we had a third person living with us in our house. I went to sleep with Penny at night, and woke up with her in the morning. I dreamed about Penny night after night. . . . (Jong, 1977, p. 47).

As we suggested throughout this chapter, there is no such thing as a "normal" response to a mate's extramarital affair. Husbands or wives who complain that they are innocent victims of their spouses' cruelty are unaware that they have been unconscious accomplices to their mates' affairs. Their reactions to their partners' affairs will always be based on the story of their lives, their unconscious id wishes, ego defenses, superego commands, and all of the other variables that comprise any complex personality.

Part IV

The Professionals' Response

Chapter 10

Can an Extramarital Affair Ever Be a Mature Form of Behavior?

Man— the object of concern—is the ever-varying cloud and psychologists are like people seeing faces in it. One psychologist perceives along the upper margin the contours of a nose and lip, and then miraculously other portions of the cloud become so oriented in respect to these that the outline of a forward-looking superman appears. Another psychologist is attracted to a lower segment, sees an ear, a nose, a chin, and simultaneously the cloud takes on the aspect of a backward-looking Epimethean. Thus, for each perceiver every sector of the cloud has a different function, name and value—fixed by his initial bias of perception.

Henry A. Murray, *Explorations in Personality*

Experts on the dynamics of human functioning are also human beings, with biases, limitations, and vulnerabilities. Consequently, their conclusions about interpersonal behavior do not rest exclusively on impartial reflection on the empirical facts but are often influenced by their own subjectivity. It has been well documented that theories of personality often tell us as much about the theorist's life history and personal problems as about psychodynamics of the human being (Stolorow and Atwood, 1979; Strean, 1975). For example, Alfred Adler, the discoverer of the "inferiority complex," was a sickly child who hated his older brother and other children for being "superior" to him (Orgler, 1963). Harry Stack Sullivan, who posited the notion that every child "needs a chum," has acknowledged that he was a very lonely boy who always yearned for a friend (Mullahy, 1948). Sigmund Freud, who idealized his own mother, discovered the Oedipus complex

185

(Jones, 1953), and Karen Horney, who never forgave her father for being away from home a great deal of the time, argued that the major etiological factor in a neurosis is the "feeling of loneliness in a hostile world" (Horney, 1950).

Further, professional judgments are frequently influenced by the compulsions to conform to the views of peers and to adhere to social norms. We must keep this in mind as we review the conclusions of experts who have researched the extramartial affair. Their positions may be influenced by emotion, prejudice, rationalization in all its forms, and challenges to their self-esteem (Jackson, 1979).

A content analysis of the major research projects on the extramarital affair yields the following sample of opinions:

> By nature most of us are varietists, and marriage, particularly over an extended period of time, smothers our varietist inclinations.
>> Psychologist J. Block, *The Other Man The Other Woman*

> From my quarter-century of counseling on marital problems, I cannot recall a single case where infidelity has strengthened the marital bond.
>> Psychiatrist A. Stone, "The Case Against Marital Infidelity," *Readers Digest*

> We can make no ironclad rules, for there are instances where it [an affair] may have saved a marriage. It may have convinced a husband that the other woman, far from being more desirable, is much less attractive than his wife.
>> Psychiatrist H. Spotnitz & journalist L. Freeman, *The Wandering Husband*

> [An extramarital affair] provides additional passion, tenderness, and stimulation for a person experiencing a good marriage.
>> Sociologist L. Meyers & H. Legitt, "A New View of Adultery," *Sexual Behavior*

> If a man has a reasonably healthy personality, is attracted to you, loves you, and has committed himself to you, you have a right to expect him to be faithful, just as he expects you to be.
>> Psychiatrist M. Bartusis, *Every Other Man*

> We are convinced that such an arrangement [an extramarital affair] can only be of benefit to people whose concern and consideration for each other and for their families are at least average.
>> Psychologist J. & M. Ziskin, *The Extramarital Arrangement*

In my own observations of adulterers. . . . I have found that there are usually both good and bad, healthy and unhealthy reasons for this type of highly unconventional behavior.

> Psychologist A. Ellis, "Healthy and Disturbed Reasons for Having Extramarital Relations," *Extramarital Relations*, ed. G. Neubeck

Infidelity, like alcoholism or drug addiction, is an expression of a deep basic disorder of character.

> Psychiatrist F. Caprio, *Marital Infidelity*

Infidelity is often a neurotic and sometimes psychotic pursuit of exactly the man or woman one imagines one needs. . . . It is primarily a return to behavior characteristic of adolescence or earlier.

> Psychiatrist L. Saul, *Fidelity & Infidelity*

The psychotherapists may be right about the infidelity they do see, but the vast mass of the unfaithful do not seek treatment and it is unjustifiable to assume that they are identical with those who do.

> Journalist M. Hunt, *The Affair*

We have inherited a morbid legacy which vigorously asserts that because of the guilt and deception involved for the participants and the feelings of humiliation and rejection experienced by the spouse, the net effect is necessarily negative to mental health. The evidence presented is invariably from clinical cases and here is probably the source of the stereotype. People who have the same experiences as the clinical cases but who don't come to "bad ends" aren't included in the sample under surveillance. Our non-clinical sample would justify almost the opposite conclusion.

> Sociologists J. Cuber and P. Harroff, *The Significant Americans: A Study of Sexual Behavior Among the Affluent*

I suddenly realize that I could fuck a different man every weekday afternoon and still not feel contented. Adultery is no solution, only a diversion.

> Novelist E. Jong, *How to Save Your Own Life*

Nothing proves more conclusively the unconscious neurotic substructure of infidelity than the "arguments" of people caught in such a conflict.

> Psychiatrist E. Bergler, "Marriage and Divorce" in *A Handbook of Psychoanalysis*, eds. H. Herma and G. Kurth

In reading these quotations, one is struck by the obvious disagreement among researchers and writers regarding the health or neurosis of persons involved in extramarital relationships. Many of the authors quoted above disagree even with themselves. For example, Albert Ellis (1969) has written that the "healthy adulterer" is one who can accept his own extramarital desires and acts but this same person may also "decide that they [affairs] are unwise."

It is interesting that most researchers who have explored adulterous relationships have avoided using the phrase "extramarital affair." It may be that expressions like "open marriage," "open-ended relationships," "intimate friendships," and "commitment with freedom" are used to conceal the anxiety and ambivalence that may be conjured up by terms such as "extramarital affair" or "adultery."

Of course, the idea of extramarital sex has induced mixed feelings in most people for some time. Of the many restrictions that organized religions place on their adherents, the tenet that husband and wife must limit themselves sexually to each other from the wedding day until "death do us part" is virtually universal. Yet religious tenets are frequently disregarded or compromised. Reviewing the data available for 185 societies, Ford and Beach (1951) reported that fewer than one-sixth of these societies consistently practiced monogamy, although virtually all of them advocated it as a mature form of marital behavior.

Four-fifths of the United States have statutes defining extramarital coitus as a crime punishable by as much as five years' imprisonment (in Maine, Oklahoma, South Dakota, and Vermont) (Rhodes, 1972); yet in *Beyond the Male Myth: What Women Want to Know About Men's Sexuality*, Pietropinto and Simenauer (1976) report that over half of approximately 4,000 men interviewed admitted that they had "cheated" on their wives and two-thirds said they "would cheat" under certain circumstances.

Paralleling the high incidence of extramarital activity among men, a significant change has been reported in the incidence of extramarital sex among American women. Kinsey in 1948 pointed out that by the age of 40, only a little over 25 percent of the married women he interviewed had had extramarital experiences. By 1974, sociologists Robert Bell and Dorothy Peltz reported that in a representative population similar to Kinsey's, over 40 percent of the married women interviewed had had extramarital sex by the time they were 40.

Many contemporary researchers have taken account of the increase in extramarital behavior in our society by devoting less attention to the emotional maturity or immaturity of the adulterer and instead claiming that an extramarital liaison is a normal form of adaptation in present-day culture. The following statement by sociologist Robert Whitehurst is typical of those of many social scientists.

> The phenomenon of [infidelity] can as easily be conceptualized as a cultural-social problem with a high probability of involvement for many males as it can be seen as either a problem in the marital relationship or in the personality of the deviant. In its essence, the behavior should be quite frequently expected, and if expected, and explained as a social-structural and cultural problem, it may then be construed much more nearly as normal rather than as abnormal behavior in the kind of society we now experience. [1969, p. 136]

In the past decade there has been a stream of articles and books claiming that sexual exclusivity in marriage is obsolescent, that monogamy is archaic, male-chauvinistic, and unsuited to modern life. Although the general public still has a tendency to condemn extramarital activities, it does so with less severity than formerly. About thirty years ago Ingrid Bergman was forced to leave the United States when her affair with Roberto Rossellini became known. Today the disclosure of an actress's infidelity does her little, if any, harm with her public (Hunt, 1977). Many prominent actresses such as Vanessa Redgrave and Catherine DeNeuve, have one or more children born out of wedlock and make no effort to conceal the fact.

IS MARITAL FIDELITY UNNATURAL?

Many students of the human being agree that people are biologically polygamous and that monogamy is an artifact of culture rather than part of the person's instinctual nature. Kinsey (1948) showed rats, monkeys, and bulls, when restricted to one partner, grew bored with copulating. However, if new females were introduced to them, they copulated with renewed vigor. Kinsey concluded that the polygamous urge observed in animals is part of the mammalian heritage and that the human animal is also subject to this same biological heritage.

Utilizing Kinsey's research to buttress their positions, many authors have concluded that marital fidelity is not an innate need but is culturally conditioned.

> The desire for newness and variety is apparently deeply rooted in us all; fidelity to a single partner is not an innate universal need. . . . We are by nature polygamous, by upbringing monogamous, and therefore perennially at war with ourselves. And this is why so many of the married—even the happily married—sometimes dream of other loves to refresh their dulled palates, to recall the taste and glow of new love. [Hunt, 1969, p. 51]

> This natural varietist tendency of human beings is well within the normal range of behaviors and is not indicative of emotional or sexual disturbance. . . . The desire for novelty and variety is apparently inherent in most human beings; long-term exclusivity with a sexual-emotional companion is not an innate human need, but a culturally induced one. Since we are by nature varietists and by social/cultural upbringing exclusivists, we are frequently in conflict. And this is why many of us—even the normal and the satisfactorily married—are so sorely tempted and sometimes act on our desires for novelty and change. [Block, 1978, pp. 59–60]

> Extramarital sex mores, which have become a part of us, rest upon a number of grounds which are either invalid or tenuous matters of faith. The fact that [extramarital sex] exists as part of the social fabric in some societies gives evidence that opposition to extramarital sex is not a "given" of human nature. It is reasonable to assume that people who might grow up in a society where extramarital sex is an openly accepted form of behavior would have no different feelings toward it than to any other normal part of their daily lives. [Ziskin and Ziskin, 1973, p. 210].

Students of human nature as dissimilar as Freud and Kinsey agree that marital fidelity has no genetic base and that mankind is biologically polygamous. People are taught from early childhood on, albeit ambivalently, that marital fidelity is a desirable form of behavior. Furthermore, because people *learn* to be faithful in marriage, they can also learn not to be.

But it does not follow from the recognition that the human being is biologically polygamous that polygamy is a mature form of behavior or will bring inner peace and happiness. On the contrary, for children to mature they have to learn to tame their impulses, give up some of their narcissism, and identify and empathize with others. It is only at birth and for the next few months that humans may be compared to rats, monkeys, or bulls because only then are they totally voracious, narcissistic, and impulsive. As infants interact with their parents and other family members, they begin to show many differences from animals. When loved and gratified, infants move from a grandiose position and accept some frustration. As they are lovingly weaned from the breast, toilet-trained, and later helped to renounce some of their incestuous and oedipal desires, they can eventually move toward a position of social consciousness and emotional intimacy with others.

If human beings governed their behavior solely by the dictates of their instincts, they would emerge as "polymorphous perverse" —i.e., egocentric, unreasonable, and impulsive individuals who would be unable to love and be loved. Rather, they would want everything in sight, strike out when frustrated, and feel no pangs of conscience when they hurt others. In addition, they would be constantly depressed becasue they would feel that they were constantly deprived of what they deserved.

Most psychoanalysts and many social scientists believe that it is invalid to compare animals with human beings. It is difficult to imagine rats having unhappy marriages because of false romantic ideals or monkeys feeling guilty becasue of unacceptable hostile fantasies toward a mate!

What is important in evaluating adulterous behavior is not so much whether it is consonant with our biological heritage but whether it is emotionally healthy or mature. Obviously, in assessing the emotional health or maturity of extramarital behavior, it is necessary to have some criteria for doing so. Many commentators on extramarital behavior have failed to state what criteria they used when they examined the maturity of adulterous behavior; others have considered a person healthy or mature if he or she was *not* in psychotherapy.

Another problem in assessing the maturity or immaturity of adultery is that researchers have frequently accepted their respondents' views of their own psychological functioning at face value. In many research projects, if those involved in extramarital behavior said they were happy, healthy, and unconflicted about the extramarital activity, their statements were not explored more fully. But human beings rationalize their behavior, and it usually takes some time to know people so that we can really understand how they feel about themselves and their life situations.

WHAT IS EMOTIONAL MATURITY?

The concept of "emotional maturity" has often been confused with the notion of adjustment to a group norm. Psychoanalysts and other mental health practitioners have frequently been criticized for helping people adjust to a sick society (Riesman, Cohen, and Pearl, 1964). It has been further alleged that the spirit governing modern psychotherapy is the "Protestant ethic," with its emphasis on rationality, "success," and individualism. Rather than enhancing individuals, psychotherapists have been accused of merely imposing a perverted middle-class value system on people (Davis, 1958).

Although some therapists may refer to a group norm in trying to help clients and patients feel more comfortable with themselves and others, in most of the mental hygiene literature, maturity is conceived as an *internal* state. Mature people are most frequently described as those who *are content with themselves* and who can make *independent* decisions, *autonomous* judgments, etc. (Erikson, 1950; Kubie, 1943). Most therapists conceive of their work as helping patients resolve certain developmental tasks so that their functioning will be more mature.

Dictionary definitions state that to "mature" is to "ripen" or "develop." But "ripen" into what? When Sigmund Freud was asked what he thought maturity was, he answered tersely, "Lieben und arbeiten" ("To love and work"). By this he meant that the person should be able to form a mutually affectionate relationship with a member of the opposite sex, pursue some socially useful and productive activity, and derive pleasure from both.

Erikson, elaborating on Freud's definition, stressed that the mature person is one who has limited hatred and can love a member of the opposite sex "with whom one is able and willing to regulate the cycle of work, procreation, and recreation, so as to secure to the offspring, too, a satisfactory development" (Erikson,

1950, p. 258). Erikson's amplification of Freud's "love and work" prescription is of course an ideal; no human being can be consistently successful in love and work without occasional regressions.

Maturity seems to imply that an individual is capable of accepting his or her own imperfections without too much guilt or shame. Furthermore, the mature person is able to accept imperfections in others as well. Though able to give and receive in a love relationship, to identify with the partner's needs, the mature person feels a sufficient sense of self-esteem so that criticisms from others do not devastate him.

In chapter 1, we referred to Reuben Fine's (1971) "analytic ideal." The "analytic ideal" can also be considered an ideal form of maturity—pursuing love, seeking pleasure that is guided by reason, gratifying sexual desires, occupying a role in the family and social order, having a rich, feeling life, and communicating with others

Utilizing Freud's, Erikson's, and Fine's definitions of maturity, we consider a mature marriage as one in which both participants have resolved several psychosexual tasks. As we discussed in chapters 1 and 2, mature people can trust each other without feeling guilty about being dependent. At the same time, they have a sense of their own identities and can take care of themselves if the other person is not available. They can enjoy feeling independent without resentment because they have a realistic sense of their own capacities; they are not busy doubting themselves. A mature husband and mature wife can love and enjoy each other sexually without making each other parental figures. They can feel attached without making excessive demands or seeking a symbiosis. They can admire the loved one without being infatuated and can enjoy intimacy and mutual devotion without engulfing or fearing that they will be engulfed.

Because a mature husband and a mature wife derive much pleasure and fulfillment from their marital interaction, they are not compelled to seek out extramarital relationships to fill emotional voids. Unlike the man or woman who needs an extramarital affair to buttress a shaky self-image or to discharge hostility, the mature husband and wife enjoy themselves and each other in a mutually trusting, intimate, and devoted relationship.

A REVIEW OF SOME RESEARCH
ON THE EXTRAMARITAL AFFAIR

Until very recently, studies of adulterous relationships have been more moralistic than analytic, more hortatory than dispassionate. In one of the earliest studies, Cuber and Harroff (1965) interviewed 437 white Americans between the ages of 35 and 55. These people constituted "a completely non-clinical sample" in that none of them had had psychotherapy in any form "or, in the opinion of the interviewers, clearly required it." These interviews with "The Significant Americans" yielded data which suggested that there were at least three types of relationships between marriage and adulterous behavior. The Type I adulterous relationship "compensated or substituted for a defective marriage," that is, the partner involved in an affair had reached the judgment that the marriage was seriously frustrating. The standardizing principle for this type of adulterous relationship was "the relationship with the spouse had some serious lack but not serious enough to terminate the marriage." Type II involved a married person of either sex who experienced "a discontinous marriage—e.g., long absence on military duty or extended residence away from home in connection with a career or profession. In Type III were people who did not accept a monogamous commitment with respect to their personal lives, although they felt committed to marriage and parenthood.

From their findings, Cuber and Harroff drew the following conclusions, which they termed "counter-generalizations" because some assumed propositions about adulterous behavior were called into question. First, the authors found that adultery is not necessarily furtive; "a considerable number of spouses have 'levelled' with their mates, who cooperated in maintaining a public pretense of monogamous marriage." Second, the authors were able to "document with a long list instances in which the spousal relationship remained at least as good qualitatively as within the average pair without adultery." In assessing marital happiness before and after adultery, they found that sometimes the marriage improved, sometimes it deteriorated, and sometimes it remained unchanged. "Overwhelmingly these people expressed no guilt," state the authors, "with respect to what they were doing, although they sometimes acknowledged regret over practical consequences."

Among the "Significant Americans," the "offended" spouses were often not offended at all, and sometimes they felt relieved that they did not have to feel responsible for their spouses' sexual gratification. The authors did find "an enormously high incidence of psychologically destructive relationships in enduring marriages." They concluded their study by tacitly advocating extramarital relationships because, according to the authors, they are often more fulfilling than enduring marriages, which are often "maintained in homage to monolithic expectations" and societal values while "adulterous relationships carry no such burden of expectation."

In the study "Five Year Effects of Altered Marital Contracts" (1969), Stephen Beltz intensively interviewed five couples who had "altered their marriage contracts during counseling." All of the couples had been married for more than ten years. They came for couseling for various reasons, but most did *not* come for help with their marriages. During the counseling each couple began either tacitly or overtly to "allow" each other to have extramarital affairs. Beltz was able, over a five-year period, to study the couples' marriages and the impact of their "altered marital contracts" on the individuals.

Of the five couples studied, four continued their extramarital affairs indefinitely, and all four eventually divorced after much unhappiness and personal instability. The one couple that discontinued extramarital activity "achieved a much higher degree of marital interaction, a return to stable family life, continuation of individual progress and happiness." Beltz concluded, "The data shed light on the prevalent notion among many laymen and professionals that extramarital sex could improve the nature of a marriage. The evidence here is overwhelmingly in the opposite direction."

Albert Ellis (1969), on the basis of clinical interviews with individuals in psychotherapy and "unofficial talks with scores of non-patients" who were "presumably a fairly random sample of well-educated middle-class adults," concluded that there are healthy and unhealthy, mature and immature reasons for extramarital activity. Although Ellis gives no information about his sample, he points out that "sexual varietism" is necessary for healthy married individuals because they will inevitably have less satisfaction after several years of marriage. He also believes that healthy people can and should love and have sex with more than one person and enjoy the adventure that is inherent in an extramarital affair. Most healthy people, according to Ellis, lead dull and routinized existences and need the escape of an affair.

Unhealthy reasons for having an affair, Ellis suggests, are low frustration tolerance, hostility to one's spouse, a need for ego bolstering to compensate for a weak self-esteem, and a need to escape from marriage. He concludes, "Just how often our millions of adulterers practice extramarital relations for good and how often for bad reasons is an interesting question."

In "A Study of Extramarital Relationships," Neubeck and Schletzer (1962) interviewed 40 married couples who were also psychologically tested to determine whether those involved in extramarital affairs were more or less "psychopathic" than those who were not. Psychopathy was defined as "an absence of deep emotional response, inability to profit from experience, and disregard of social mores." The interviews and tests seemed to demonstrate that adulterers *were* more psychopathic than nonadulterers.

Through referrals, Whitehurst (1974) located and gave questionnaires to 35 couples in open relationships; 23 were legally married and 12 were not. The respondents' ages ranged from 22 to 62, and most of them were upper-middle-class professionals. Those participating in the study viewed their sexually open relationships as "a compromise way of living which merged freedom to pursue personal growth and autonomy." They rejected the restrictiveness of traditional marriage and sought "variety, complexity, romance, courtship, and even problems to keep things lively."

In analyzing responses to his questionaires, Whitehurst learned that virtually no respondent had any desire to return to a conventional marital relationship. Sexual problems were rare, and respondents "seemed more natural and less rigid in their views of sex, which was considered fun and vital, than conventional persons who might approach sex less playfully." The arrangement "exacted a price in uncertainty, anxiety and a degree of emotional pain. Tranquility and stability were at times traded for growth and ego-enhancement from outside relationships." In the sample, the women had more outside contacts than the men.

The problem most of the respondents shared was "a limited potential for honest social interaction and friendship." They found it "painful to have to exclude more conservative friends, relatives and coworkers from knowledge of their sexually open life style" and it was difficult for them to accept that their views and behavior probably would be rejected within their own social networks.

The marital partners found that reaching agreement about their sexually open marriages required "intense, honest communication and endurance" that Whitehurst speculated "would be too difficult for many people conventionally reared in a jealous, possessive, male-dominated society." Jealousy most often involved fear of loss and "lingering feelings of possessiveness or desire to control the mate." Though the couples worked toward equality, occasionally marital partners discovered they had a different commitment to or involvement in a sexually open marriage, and this led to conflict, particularly in regard to sharing free time. The partner who was "left out" often felt resentful and lonely. Sometimes "freedom" and "openness" were abused as in the cases of some couples who used outside relationships as a means to escape their spouses.

Whitehurst concluded that sexually open marriages are inadvisable for people who are not emotionally equipped to handle freedom, time alone, complex interrelationships, high intensity or the struggle of possessiveness versus autonomy.

Knapp (1974, 1975, 1976) studied 17 legally married couples who also defined their marriages as sexually open. Of the couples participating in the project, one or both spouses had had or were currently having outside sexual relationships, and these couples all indicated that they preferred independent functioning to exchanging partners as in "swinging." Knapp's couples were located primarily through referrals from mutual acquaintances. Each interviewee answered 51 open-ended questions regarding personal history, "open marriage attitudes," and sexual experiences.

Wives again prevailed in the extent of outside extramarital activity; they had 81 satellite partners or 57 percent of the combined total, while their spouses had 60 partners or 43 percent of the total. The duration of extramarital relationships varied from a month to one or two years or more. Most of the spouses emphasized that they did not share all the details or feelings about their extramarital relationships, though they were strongly against lying to their partners or withholding information when asked for it. The respondents' children were mostly under ten years of age, and Knapp thought that the parents' nontraditional marital style was not very visible to their offspring. The youngsters "did not raise any questions that would indicate worry or curiosity."

The most frequently reported benefits of the sexually open marriage, according to Knapp's respondents, included: better fulfillment of personal needs; the excitement of new experiences leading to feelings of increased vitality; an eventual lessening of jealousy and possessiveness; freedom and security together; and the opportunity to be fully oneself. Seven respondents could think of no particular disadvantages of the sexually open marriage but others mentioned jealousy and time-sharing as problems. Resentment over the importance of an outside partner was another problem that was occasionally reported. Knapp found that her respondents as a group could not be judged significantly more neurotic, antisocial, or "personality disordered" than the general population of the United States. If anything, the author felt that they were less neurotic and more self-assured and non-defensive. Knapp concluded that her respondents were imaginative, individualistic, adventurous, and rather than being destructively antisocial or lacking in social conscience, they were "variant," not "deviant," and "socially innovative".

In research for *The Affair*, Morton Hunt (1969) conducted 91 tape recorded interviews running from one to 15 hours with men and women who had or were still having extramarital affairs. In addition, Hunt was able to examine diaries that some of his subjects kept which described their reactions to their affairs. Finally, he examined 360 completed questionnaires from respondents all over the country, designed by a university social-science research team.

From his data Hunt concluded that different kinds of affairs interact with different kinds of marriages in patterned ways—some extremely damaging to the marriages, others relatively innocuous and still others distinctly beneficial. Although Hunt continually points out that few people are exempt from feeling ambivalent about adultery, his final conclusion is as follows:

While I agree with those authorities on marriage and sex who believe that an occasional minor affair may benefit marriage, I feel this is true only of marriages that need benefitting: the distant, the boring, the conflict-ridden. I have heard of marriages said to be loving, satisfying, and close, in which one partner or both have casual affairs that benefit the marriage or at least do it no harm, but each time I have been able to investigate such a case, it has seemed to me that the marriage is amiable rather than loving, tolerable rather than satisfying, and comfortable rather than close. . . . I have not yet seen any evidence that the loving, satisfying, and close marriage can be improved—or even that it can remain unthreatened—by affairs. [1969, pp. 165–166]

In another study, Hunt (1974) again conducted in-depth interviews with close to 100 people and also gave several hundred people involved in extramarital affairs questionnaires to answer. Hunt points out in this study that the seeming permissiveness of Americans today concerning extramarital sex is apparently more a matter of public attitude than real conviction. Most people, according to him, continue to disapprove of such behavior because they believe that when it becomes a reality rather than a fantasy, "it undermines and endangers the most important human relationship in their lives."

A generalization that evolved from Hunt's *Sexual Behavior in the 1970's* is that

. . . by far the largest part of extramarital activity is secret and furtive, violative of the emotional entente existing between the spouses, productive of internal conflict and guilt feelings on the part of the one engaging in such acts, and anywhere from infuriating to shattering to the other if he or she discovers the truth. . . . Our data indicate that there is still a very great emphasis on secrecy based on the clear recognition that extramarital acts will be perceived by the spouse as disloyalty, partial abandonment, and a repudiation of marital love [1974, p. 255].

From in-depth interviews with many subjects and work with clients in marital counseling, Block (1978) concluded that "all monogamy is not blissful and healthy and . . . all adultery is not painful and sick." He contends that it is "a myth" that adultery must adversely affect a marriage or that it is always a symptom of a troubled marriage or troubled psyche. "It is not having an affair in itself that counts but the state of the marriage, the motivation of the adulterer, the self-image of the non-involved spouse and the meaning of the affair for both spouses." Yet he concludes, that prolonged extramarital experiences result "in decidedly more negative than positive effects on marriage."

Ziskin and Ziskin (1973) interviewed 134 couples practicing extramarital sex by agreement. Each interview was approximately two hours and "was marked by a high degree of candor." The interviews revealed that the subjects were happy people who had a considerable zest for living and confidence in what they were doing. Having mutually agreed to practice adultery, many couples felt that their extramarital affairs helped them feel warmer and closer to their spouses and "generally increased their enjoyment of their life together." Most of these couples reported either increased frequency and enjoyment of marital sex or maintenance of marital sex at a previously high level. Prior to their study the authors had anticipated that jealousy would be a very difficult problem for the couples but the small amount of jealousy demonstrated by these couples represented another unexpected finding.

The Ziskins conclude that society would benefit if comarital arrangements were sanctioned by major institutions such as the church, school, etc., because, they believe, extramarital arrangements sustain marriages.

A CRITIQUE OF THE RESEARCH

A review of the conclusions emanating from the research cited reveals again that the experts are in much disagreement about the emotional health or maturity of an extramarital affair. Some conclude that it enhances marriage, while others contend that it can destroy the marital bond. Some researchers conclude that participation in an extramarital affair is a sign of maturity and autonomy, while others see it as a sign of psychopathy or neuroses. Finally, many authors like Ellis believe that there are mature and immature motives that can spark and sustain an extramarital affair.

What must be questioned about the research we have reviewed is the methodology utilized to gather the data that helped the researchers form their conclusions. For those of us who view the human being as a complex biological, psychological, and social organism, measurement poses problems. If the researcher believes that hopes, dreams, emotions, fantasies, anxieties, defenses, and other internal states exist, research activities must take these phenomena into account. If one human being asks another a question, the answer is a variable one, depending on the question, the relationship between the questioner and subject, and a host of unconscious factors.

Few theories of the human being, with the exception of psychoanalytic theory, take the measurement problem into account (Fine, 1960). As we have demonstrated in previous chapters, the psychoanalytic perspective allows for internal motives and recognizes that what a subject tells a researcher depends heavily on the relationship between the two, i.e., transference and countertransference reactions.

Because almost none of the studies on extramarital behavior takes into account the motivation of the subjects, their transferences to the real or imagined interviewer, their histories, their defenses, etc, their observations are contaminated. The fact that certain types of behavior and certain statements can be enumerated tells us little. Statements can be rationalizations and their full meaning cannot be understood unless we know the subject for some time. Behavior, as we have seen, tells us little until we know the many unconscious motives of the actor. Because so many of the examinations of the extramarital affair have failed to include an appraisal of the subjects' internal evaluation of the relationship between the subject and the investigator, as well as other unconscious factors discussed throughout this book, the results from the research have to be questioned.

A well-known axiom from physics, the Heisenberg principle, states that the act of observation affects the data observed, and this principle seems to be quite applicable in observing people. When a human being is a subject of an observation, he has feelings about being a subject, wishes to please or displease the interviewer, perhaps has certain exhibitionistic fantasies. Certainly many unconscious wishes, defenses, and anxieties are operating in the experiment, all of which affect his responses to the study.

As R. D. Laing, the British psychiatrist, said in his book *Self and Others* (1969), "If I want to get to know you, it is unlikely that I shall proceed as though I were studying nebulae and rats. You will not be inclined to disclose yourself to me. If one says that all one is interested in is behavior pure and simple, then one is not studying persons."

Because we are arguing for the superiority of the psychoanalytic approach to research that we have presented in this book, we also have to address the argument of many professional and laymen that a "clinical" population is a skewed sample. Indeed it is. As was stated in the prologue, those individuals who involve themselves in psychoanalytic therapy usually have more courage to face themselves than nonanalysands. Most of them have the capacity to trust another human being to help them make their unconscious conscious; in addition, they usually have the capacity to take responsibility for their life situations. Individuals in analysis are able, eventually, to acknowledge, for example, that the complaints of their spouses are unconscious wishes and that much of their feeling of malaise is self-created.

Many of the researchers on the extramarital affair view patients in psychotherapy as deviants, and in some cases this is true. However, it has been demonstrated time and time again that "nonpatients" are no less neurotic and conflicted than those in therapy, if not more so (Fine, 1975). Most people have neurotic anxieties, phobias, feelings of inferiority, unexplained angers, guilts, etc. Those who are willing to examine the internal factors that cause their difficulties cannot and should not be considered to be more conflicted than those who are not in therapy.

LOVE'S LABOR LOST

On the basis of my own observation and research, I am firmly of the opinion that an extramarital affair is *never* a healthy or mature act. If a man or woman can be dependent on someone without wishing for a merger, can accept frustration without feeling sadistic or masochistic, can enjoy sex without being bombarded with competitive or incestuous fantasies, can admire a partner without overidealizing, and can be autonomous without resentment, he or she is a relatively happy human being who will want to devote him or herself to another happy human being.

As we have constantly reiterated, a happy marriage consists of two happy human beings. Most of those who advocate extramarital sex argue from the observation that many married people are unhappy, that there is something wrong with the institution of marriage. I disagree. I believe that many people who get married are psychologically still children, seeking gratification of childish wishes—to merge, to dominate, to rescue, to be demeaned, to compete, etc. Furthermore, because unresolved childish wishes cause anxiety, many married individuals must defend themselves against intimacy because it conjures up wishes that they cannot tolerate.

Although I believe that an occasional one-night stand or short-term extramarital affair can sometimes be viewed as a harmless regression, a prolonged extramarital affair always implies that the adulterer is involved in a conflicted marriage and therefore is a conflicted person who probably can profit from psychotherapy.

As we stated in chapter 1, a marital relationship in this day and age is not easy to sustain. There are so many stimuli in our environment that tempt us to regress and be narcissistic children. Successful marriage requires frustration tolerance, empathy, autonomy, and relative freedom from anxiety. It requires the resolution of certain psychosocial tasks—oral, anal, and phallic-oedipal conflicts. When people have resolved these tasks, they can and do enjoy loving a person of the opposite sex and will want to devote themselves to that person in a monogamous marriage.

I believe that marriage is a workable, irreplaceable, and unique institution for healthy and mature people. Neurotic people are poor material for marriage; they go through the motions but have to fail, not because marriage is "antiquated" but because of their own unconscious conflicts. All stories about a "normal" woman who becomes the victim of a neurotic man, or vice versa, are fairy tales. Real life demonstrates that two neurotic individuals look for and find each other with uncanny regularity (Bergler, 1963).

The fate of an unhappy marriage is decided long before the marriage occurs. The human psyche is formed in early childhood and the result is enshrined in the person without his conscious knowledge. To ward off the anxiety that unresolved childish wishes create, marital partners can do many things—withdraw, fight, murder, divorce, or have an extramarital affair. I take issue with those writers who believe that when marital partners mutually agree that both will participate in independent affairs, they are acting maturely and lovingly. I believe that these are individuals who are afraid to be full men and women with their spouses and who have many unresolved sexual conflicts. I also believe that it is a neurotic person who is attracted to an adulterer. A mature person with high self-esteem will not be satisfied with a part-time lover.

One of the rationalizations utilized by advocates of the extramarital affair is that after a while any two people in a marriage grow apathetic and tired of each other. Neurotics do grow tired of each other because they are unable to fuse tender and sensual feelings onto one person for a long period of time. They avoid confronting their inhibitions and anxieties by trying to prove that a marital relationship fosters boredom while an extramarital affair creates stimulation and excitement. They fail to realize that much of the excitement they feel in an affair is not sexual excitement but evolves from the defiant fantasies that they are gratifying by spiting their spouses, whom they experience unconsciously as parental figures.

To call monogamy the result of puritanical teaching and preaching is also a convenient rationalization but does not conform to clinical experience. Any therapist who has worked with men and women in prolonged extramarital affairs comes to recognize that these are basically unhappy people who need two part-time relationships; a singly mutually loving relationship frightens them, although they are the last to recognize it. They choose the route of an extramarital affair and tell themselves that they need greater sexual enjoyment. What they don't want to confront is that they cannot enjoy sex in marriage.

The observations and conclusions set forth in this book will not please all of my readers. To some, my conclusions will be too close to home to feel comfortable; others will experience me as a prudish conservative. Many of the assertions made by psychoanalysts are unpopular because they activate anxiety. It often takes an analysand many years of treatment to accept the emotional truth about his or her neurosis. It is extremely difficult for many adults to acknowledge that a prolonged extramarital affair is a neurotic symptom. Often people cringe when they hear that an extramarital liaison is an expression of unresolved homosexual, incestuous, dependency, and sadomasochistic conflicts.

Whether or not my contentions are accepted, they are intended to illuminate and provide guidance for the many unhappy people who are involved in or constantly fantasize having extramarital affairs. These people will not find sustained pleasure in an affair nor will they derive comfort if they struggle to cease and desist. It is my opinion that only psychotherapy will help them resolve those emotional conflicts and immaturities that provoke their marital distress and precipitate their extramarital affairs.

Most individuals who rebel against marriage and monogamy are angry and unhappy people who understandably rationalize their objections. They know nothing about the forces that make them miserable. They need therapeutic help so that they can mature and derive genuine pleasure from living.

Bibliography

ABLES, B. 1977. *Therapy for Couples.* San Francisco: Jossey-Bass.

ABRAHAM, K. 1927. "The Influence of Oral Eroticism on Character Formation." In *Selected Papers of Karl Abraham.* London, England: Institute of Psychoanalysis and Hogarth Press.

ACKERMAN, N. 1958. *The Psychodynamics of Family Life.* New York: Basic Books.

ALEXANDER, F., and Ross, H. 1952. *Dynamic Psychiatry.* Chicago: University of Chicago Press.

AUSTIN, L. 1958. "Dynamics and Treatment of the Client with Anxiety Hysteria." In *Ego Psychology and Dynamic Casework,* ed. H. Parad. New York: Family Service Association of America.

BACH, G. 1969. *The Intimate Enemy: How to Fight Fair in Love and Marriage.* New York: Avon.

BARRIE, J. 1950. *Peter Pan.* New York: Charles Scribners' Sons.

BARTUSIS, M. 1978. *Every Other Man.* New York: E. P. Dutton.

BELL, R., and PELTZ, D. 1974. "Extramarital Sex Among Women." *Medical Aspects of Sexuality,* vol. 8.

BELTZ, S. 1969. "Five Year Effects of Altered Marital Contracts." *In Extramarital Relations,* ed. G. Neubeck. Englewood Cliffs, N.J.:Prentice-Hall.

BERGLER, E. 1969. *Selected Papers of Edmund Bergler.* New York: Grune and Stratton.

——. 1963. "Marriage and Divorce." In *A Handbook of Psychoanalysis,* eds. H. Herma and G. Kurth. Cleveland, Ohio: World.

——. 1960. *Divorce Won't Help.* New York: Liveright.

BETTLEHEIM, B. 1971. "Obsolete Youth: Toward a Psychograph of Adolescent Rebellion." In *Adolescent Psychiatry,* vol. 1, eds. S. Feinstein, P. Giovacchini, and A. Miller. New York: Basic Books.

BIRNER, L. 1971. "The First Foreign Land." *Psychoanalytic Review,* vol. 58, no. 2.

BLANCK, R., and BLANCK, G. 1968. *Marriage and Personal Development.* New York: Columbia University Press.

BLOCK, J. 1978. *The Other Man, The Other Woman.* New York: Grosset and Dunlap.

BLOS, P. 1967. "The Second Individuation Process of Adolescence." In *The Psychoanalytic Study of the Child,* vol. 22. New York: International Universities Press.

————. 1953. "The Treatment of Adolescents." In *Psychoanalysis and Social Work,* ed. M. Heiman. New York: International Universities Press.

BOLTON, C. 1961. "Mate Selection as the Development of a Relationship." In *Marriage and Family Living,* vol. 23, no. 4.

BONAPARTE, M. 1953. *Female Sexuality.* New York: International Universities Press.

BOWLBY, J. 1973. *Attachment and Loss,* vol. 2. New York: Basic Books.

BOWMAN, H. 1974. *Marriage for Moderns.* New York: McGraw-Hill.

BREEDLOVE, W. and BREEDLOVE, J. 1964. *Swap Clubs: A Study in Contemporary Sexual Mores.* Los Angeles: Sherbourne Press.

CAMERON, N. 1963. *Personality Development and Psychopathology.* New York: Houghton Mifflin.

CAPRIO, F. 1953. *Marital Infidelity.* New York: Citadel Press.

CLANTON, G., and SMITH, L. 1977. *Jealousy.* Englewood Cliffs, N.J.: Prentice-Hall.

CUBER, J., and HARROFF, P. 1965. *The Significant Americans.* New York: Appleton-Century.

DAVIS, K. 1958. "Mental Hygiene and the Class Structure." In *Social Perspectives on Behavior,* eds. H. Stein and R. Cloward. New York: Free Press.

DEBURGER, J. 1978. *Marriage Today.* Cambridge, Mass.: Schenkman.

DELL, F. 1926. *Love in Greenwich Village.* New York: George H. Doran.

DEUTSCH, H. 1965. "Some Forms of Emotional Disturbance and Their Relationship to Schizophrenia." In *Neuroses and Character Types,* ed. H. Deutsch. New York: International Universities Press.

DURBIN, K. 1977. "On Sexual Jealousy." In *Jealousy,* eds. G. Clanton and L. Smith, Englewood Cliffs, N.J., Prentice-Hall.

EIDELBERG, L. 1956. "Neurotic Choice of Mate." In *Neurotic Interaction in Marriage,* ed. V. Eisenstein. New York: Basic Books.

EISENSTEIN, V. 1956. "Sexual Problems in Marriage." In *Neurotic Interaction in Marriage,* ed. V. Eisenstein. New York: Basic Books.

ELLIS, A. 1969. "Extramarital Problems in Modern Society." In *Extramarital Relations*, ed. G. Neubeck. Englewood Cliffs, N.J.: Prentice-Hall.

ENGLISH, O., and PEARSON, G. 1945. *Emotional Problems of Living*. New York: W. W. Norton.

ERIKSON, E. 1956. "The Problem of Ego Identity." *Journal of American Psychoanalytic Association*, vol. 4.

———. 1950. *Childhood and Society*. New York: W. W. Norton.

ESMAN, A. 1975a. "The Latency Period." In *Personality Development and Deviation*, ed. G. Wiedeman. New York: International Universities Press.

———. 1975. *The Psychology of Adolescence*. New York: International Universities Press.

EVANS, R. 1964. *Conversations with Carl Jung*. Princeton, N.J.: Van Nostrand Reinhold.

FELDMAN, S. 1964. "The Attraction of 'The Other Woman.'" *Journal of the Hillside Hospital*, vol. 13, no. 1.

FENICHEL, O. 1945. *The Psychoanalytic Theory of Neurosis*. New York: W. W. Norton.

FINE, R. 1975. *Psychoanalytic Psychology*. New York: Jason Aronson.

———. 1973. "Psychoanalysis." In *Current Psychotherapies*, ed. R. Corsini. Itasca, Ill.: F. E. Peacock.

———. 1971. *The Healing of the Mind*. New York: David McKay.

———. 1960. "The Measurement Problem." *The Psychoanalytic Review*, vol. 47, no. 3.

FORD, C., and BEACH, F. 1951. *Patterns of Sexual Behavior*. New York: Harper and Bros.

FRAIBERG, S. 1977. *In Defense of Mothering*. New York: Basic Books.

FRANCE, A. 1933. *Penguin Island.* New York: The Modern Library.

FREUD, A. 1965. *Normality and Pathology in Childhood: Asessment of Development*. New York: International Universities Press.

———. 1937. *The Ego and Mechanisms of Defense*. London: Hogarth Press.

FREUD, S. 1939. *An Outline of Psychoanalysis, Standard Edition*, vol. 23. London: Hogarth Press, 1964.

———. 1932. *The Anatomy of the Mental Personality*. In New *Introductory Lectures on Psychoanalysis*, standard edition, vol 22. London: Hogarth Press, 1964.

———. 1923. *Beyond the Pleasure Principle*, standard edition, vol. 18. London: Hogarth Press, 1961.

———. 1918. *The Taboo of Virginity*, standard edition, vol. 14. London: Hogarth Press, 1957.

———. 1916. *Some Analytic Character Types Met in Psychoanalytic Work*, standard edition, vol. 14. London: Hogarth Press, 1957.

———. 1914. *On Narcissism*, standard edition, vol. 14. London: Hogarth Press, 1957.

———. 1910a. *Contributions to the Psychology of Love: The Most Prevalent Form of Degradation in Erotic Life*, Standard Edition, Vol. 11, London, Hogarth Press, 1957.

———. 1910b. *A Special Type of Choice of Object Made by Men*, standard edition, vol. 11. London: Hogarth Press, 1957.

———. 1909. *Analysis of a Phobia in a Five Year Old Boy*, standard edition, vol. 10. London: Hogarth Press, 1955.

———. 1905. *Three Essays on the Theory of Sexuality*, standard edition, vol. 7. London: Hogarth Press, 1957.

———. 1900. *The Interpretation of Dreams*, standard edition, vols. 4 and 5. London: Hogarth Press, 1953.

FROMM, E. 1956. *The Art of Loving*. New York: Harper.

GIOVACCHINI, P. 1972. *Tactics and Techniques in Psychoanalytic Theory*. New York: Jason Aronson.

GRUNEBAUM, H., and CHRIST, J. 1976. *Contemporary Marriage*. Boston: Little, Brown.

HARTMANN, H. 1964. *Essays on Ego Psychology*. New York: International Universities Press.

———. 1958. *Ego Psychology and the Problem of Adaptation*. New York: International Universities Press.

HENDIN, H. 1975. *The Age of Sensation*. New York: W. W. Norton.

HITE, S. 1976. *The Hite Report*. New York: Macmillan.

HORNEY, K. 1950. *Neurosis and Human Growth*. New York: W. W. Norton.

HOWARD, J. 1978. *Families*. New York: Simon and Schuster.

———. 1970. *Please Touch*. New York: McGraw-Hill.

HUNT, M. 1977. "Is Marriage in Trouble?" In *Marriage Today*, ed. J. Deburger. New York: John Wiley & Sons.

———. 1974. *Sexual Behavior in the 1970's*. New York: Dell.

———. 1969. *The Affair*. Bergenfield, N.J.: The New American Library.

JACOBS, E. 1978. "Neverland." *Issues in Ego Psychology*, vol. 1, no. 1. New York: Washington Square Institute for Psychotherapy.

JACKSON, J. 1979. "Sages and/or Scientists?" Op. Ed. Page, *New York Times*, March 19, 1979.

JONES, E. 1953. *The Life and Work of Sigmund Freud*, vol. 1. New York: Basic Books.

———. 1922. "Some Problems of Adolescence." In *Papers on Psychoanalysis*, ed. E. Jones. London, England: Bailliere, Tindall, and Cox.

JONG, E. 1977. *How to Save Your Own Life*. New York: Holt, Rinehart, and Winston.

———. 1973. *Fear of Flying*. New York: Holt, Rinehart, and Winston.

JOSSELYN, I. 1971. "Etiology of Three Current Adolescent Syndromes." In *Adolescent Psychiatry*, vol. 1, eds. S. Feinstein, P. Giovacchini, and A. Miller. New York: Basic Books.

———. 1948. *Psychosocial Development of Children*. New York: Family Service Association of America.

KAUFMAN, B. 1977. *To Love is to Be Happy With*. New York: Coward, McCann, and Geoghegan.

KIELL, N. 1964. *The Universal Experience of Adolescence*. New York: International Universities Press.

KINSEY, A.; WARDELL, B.; POMEROY, B.; and MARTIN, C. 1948. *Sexual Behavior in the Human Male*. Philadelphia: W. B. Saunders.

KLEIN, M. 1957. *Envy and Gratitude*. New York: Basic Books.

KNAPP, J. 1976. "An Exploratory Study of Seventeen Sexually Open Marriages." *Journal of Sex Research*. vol. 12.

———. 1975. "The Myers-Briggs Type Indicator as a Basis for Personality Description of Spouses in Sexually Open Marriage." Paper presented at First National Conference on the Uses of the MBT1, Gainesville, Fla.

———. 1974. "Co-Marital Sex and Marriage Counseling. Sexually 'Open' Marriage and Related Attitudes and Practices of Marriage Counselors." Doctoral Dissertation, University of Florida.

KUBIE, L. 1956. "Psychoanalysis and Marriage: Practical and Theoretical Issue." In *Neurotic Interaction in Marriage*, ed. V. Eisenstein. New York: Basic Books.

———. 1943. "The Nature of Psychotherapy." *Bulletin of the New York Academy of Medicine*, vol III.

LAING, R.D. 1969. *The Self and Others*. New York: Penguin Publishers.

LANGLEY, R., and Levy, R. 1977. *Wife Beating: The Silent Crisis*. New York: Dutton Publishers.

LINTON, R. 1936. *The Study of Man*. New York: D. Appleton-Century.

LOBSENZ, N. 1975. "Taming the Green-Eyed Monster." *Redbook*, March 1975.

LUTZ, W. 1964. "Marital Incompatibility." In *Social Work and Social Problems*, ed. N. Cohen. New York: National Association of Social Workers.

MAHLER, M.; PINE, F.; and BERGMAN, A. 1975. *The Psychological Birth of the Human Infant*. New York: Basic Books.

MAHLER, M. 1968. *On Human Symbiosis and the Viscissitudes of Individuation*. New York: International Universities Press.

MALINOWSKI, M. 1963. "Marriage." Encyclopedia Britannica.

———. 1923. "Psychoanalysis and Anthropology." *Psyche*, vol. 4.

MARASSE, H., and HART, M. 1975. "The Oedipal Period." In *Personality Development and Deviation*, ed. G. Wiedeman. New York: International Universities Press.

MAUGHAM, W. S. 1954. *Of Human Bondage*. Garden City, New York: Doubleday.

MEAD, M. 1967. "Sexual Freedom and Cultural Change." Paper delivered at forum, "The Pill and the Puritan Ethic," San Francisco State College, February 10, 1967.

"Marriage and Divorce Today: The Professionals' Newsletter," March 12, 1979.

MEISSNER, W. 1978a. "The Conceptualization of Marriage and Family Dynamics from a Psychoanalytic Perspective." In *Marriage and Marital Therapy*, eds. T. Paolino and B. McCrady. New York: Brunner-Mazel.

———. 1978b. *The Paranoid Process*. New York: Jason Aronson.

MEYERS, L., and LIGGITT, H. 1970. "A New View of Adultery." *Sexual Behavior*, vol 2.

MILLER, A. 1964. *After the Fall*, New York: Viking Press.

MILLS, C. 1959. *The Sociological Imagination*. New York: Oxford University Press.

MONTAGU, A. 1956. "Marriage: A Cultural Perspective." In *Neurotic Interaction in Marriage*, ed. V. Eisenstein. New York: Basic Books.

MUENSTERBERGER, W. 1961. "The Adolescent in Society." In *Adolescence*, eds. S. Lorand and H. Schneer. New York: Paul B. Hoeber, Inc.

MULLAHY, P. 1948. *The Contributions of Harry Stack Sullivan*. New York: Heritage House, 1948.

MURDOCK, G. 1949a. *Social Structure*. New York: Macmillan.

———. 1949b. "The Social Regulation of Sexual Behavior." In *Psychosexual Development in Health and Disease*, eds. P. Hoch and J. Zubin. New York: Grune and Stratton.

MURRAY, H. 1938. *Explorations in Personality*. New York: Science Editions, 1962.

MURSTEIN, B. 1976. "The Stimulus-Value-Role Theory of Marital Choice." In *Contemporary Marriage*, eds. H. Grunebaum and J. Christ. Boston: Little, Brown.

NEUBECK, G. 1969. *Extramarital Relations*. Englewood Cliffs, N.J.: Prentice-Hall.

———. and SCHLETZER, V., 1969. "A Study of Extramarital Relationships." In *Extramarital Relations*, ed. G. Neubeck. Englewood Cliffs, N.J.: Prentice-Hall.

NEWMAN, M., and BERKOWITZ, B. 1977. *How to Take Charge of Your Life* New York: Harcourt Brace Jovanovich.

O'NEILL, N. and O'NEILL, G. 1972a. "Open Marriage: A Synergic Model." *The Family Coordinator*, vol. 21.

———. 1972b. *Open Marriage*. New York: M. Evans Publishers.

ORGLER, H. 1963. *Alfred Adler: The Man and His Work*. New York: The New American Library.

PACKARD, V. 1968. *The Sexual Wilderness*. New York: David McKay.

PIKE, J. 1967. *You and the New Morality*. New York: Harper and Row.

PERRY, S. 1958. "The Conscious Use of Relationship with the Neurotic Client" in *Ego Psychology and Dynamic Casework*. ed. H. Parad, New York: Family Service Association of America.

PIETROPINTO, A., and SIMENAUER, J. 1976. *Beyond the Male Myth: What Women Want to Know About Men's Sexuality: A National Survey*. New York: Times Books.

RANK, O. 1926. *Will Therapy and Truth and Reality*. New York: Alfred A. Knopf, 1972.

REICH, I. O. 1970. *Wilhelm Reich: A Personal Biography*. New York: Avon

REIK, T. 1949. *Listening with the Third Ear*. New York: Farrar Strauss.

———. 1941. *Masochism in Modern Man*. New York: Grove Press.

REISMAN, D. 1956. *The Lonely Crowd*. New York: Doubleday, Anchor Books.

RHODES, R. 1972. "Sex and Sin in Sheboygan." *Playboy*, August.

RIBBLE, M. 1943. *The Rights of Infants*. New York: Columbia University Press.

RIESMANN, F., COHEN, J. and PEARL, A. 1964. *Mental Health of the Poor*. New York: The Free Press.

RIMMER, R. 1966. *The Harrod Experiment*. Los Angeles: Sherbourne Press.

RINGER, R. 1977. *Looking Out for Number One*. New York: Funk and Wagnalls.

ROHEIM, G. 1932. "Psychoanalysis of Primitive Cultural Types." *International Journal of Psychoanalysis*, vol. 13, no. 1.

ROTH, P. 1969. *Portnoy's Complaint*. New York: Random House.

SALINGER, J. 1945. *Catcher in the Rye*. New York: Little Brown.

SAPIRSTEIN, M. 1948. *Emotional Security*. New York: Crown.

SAUL, L. 1967. *Fidelity and Infidelity*. Philadelphia: Lippincott.

SOKOLOFF, B. 1947. *Jealousy: A Psychiatric Study*. New York: Howell, Soskin.

SILVERBERG, W. 1952. *Childhood Experience and Personal Destiny*. New York: Springer Publishing Company.

SMITH, J., and SMITH, L. 1974. *Beyond Monogamy*. Baltimore, Md: The Johns Hopkins University Press.

SOCARIDES, C. 1977. "On Vengeance: The Desire to 'Get Even'" In *The World of Emotions*. New York: International Universities Press.

SPOTNITZ, H., and FREEMAN, L. 1964. *The Wandering Husband*. Englewood Cliffs, N.J.: Prentice-Hall.

STOLLER, R. 1975. *Perversion: The Erotic Form of Hatred*. New York: Pantheon Books.

STOLOROW, R., and ATWOOD, G. 1979. *Faces in a Cloud: Subjectivity in Personality Theory*. New York: Jason Aronson.

STONE, A. 1954. "The Case Against Marital Infedelity." *Readers Digest*, May.

STREAN, H. 1970. *New Approaches in Child Guidance*. Metuchen, N.J.: Scarecrow Press.

———. 1975. *Personality Theory and Social Work Practice*. Metuchen, N.J.: Scarecrow Press.

TOFFLER, A. 1970. *Future Shock*. New York: Random House.

UPDIKE, J. 1979. *Too Far to Go*. New York: Fawcett Crest.

WAELDER, R. 1941. "The Scientific Approach to Casework with Special Emphasis on Psychoanalysis." *Journal of Social Casework*, vol. 22.

WERTHAM, F. 1969. *A Sign for Cain.* New York: Macmillan.

WHEELIS, A. 1958. *The Quest for Identity.* New York: W. W. Norton.

WHITEHURST, R. 1969. "Extramarital Sex: Alienation of Extension of Normal Behavior" in *Extramarital Relations,* ed. G. Neubeck, Englewood Cliffs, N.J. Prentice-Hall.

WILLIAMSON, D. 1977. "Extramarital Involvements in Couple Interaction." In *Counseling in Marital and Sexual Problems,* eds. R. Stahmann and W. Hiebert. Baltimore, Md.: Williams and Wilkins.

ZISKIN, J., and ZISKIN, M. 1973. *The Extramarital Arrangement.* London: Abelard-Schuman.

Index